"Drawing on his many years of studying th
look at these foundational works in canonical
intertestamental and theological connections, which lead to applicable observations
regarding faithful living in the presence of God. Readers will join me in offering genu-
ine gratitude to Professor Hays for providing this wonderful resource for all of us."

—**David S. Dockery**, president and distinguished professor of theology,
Southwestern Baptist Theological Seminary

"*The Pentateuch* is evangelical in its orientation, robust in its discussion, interactive
in its approach, balanced in its tone, and engaging in its style. I found the appendix,
'How to Interpret and Apply the Old Testament Law,' particularly valuable!"

—**Gordon H. Johnston**, professor of Old Testament studies,
Dallas Theological Seminary

"This is an excellent introduction to the Pentateuch. Hays writes in a clear and
engaging style, making complex issues accessible without being simplistic. Fair and
evenhanded on issues of date, authorship, and historical and literary context, *The
Pentateuch* will appeal to a broad Christian readership. Additional sections on relevance and application for modern Christians make it ideal for classroom use."

—**Catherine McDowell**, associate professor of Old Testament,
Gordon-Conwell Theological Seminary

"J. Daniel Hays has written a solid textbook on the Pentateuch, offering standard introductory material within the story line of life in God's presence and covering matters
of debate with judicious wisdom. His work will surely benefit students of Scripture."

—**L. Michael Morales**, professor of biblical studies,
Greenville Presbyterian Theological Seminary

"J. Daniel Hays has provided a good, readable introduction of the Pentateuch's message. This will be an eminently usable addition to the Old Testament professor and
students in the seminary classroom."

—**Eric Mitchell**, professor of Old Testament and biblical backgrounds,
Southwestern Baptist Theological Seminary

THE
PENTATEUCH

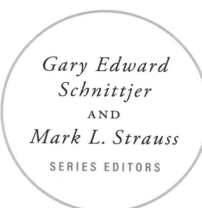

Gary Edward Schnittjer
AND
Mark L. Strauss
SERIES EDITORS

THE
PENTATEUCH

— LIFE IN THE PRESENCE OF GOD —

J. Daniel Hays

SCRIPTURE CONNECTIONS

B&H
ACADEMIC
BRENTWOOD, TENNESSEE

The Pentateuch: Life in the Presence of God
Copyright © 2024 by J. Daniel Hays

Published by B&H Academic
Brentwood, Tennessee

All rights reserved.

ISBN: 978-1-0877-4221-2

Dewey Decimal Classification: 222.1
Subject Heading: BIBLE. O.T. PENTATEUCH \ GOD
\ MOSES (BIBLICAL CHARACTER)

Unless otherwise noted, all Scripture quotations are taken from the Christian Standard Bible®, Copyright © 2017 by Holman Bible Publishers. Used by permission. Christian Standard Bible® and CSB® are federally registered trademarks of Holman Bible Publishers. Bold text in the New Testament represents words quoted from the Old Testament.

Other translations cited: The Holy Bible, English Standard Version. ESV® Text Edition: 2016. Copyright © 2001 by Crossway Bibles, a publishing ministry of Good News Publishers; Holy Bible, King James Version (public domain); New American Standard Bible®, Copyright © 1960, 1971, 1977, 1995, 2020 by The Lockman Foundation. All rights reserved; NET Bible® copyright ©1996–2017 by Biblical Studies Press, L.L.C. http://netbible.com All rights reserved; Holy Bible, New International Version®, NIV® Copyright ©1973, 1978, 1984, 2011 by Biblica, Inc.® Used by permission. All rights reserved worldwide; *Holy Bible*, New Living Translation, copyright © 1996, 2004, 2015 by Tyndale House Foundation. Used by permission of Tyndale House Publishers, Inc., Carol Stream, Illinois 60188. All rights reserved; New Revised Standard Version Bible, copyright © 1989 National Council of the Churches of Christ in the United States of America. Used by permission. All rights reserved worldwide; New Revised Standard Version, Updated Edition. Copyright © 2021 National Council of Churches of Christ in the United States of America. Used by permission. All rights reserved worldwide.

The web addresses referenced in this book were live and correct at the time of the book's publication but may be subject to change.

Cover design by Derek Thornton / Notch Design and Emily Keafer Lambright. Cover image: *Moses Breaks the Ten Commandments* by Julius Schnorr von Carolsfeld; sourced from ivan-96/iStock. Additional images by Rubanitor/Shutterstock and Balefire/Shutterstock.

Printed in China

29 28 27 26 25 24 RRD 1 2 3 4 5 6 7 8 9 10

To Liam, Reed, and Daniella

"Only be on your guard and diligently watch yourselves, so that you don't forget the things your eyes have seen and so that they don't slip from your mind as long as you live. Teach them to your children and your grandchildren."
—Deuteronomy 4:9

CONTENTS

LIST OF ABBREVIATIONS

AB	Anchor Bible
ABD	*Anchor Bible Dictionary*. Edited by David Noel Freedman. 6 vols. New York: Doubleday, 1992.
ANE	Ancient Near East
ANET	James B. Pritchard, ed. *Ancient Near Eastern Texts Relating to the Old Testament*. 3rd ed. Princeton: Princeton University Press, 1969.
AOTC	Apollos Old Testament Commentary
ASV	American Standard Version
BBR	*Bulletin for Biblical Research*
BBRSup	*Bulletin for Biblical Research, Supplements*
BCOT	Baker Commentary on the Old Testament
BIBBC	J. Scott Duvall and J. Daniel Hays, eds. *The Baker Illustrated Bible Background Commentary*. Grand Rapids: Baker, 2020.
BIBH	J. Daniel Hays and J. Scott Duvall, eds. *The Baker Illustrated Bible Handbook*. Grand Rapids: Baker, 2011.
BR	*Bible Review*
BSac	*Bibliotheca Sacra*
BZAW	Beihefte zur Zeitschrift für die alttestamentliche Wissenshaft
CSB	Christian Standard Bible
COS	William W. Hallo and K. Lawson Younger, eds. *The Context of Scripture*. 3 vols. Leiden: Brill, 1997–2003.
ECC	Eerdmans Critical Commentary

ESBT   Essential Studies in Biblical Theology
ESV   English Standard Version
FAT   Forshungen zum Alten Testament
ICC   International Critical Commentary
JETS   *Journal of the Evangelical Theological Society*
JBL   *Journal of Biblical Literature*
JSOT   *Journal for the Study of the Old Testament*
JSOTSS   Journal for the Study of the Old Testament Supplement Series
KJV   King James Version
NAC   New American Commentary
NASB   New American Standard Bible
NET   New English Translation
NIBC   New International Biblical Commentary
NICNT   New International Commentary on the New Testament
NICOT   New International Commentary on the Old Testament
NIDOTTE   Willem A. VanGemeren, ed. *New International Dictionary of Old Testament Theology and Exegesis*. 5 vols. Grand Rapids: Zondervan, 1997.
NIV   New International Version
NIVAC   NIV Application Commentary
NKJV   New King James Version
NLT   New Living Translation
NRSV   New Revised Standard Version
NRSVue   New Revised Standard Version updated edition
NSBT   New Studies in Biblical Theology
OTL   The Old Testament Library
SGBC   The Story of God Bible Commentary
SSBT   Short Studies in Biblical Theology
TDOT   G. Johannes Botterweck and Helmer Ringgren, eds. *Theological Dictionary of the Old Testament*. Translated by John T. Willis et al. 16 vols. Grand Rapids: Eerdmans, 1974–2018.
TOTC   Tyndale Old Testament Commentaries
TTCS   Teach the Text Commentary Series
VT   *Vetus Testamentum*
WBC   Word Biblical Commentary
ZAW   *Zeitschrift für die alttestamentliche Wissenschaft*
ZIBBC   John H. Walton, ed. *Zondervan Illustrated Bible Backgrounds Commentary*. 5 vols. Grand Rapids: Zondervan, 2009.

A NOTE TO PROFESSORS
FROM THE EDITORS

The textbooks in the Scripture Connections series feature somewhat shorter page counts than many traditional survey texts. Professors in traditional courses can use these textbooks to provide room in their courses for other targeted readings. Professors teaching courses in more concise formats can assign the entire textbook. In sum, the short page count is meant to offer maximal flexibility in course design.

Professors who adopt this book as a required text are welcome to access its supplemental professor's materials at no cost. Please go to bhacademic.com/requests.

Gary Edward Schnittjer, editor of Old Testament
Mark L. Strauss, editor of New Testament

INTRODUCTION TO THE PENTATEUCH (THE FIVE BOOKS OF MOSES)

This book of instruction must not depart from your mouth; you are to meditate on it day and night so that you may carefully observe everything written in it.

—JOSHUA 1:8

"Everything written about me in the Law of Moses, the Prophets, and the Psalms must be fulfilled."

—LUKE 24:44

The way that a story begins is usually important to the meaning of the story. This is certainly true for the Bible. Placed at the front of the Holy Scriptures as a foundational introduction to God's written revelation to us, the Pentateuch, those amazing first five books of the Bible, have inspired, taught, challenged, and led God's people in knowing him and understanding his word for over three thousand years. Welcome! We are going to engage in studying and grappling with a fascinating part of God's Word. My prayer for you is that you benefit greatly from this study, not only in your personal walk with the Lord, but also in the work to which God calls you— that this study will help you to know God better, to walk in obedience to his Word, and to proclaim and teach his Word with accuracy and power that the church might be strengthened and that all nations of the world might know Jesus Christ.

What Do We Call the First Five Books of the Bible?

The English word *Pentateuch* is a term commonly used by English-speaking Christians to refer to the first five books of the Bible: Genesis, Exodus, Leviticus, Numbers, and Deuteronomy. Many other languages around the world (e.g., French, Spanish, German) use a similar term. This word was derived from combining the two Greek words *pente*, which means "five," and *teuchos*, which means, "scroll, book, scroll case." Thus, the term *Pentateuch* refers to a five-scroll or five-book collection. Mark 12:26 implies that in the first-century-AD synagogue all five books were included in one scroll.

The term *Pentateuch* is never used in the Bible itself but was widely used by Greek and Latin Christian writers by the end of the second century AD. Some examples of early Christian writers who used the term *Pentateuch* include Tertullian (AD 155–220; *Adversus Marcionem* 1.10), Hippolytus (AD 170–235; Ref. 8.7); and Origen (AD 184–253; *Commentary on John* 5.4; *Commentary on Matthew* 11.10).

In Jewish tradition, however, the first five books of the Hebrew Bible are generally referred to as the *Torah*, a Hebrew word that means "teaching" or "instruction." When referring to the Hebrew Bible as a whole, Jews often use the acronym *Tanak*, which reflects the three major divisions of their Bible. The T represents *Torah* (the five books of Moses), the N represents *Nevi'im* (the Prophets, including the Former and Latter prophets), and the K stands for *Ketuvim* (the Writings).[1] Occasionally, Jews also use the term *Chumash* (or *Ḥumash*), which comes from the Hebrew word for "five," when referring to one or all of the first five books, especially when it is in a "book" (i.e., codex) form rather than a scroll form.

Some languages, such as the Scandinavian languages, refer to the first five books of the Bible with a term that means the "Books of Moses" and then refer to each of the books with number references (e.g., Genesis as the "first book of Moses"). The Japanese language uses two terms, one meaning "the five books of Moses" and the other meaning "the five books." Chinese primarily uses a term that means "the five

---

[1] Thus in the *Tanak*, the "Former Prophets" include Joshua, Judges, 1–2 Samuel, and 1–2 Kings; the "Latter Prophets" include Isaiah, Jeremiah, Ezekiel, and the Twelve (the Minor Prophets); and the "Writings" include Psalms, Proverbs, Job, Song of Songs, Ruth, Lamentations, Ecclesiastes, Esther, Daniel, Ezra, Nehemiah, and 1–2 Chronicles.

scriptures." A few other languages, such as Swahili (East Africa), use a term related to the Hebrew word *torah*.

Throughout the Old Testament itself, the Hebrew word *torah* is often used to refer to these first five books or to various parts of these books (e.g., Josh 1:7–8; 1 Kgs 2:3; 2 Kgs 10:31; Ps 119:1–174; Isa 1:10; Jer 9:13; Amos 2:4; Mal 4:4). This term, carrying the nuance of teaching or instruction is much more descriptive of the actual content of the first five books than is the term *Pentateuch*. Throughout the Old Testament we also frequently find references to the "*torah* of Moses," often translated in English Bibles as the "law of Moses," although the concept of teaching or instruction perhaps captures more of the nuanced meaning than the word *law*. Sometimes the word for "scroll" is used, often translated into English as "book" when referencing either one of the specific books (e.g., Deuteronomy) or to the entire collection. Keep in mind that, speaking physically, in the early days these ancient manuscripts were scrolls; bound "books" (codices) did not start appearing until the second century AD. Examples of Old Testament references to all or part of the first five books of the Bible include Josh 1:7–8 ("Be careful to obey all the law my servant Moses gave you. . . . Keep this Book of the Law always on your lips," NIV); 8:31–32 ("what is written in the Book of the Law of Moses. . . . Joshua wrote on stones a copy of the law of Moses," NIV); 22:5 ("the law that Moses the servant of the Lord gave you," NIV); 1 Kgs 2:3 ("as written in the Law of Moses," NIV); 2 Kgs 14:6 ("what is written in the Book of the Law of Moses," NIV); 21:8 ("keep the whole Law that my servant Moses gave them," NIV); Ezra 6:18 ("according to what is written in the Book of Moses," NIV); 7:6 ("Ezra . . . was a teacher well versed in the Law of Moses, which the Lord, the God of Israel, had given," NIV); Dan 9:11–13 ("written in the Law of Moses," NIV); and Mal 4:4 ("Remember the law of my servant Moses," NIV). Thus we see that the interrelated terms that repeat throughout the Old Testament in reference to this part of Scripture are "law" (i.e., *torah*, instruction), "Moses," and "book" (i.e., scroll or scrolls).

References to this material in the New Testament are similar: Matt 7:12; 22:40 ("the Law and the Prophets," NIV); 11:13 ("the Prophets and the Law," NIV); Mark 10:5 ("Moses wrote you this law," NIV); 12:26 ("the Book of Moses," NIV); Luke 2:22–23 ("the purification rites required by the Law of Moses . . . as it is written in the Law of the Lord," NIV); 10:26 ("What is written in the Law?," NIV); 16:16 ("the Law and the Prophets," NIV); 24:27 ("Beginning with Moses and all the Prophets," NIV); 24:44 ("the Law of Moses, the Prophets and the Psalms," NIV); John 1:17 ("For the law was given through Moses," NIV); 5:46 ("If you believed Moses, you would believe me, for he wrote about me," NIV); 7:19 ("Has not Moses given you the law?," NIV); Acts 13:15 ("After reading from the Law and the Prophets," NIV);

13:39 ("a justification you were not able to obtain under the law of Moses," NIV); Rom 10:5 ("Moses writes this about the righteousness that is by the law," NIV); 1 Cor 9:9 ("For it is written in the Law of Moses," NIV); and Gal 3:10 ("everything written in the Book of the Law," NIV).

In Acts and throughout the letters of Paul the term *law* (Greek, *nomos*) is used dozens of times referring primarily to the legal material in Exodus, Leviticus, and Deuteronomy. But note that in 1 Cor 14:21 Paul states, "In the Law, it is written" and then quotes from Isaiah 28, indicating the term *law* is fairly fluid in Paul's writings and can be used to refer to the Old Testament Scriptures in general.

In this book we will primarily use the term *Pentateuch* in reference to Genesis, Exodus, Leviticus, Numbers, and Deuteronomy, while recognizing that designations like "the Books of Moses" or "the Torah" are equally valid terms to use.

Genre

The Pentateuch is probably best described not so much as being composed of five books as being one book with five interrelated sections. Scattered across the pages of the Pentateuch, however, is quite a range of different genres, or types, of literature. Thus, we find narratives with sequential time-action, plot, characters, and dialogues; travel narratives; poems and songs; blessings and prayers; prophecies; a wide range of laws and legal material; census results (name lists); and directions for how to construct the tabernacle and how to worship God. Yet stretching across the Pentateuch from Genesis to Deuteronomy is a coherent and generally chronological narrative story. All these various genres or literary types are incorporated or embedded into the overarching master narrative. So, while a lot of laws and legal material appear in the Pentateuch, this material is not presented in timeless, nonhistorical isolation, but rather it is presented as part of the story, embedded into the narrative at particular points in that narrative.

One of the fascinating aspects of the Pentateuch is that God himself shows up repeatedly in the story. Indeed, although Moses plays a very important role, God is the actual central character.

The Basic Storyline of the Pentateuch

Genesis 1–11

In the beginning God creates the world and all that is in it, including people. That establishes right from the start who he is—the Creator, and who we are—the created beings. God creates a wonderful garden for his created people to live in, who are blessed especially by his presence there in the garden. Things are very good. However, we next read four stories of foolish human disobedience. Adam and Eve eat the forbidden fruit and are kicked out of the garden, away from the presence of God and the tree of life. Then Cain kills his brother Abel. Next, the people become so bad that God has to destroy the world with a flood (reversing the creation) and, in essence, start over. Then the next story shows people once again rebelling against God, building a tower to create a name for themselves, and thus they are scattered by God. These four stories illustrate that the human race is not off to a good start. This underscores the problem of humanity—sin and rebellion that separates them from God and results in death.

Genesis 12–50

The rest of the Bible, from Genesis 22 to Revelation 22, is about how God works to restore the relationship. Indeed, at the end of the story, we see God's people back in a garden, enjoying the blessings of God's presence once again (Revelation 22). This story of redemption, of God working to bring people back into relationship with him (and especially into the blessings that result from his close presence), begins in earnest with Abraham in Genesis 12. God calls Abraham and makes a covenant with him, promising him a land, numerous descendants, and blessing (God even states that he would bless those who bless you [family of Abraham] and curse those who curse you). He then adds that the whole world would be blessed through Abraham. God also promises to be with Abraham, reestablishing, in part, the relationship lost in Genesis 2–3. Abraham has a son named Isaac; then Isaac has a son named Jacob. The promises God made to Abraham are repeated to each of these descendants of Abraham. Jacob has twelve sons, one of which is Joseph. These become the tribes of Israel. Joseph's brothers sell him into slavery and he is taken to Egypt, where under God's sovereign guidance he rises to power. A famine occurs, and Jacob and his sons eventually also travel to Egypt to escape the famine. Joseph graciously forgives his brothers and cares for them. As the book of Genesis ends, the family is in Egypt.

Exodus 1–2

The story opens with the descendants of Abraham still in Egypt, thus connecting the beginning of Exodus to the ending of Genesis. Time has passed, and God has been working to fulfill his promises to Abraham. In fact, the fulfillment of God's promise to Abraham regarding numerous descendants creates the crisis in the opening of Exodus. Pharaoh tries to stop the increase in Abraham's descendants, not only by overworking them, but even to the point of throwing the baby Hebrew boys into the Nile River. The people cry out in their anguish and God hears them, acknowledging his covenant with Abraham, particularly his promise "I will bless those who bless you and curse those who curse you." Pharaoh and the Egyptians will experience the negative consequences for their terrible actions (cursing Israel rather than blessing them), as well as for their failure to acknowledge God.

Exodus 2–24

God raises up Moses, calling him through a powerful, personal encounter of divine presence (at the burning bush), and sends him back to Egypt to deliver the people. Pharaoh defiantly refuses to acknowledge Yahweh, the God of Israel. Therefore, through the plagues and the destruction of Pharaoh's army in the Red Sea, God crushes Egypt while delivering Israel. This deliverance, however, is not just deliverance and freedom from Egypt, but, even more significantly, a deliverance that brings the Israelites into a special relationship with the very presence of God. Indeed, the exodus event will become the paradigmatic story of deliverance/salvation in the Old Testament. God brings the Israelites to Mount Sinai, where he comes crashing down dramatically from heaven to enter into a close, relational, covenant agreement with them, summarized by three central promises: (1) I will be your God, (2) you will be my people, and (3) I will dwell in your midst.

Exodus 25–40

If God is going to dwell in their midst, then he needs a place to stay. Most of Exodus 25–40, a huge portion of the book of Exodus, consists of instructions from God on how to build the tabernacle (the dwelling place of God), followed by Moses's faithful obedience in actually constructing the tabernacle. There is an ominous interruption in Exodus 32–34 (the golden calf incident), foreshadowing future disobedience. But climactically, at the end of Exodus, after Moses and the Israelites have obediently constructed the tabernacle, God's glory fills the tabernacle. That is, he takes up residence in the tabernacle, fulfilling the covenant promise to "dwell in your midst," a huge step toward the recovery of the divine presence lost in the garden back in Genesis 3.

Leviticus

Leviticus connects seamlessly to Exodus. Now that the holy, awesome God who has created the heavens and earth has come down to dwell in the tabernacle, residing physically right in the midst of his people, *everything in their life will change.* This is what Leviticus is about. How can sinful people live with the holy, awesome God dwelling right there among them? How can they deal with their sin that is utterly incompatible with the holiness of his presence? How can they worship him? Leviticus covers these issues. Now that the holy God dwells right there among the Israelites, their lives will be dramatically different, now to be lived in light of his holy presence, always conscious of this holy presence of God and his blessings, as well as the demands on their life that this presence brings.

Numbers 1–14

As Numbers opens, the Israelites are still at Mount Sinai. So, the narrative story picks back up from the end of Exodus. God has come down to live in the tabernacle and to dwell in their midst. He has given them directions for how to live with his holy presence among them (Leviticus). Now it is time to pack up and head for the land that God promised to Abraham, with God traveling with them. Yet after they arrive at the Promised Land, the unthinkable happens. The people of Israel refuse to enter the land! This is highly ironic, because settling in the Promised Land was one of God's central goals and purposes of the exodus. God not only wanted to deliver them from the Egyptians and then to enter into covenant relationship with them at Mount Sinai, but then he wanted to move them into the Promised Land, where they would live under this relational covenant with his presence residing in their midst, and where they would find blessing. The faithless people say that they cannot conquer the land; in fact, they foolishly say that they wished they had died in the wilderness. Fine, God says. Go die in the wilderness.

Numbers 15–36

The disobedient Israelites spend the next forty years wandering in the wilderness (in God's grace they are still protected by him), until the entire generation of disobedient people dies off. God then takes the next generation of Israelites and brings them back to the edge of the Promised Land to try it again.

Deuteronomy 1–34

Now that the Israelites are back near the edge of the Promised Land and about to enter, God gives them the material recorded in the book of Deuteronomy. He revisits their history together, and then he restates the covenant terms that he first gave them in Exodus at Mount Sinai. Deuteronomy presents the terms by which Israel could live and be blessed in the Promised Land with the holy, awesome God dwelling in their midst. God explains the wonderful blessings they will receive if they are obedient and faithful to him, along with a stark description of the curses they will experience if they turn to other gods in disobedience. The people agree to the terms, in essence renewing their pledge to the covenant. Joshua is appointed as the new leader, and Moses dies. They are now ready to enter the Promised Land, an event described in the following book, Joshua.

The question echoing from Deuteronomy across the entire rest of the Old Testament is this: Will the Israelites be faithful to God and keep the terms of Deuteronomy? This question drives the story to the end of 2 Kings and throughout the Prophets. The sad answer, of course, is no, they won't stay faithful or be obedient. Thus, at the end of 1–2 Kings, they are kicked out of the Promised Land, just as Adam and Eve were kicked out of the garden, away from the life-giving presence of God. This underscored the need for a new covenant, one based on grace, foreshadowed and prophesied dramatically throughout the rest of the Scriptures, and fulfilled climactically in Jesus Christ.

Issues of Authorship: Who Wrote the Books of Moses?

As already indicated, throughout both the Old Testament and the New Testament, Moses is closely associated with the first five books of the Old Testament. These books are not only frequently called the "books of Moses," but both the Old Testament and the New Testament claim that God gave the Law (Hebrew, *torah*; Greek, *nomos*) through his servant Moses. This is stressed in the biblical witness. Several texts also mention the act of writing, which in the biblical narrative will also become a very important feature of this revelation from God.

Let's look at what the books of the Pentateuch themselves say about their literary composition. The first mention of writing down an episode or portion of the Pentateuch is found in Exod 17:14. God has just given the Israelites a victory over the Amalekites, and he tells Moses, "Write this down on a scroll as a reminder and recite it to Joshua."

More central to the production of the book of Exodus, however, are the events that take place at Mount Sinai. After God brings the Israelites out of Egypt, he takes them to Mount Sinai, where he descends onto the mountaintop with fire and smoke and engages in conversation with Moses. Then, with Moses as the mediator, God enters into a covenant agreement with the Israelites. After God gives Moses the basic aspects of the covenant (Exodus 20–23), Moses, as mediator, declares the terms of the covenant to the people. After they accept the covenant terms (Exod 24:3), the text declares, "And Moses wrote down all the words of the Lord" (24:4). In Exod 24:7, this document, probably written on a papyrus scroll, is called the "covenant scroll" (NIV, "Book of the Covenant"). God himself then writes down the Ten Commandments on stone tablets (Exod 24:12; Deut 9:10). Later, upon seeing Israel worshipping the golden calf, Moses breaks the original stone tablets (Exod 32:19; Deut 9:17), but then God himself writes them down again (Exod 34:28 [the pronoun "he" in the second half of 34:28 undoubtedly refers to God and not Moses]; Deut 10:2–4). Then in Exod 34:27 God tells Moses, "Write down these words, for I have made a covenant with you and with Israel based on these words." The phrase "these words" here probably does not refer only to the Ten Commandments but to all of the revelation Moses has just recently received, especially in regard to the construction of the tabernacle (Exodus 25–31). The written Ten Commandments are then placed in the ark of the covenant, which is in turn located in the holy of holies in the tabernacle, and God himself comes down to live in the tabernacle as part of the covenant relationship.

It is important to note the significant and foundational role that the written word of God plays in this covenant relationship, both the words Moses writes based on what God tells him and shows him, and the words God himself writes. Thus, before the Israelites even leave Mount Sinai, we have a clear indication that a significant portion of Exodus, roughly Exodus 20–31 at least, is already completed. We can speculate and envision that this was the beginning of the written Pentateuch and that over the next forty years Moses adds to and expands this material to produce the Pentateuch (or, at least, *most* of the Pentateuch).[2]

Numerous texts describe the ongoing interaction between God in the tent of meeting and Moses (e.g., Exod 33:11; Lev 1:1; Num 7:89). The typical pattern is that God reveals material to Moses, and then Moses transmits (and probably also records) this material to the Israelites immediately afterward.

---

[2] Stephen Dempster, "The Production and Shaping of the Old Testament Canon," *BIBH*, 1010–11.

In Num 1:1–2 and 26:1–2 God instructs Moses and Aaron (Eleazar in 26:1–2) to take a census of all males over the age of twenty. The strong implication is that the list of names and the numbers of people listed right after that in Numbers 1 and 26 reflect a written record of that census. Also, in Num 33:2, just before the speeches Moses delivers in the book of Deuteronomy, God instructs Moses to write down the stages of the long trip from Egypt to the plains of Moab (33:3–49).

In Deut 4:44–45, the large section that follows (probably at least 4:44–28:68, perhaps even the entire book of Deuteronomy) is introduced like this: "This is the law (*torah*) Moses gave the Israelites. These are the decrees, statutes, and ordinances Moses proclaimed to them after they came out of Egypt." At the end of Deuteronomy, just before Moses's death, there are several more important references about Moses's involvement in writing parts of the *torah* (law) (31:9, 19). Deuteronomy 31:24–26 states, "When Moses had finished writing down on a scroll every single word of this law [*torah*], he commanded the Levites who carried the ark of the LORD's covenant, 'Take this book of the law [*torah*] and place it beside the ark of the covenant.'" Scholars are divided over whether this refers to just a small part of Deuteronomy (e.g., the song of 32:1–43; cf. 31:19), most of Deuteronomy (all except Deuteronomy 34), or most or all of the Pentateuch. At any rate, it is primarily from this text that the Jewish tradition, later inherited by Christianity, of ascribing Moses as the author of the Pentateuch arose.

As the biblical story moves from Deuteronomy to the book of Joshua, it is clear that Joshua has an authoritative, written document called "the book of instruction [*torah*]" that came from God via Moses to the people of Israel (Josh 1:7–8). An important observation in the transition from Moses to Joshua is that while Joshua replaces Moses as the military leader of Israel, he does not replace Moses as the great mediator between God and the people. In this role, Moses is replaced by the written Word of God, the *Torah* (the Pentateuch).

While the Bible clearly presents the material in the Pentateuch as being an authoritative revelation from God mediated to Israel through Moses, note that the books of the Pentateuch do not claim or insist that Moses authored *all* the material in the Pentateuch. In fact, there are several indications that some later, minor additions and updates were possibly added. For example, the death of Moses is described in Deuteronomy 34. While it certainly is possible for God to have given Moses the details of his own death in advance, it is highly unlikely. It is much more likely that someone else wrote the account of the death of Moses.

There are also occasional comments in the text that seem to indicate some reflection being made at a time after the time of Moses. For example, Deut 34:10 states, "No prophet has arisen again in Israel like Moses." Likewise, while Deut 34:6 records the burial of Moses, it also states, "And no one *to this day* knows where his grave is" (emphasis added). Genesis 36:31 also seems to indicate a later time of reflection: "These are the kings who reigned in the land of Edom before any king reigned over the Israelites." Similarly, Deut 2:12 states "the descendants of Esau drove them out, destroying them completely and settling in their place, just as Israel did in the land of its possession the LORD gave them," implying a reflection from after the conquest of the land.

This later reflection shows up in other texts as well. Sometimes these seem to involve name changes or updates. Deuteronomy 3:13–14, for example, explains that Jair, a descendant of Manasseh, captured the region of Bashan, and that "he called Bashan by its own name, Jair's Villages [the settlements of Jair], *as it is today*" (emphasis added). Likewise, Deut 29:28 states, "The LORD uprooted them from their land in his anger, rage, and intense wrath, and threw them into another land *where they are today*" (emphasis added). The comment "where they are today" appears to represent a later reflection, perhaps an editorial updating. This same thing also occurs in Genesis (26:33; 32:32; 47:26) as well as elsewhere in Deuteronomy (2:22; 10:8).[3]

Another interesting text suggesting that some editing occurred later than the events reported is Gen 14:14. Abraham's nephew Lot had been captured. In this passage, Abraham gathered his trained men and "went in pursuit *as far as Dan*" (emphasis added). In Moses's day, however, this region was not yet called Dan. The area only becomes known as Dan after the conquest, well after the time of Moses. Previously, it was known as Laish (see Judges 18). Although we cannot be certain, in all probability, Moses referred to the place as Laish, and a later editor (Ezra?) realized that no one knew where Laish was anymore and updated the place to Dan. Similar updates for the location of Dan would have occurred in Deut 33:22 and 34:1.[4]

Also keep in mind that languages change and evolve over the centuries. Consider, for example, the opening lines of Chaucer's *Canterbury Tales* (AD 1387–1400); notice how different the English language was back then from what we know today.

> Whan that Aprill with his shoures soote
> The droghte of March hath perced to the roote,
> And bathed every veyne in swich licuor
> Of which vertu engendered is the flour.[5]

---

[3] Michael A. Grisanti, "Inspiration, Inerrancy, and the OT Canon: The Place of Textual Updating in an Inerrant View of Scripture," *JETS* 44, no. 4 (2001): 585.

[4] Grisanti, 584.

[5] Geoffrey Chaucer, *Canterbury Tales; Part I, General Prologue*, in *The Complete Poetry and Prose of Geoffrey Chaucer*, 2nd ed., ed. John H. Fisher (New York: Holt, Rinehart and Winston, 1989), 9.

The Hebrew language likewise underwent numerous changes in grammar, spelling, and the shapes of the letters from the time Moses first wrote the Pentateuch until the earliest Hebrew manuscripts we have now (the Dead Sea Scrolls). So, in all probability, while the content and meaning of the Pentateuch stayed the same, the Hebrew language, which conveyed that meaning, underwent numerous updates and modifications in spelling, grammar, the shapes of letters, and perhaps some place names.

In conclusion, the Bible itself attributes (or strongly implies attribution) the writing of most (practically all) of the Pentateuch to Moses. Yet someone else probably writes the last chapter of Deuteronomy, describing the death of Moses. Likewise, some minor updating of spelling, grammar, letter shapes, and place names probably occurred through the centuries. This finished product in whole was referred to in the New Testament as the "law of Moses" and was treated as authoritative.[6] This will be the viewpoint reflected in this textbook and is the view held by many evangelical scholars.[7]

Outside of evangelicalism is a range of ever-evolving, often disparate views on the composition of the Pentateuch, united loosely by the common rejection of Mosaic authorship and the dating of the composition well after the time of Moses. For much of the nineteenth and twentieth centuries, Old Testament scholarship outside of evangelicalism was dominated by what has been called the *Documentary Hypothesis* or variations of this approach. The premise of this approach is the belief that there were various sources—that is, separate written documents by separate authors or schools of authors at different times (although all of whom were much later in Israel's history than Moses) that lie behind the actual books of the Pentateuch. For evidence of these different sources, these advocates noted the different Hebrew names used for God (Yahweh or Elohim), duplicate stories, a supposed lack of chronology, and a supposed contradiction of content. The advocates of this documentary approach then tried to identify the original sources and to determine how these sources were created and how they were combined into more complex units. They based this primarily

---

[6] The New Testament writers attribute references and citations from all five books of the Pentateuch as being written by Moses or part of the "law of Moses." For examples, note the following New Testament texts with the pentateuchal reference in parentheses: Matt 22:40 (Lev 19:18; Deut 6:5); Mark 10:4 (Deut 24:1–4); Mark 10:5 (Gen 1:27); Mark 12:19 (Deut 25:5); Mark 12:26 (Exod 3:1–17); Luke 2:22–24 (Exod 13:2–15; Lev 12:2–8; Num 3:13); Luke 10:26–28 (Lev 19:18; Deut 6:5); Rom 10:5 (Lev 18:5); and 1 Cor 9:9 (Deut 25:4).

[7] Duane Garrett, *Rethinking Genesis: The Sources and Authorship of the First Book of the Pentateuch* (Grand Rapids: Baker, 1991); Andrew E. Steinmann, *Genesis*, TOTC (Downers Grove, IL: InterVarsity, 2019), 2–15.

on their view of the changing historical context of ancient Israel, presupposing that the religious understanding of Israel was constantly evolving. A widely held form of the Documentary Hypothesis, often called the JEPD Theory, argued that four main sources could be identified: a "J" source (which used the name *Yahweh* for God; in German, Yahweh was spelled *Jahweh*); an "E" source (which used the name *Elohim* for God); a "P" source (primarily comprised of priestly related material); and a "D" source (composed primarily of Deuteronomy). J and E were supposedly composed during the early to mid-monarchy period (tenth to ninth centuries BC). D was supposedly composed during the reform of Josiah near the end of the monarchy (late seventh century BC), and P was supposedly composed in the postexilic period (sixth to fifth centuries BC).[8]

Toward the end of the twentieth century, although still very influential, the Documentary Hypothesis was challenged on numerous fronts by a wide range of scholars, including many scholars outside of evangelicalism, who pointed out a variety of weaknesses of this approach. These critics noted that this approach did not take into account other literature of the ANE (no other literature in the ANE can be demonstrated to have come together like this) nor had it dealt seriously with the role of oral tradition. In addition, those advocating the Documentary Hypothesis had assumed a certain "progressive" development of religious ideas based on modern perceptions that could not be verified without circular reasoning. Furthermore, it assumed that repetitions and doublets reflected separate sources rather than ancient literary practices that incorporated these features as aesthetic and poetic elements. Finally, it assumed that the later scribes who put the sources together were rather wooden and clumsy, without any creativity or adaptation to new situations.[9]

Thus, at the end of the twentieth century and into the first two decades of the twenty-first century, numerous nonevangelical Old Testament scholars around the world rejected many of the specific conclusions of the Documentary Hypothesis as it had been taught for most of the twentieth century. They did not, however, turn back

---

[8] Thomas B. Dozeman, *The Pentateuch: Introducing the Torah* (Minneapolis: Fortress, 2017), 62–73.

[9] Dozeman, *The Pentateuch*, 74–75, 144–47. For a convincing critique of the methodology that dominated historical-critical approaches in the nineteenth and twentieth centuries that produced the Documentary Hypothesis, see Joshua A. Berman, *Inconsistency in the Torah: Ancient Literary Convention and the Limits of Source Criticism* (New York: Oxford University Press, 2017). Likewise critiquing the old historical-critical approaches underlying the Documentary Hypothesis, as well as exploring some possible ways forward, is L. S. Baker Jr., Kenneth Bergland, Felipe A. Masotti, and A. Rahel Wells, eds., *Exploring the Composition of the Pentateuch*, BBRSup 27 (University Park, PA: Eisenbrauns, 2020).

to Mosaic authorship, still advocated by most evangelical Old Testament scholars. Numerous new theories and variations regarding how the Pentateuch was composed were proposed and debated, without any clear consensus being formed.[10] This has continued to the present. Although there is no consensus, and a diverse range of often disparate approaches and conclusions exists, some general features that characterize the trends in pentateuchal composition theories today are: (1) more concern with the present form of the text and less concern with oral history (which focused on an assumed lengthy oral stage of transmission, before the text was written down), form criticism (which tried to identify composition chronology by determining a chronological development of literary form), tradition history (which assumed that biblical texts were formed and shaped over numerous generations of oral and written transmission, often within different contexts), or history of religious ideas (which assumed that religious thought evolved from simple to complex and sought to track this development throughout the region and use it to date biblical texts); (2) a much greater attribution of theological shaping and final literary shaping to later redactors (scribes who combined texts while editing and revising them); and (3) a tendency to push more and more composition to later periods, especially the postexilic period.[11]

Some evangelical Old Testament scholars maintain a middle position, positing that the biblical claim of Mosaic authorship for the "Book of the Law" most likely only refers to Deuteronomy, or a large portion of Deuteronomy. The rest of the Pentateuch, they suggest, only existed in "traditions," some written and some oral, until the postexilic period, when these traditions were redacted together into the Pentateuch as we know it today. Often these writers still advocate for the divine, inspired authority of the books of the Pentateuch, but they see postexilic redactors (especially Ezra) as playing an important role in composing or redacting the inspired text of the Pentateuch.[12]

Many evangelical Old Testament scholars, however, along with some conservative Jewish scholars, have continued to take seriously the biblical claim of Mosaic authorship for the "Books of Moses." They have argued that the different names for God do

---

[10] See the various regional schools of thought—North American, Israeli, European—in Thomas B. Dozeman, Konrad Schmid, and Baruch J. Schwartz, *The Pentateuch: International Perspectives on Current Research*, FAT 78 (Tübingen: Mohr Siebeck, 2011).

[11] For a good, thorough discussion of nonevangelical pentateuchal compositional theories over the last 200 years, see Dozeman, *The Pentateuch*, 33–199.

[12] See, for example, T. D. Alexander, "Authorship of the Pentateuch," in *Dictionary of the Old Testament: Pentateuch*, ed. T. Desmond Alexander and David W. Baker (Downers Grove, IL: InterVarsity Press, 2003), 61–72.

not reflect different underlying literary sources but rather reflect different theological nuances in God's relationship with his people. They have also posited that the theological and narrative story across the Pentateuch is not only coherent but that it serves as a clear and powerful introduction to the rest of the Old Testament. They have recognized that repetition and duplication are common artistic features in the literature of the ANE, used for rhetorical or artistic effect (e.g., chiasm or bracketing[13]). They have pointed out that the complex priestly issues discussed in the Pentateuch were not late (i.e., late first-millennium-BC ideas) but were, in fact, common in the second millennium BC. They have also noted that the literary form of Deuteronomy has numerous parallels with Hittite treaties that date to the mid-second millennium. Some of them recognize the *possibility* that Moses used earlier sources (perhaps portions of Genesis were written down before Moses), as well as the likelihood of some later very minor editorial updating.[14]

Yet always keep in mind that at the heart of the evangelical approach to the composition of the Pentateuch is the belief that God himself is the ultimate primary author who inspired Moses, incorporating the skills, experiences, and education of Moses to produce the first five books of his written revelation to people that we know as the Bible.

The Date of Composition for the Pentateuch

If, along with many evangelical Old Testament scholars, we accept Moses as the primary human author of the Pentateuch, the date of composition is tied to the life and times of Moses. That is, various parts of the Pentateuch would have been written during the initial months of the exodus event, during the forty years of wilderness wandering, or immediately before entering the Promised Land. The date of Moses and thus for the composition of the Pentateuch, therefore, is tied to the date for the exodus event. While there is no agreement on the dating of the exodus event (see the discussion in chapter 2, "Exodus"), the two primary options place the date at either

---

[13] Chiasm is a literary device that uses parallel comparisons for lines of text or for story events but in inverse order. That is, if there are six lines of texts, then line one parallels line 6, line 2 parallels line 5, and line 3 parallels line 4.

[14] For good discussions on the evangelical view that recognizes Mosaic authorship for much of the Pentateuch, see Tremper Longman III and Raymond B. Dillard, *An Introduction to the Old Testament*, 2nd ed. (Grand Rapids: Zondervan, 2006), 40–51; Bill T. Arnold and Bryan Beyer, *Encountering the Old Testament*, 3rd ed. (Grand Rapids: Baker, 2015), 43–49; and Peter T. Vogt, *Interpreting the Pentateuch* (Grand Rapids: Kregel, 2009), 130–36.

1446 BC or 1270 to 1260 BC. If the exodus started at one of these two dates, the composition of the Pentateuch occurred during the forty years immediately following the exodus event. Thus, the composition of the Pentateuch took place during between 1446 and 1406 BC or 1270/1260 and 1230/1220 BC.

ANCIENT CONNECTIONS SIDEBAR I.1: MOSES, THE ALPHABET, AND WRITING IN ANCIENT EGYPT

Exodus 2:10 implies that Moses grew up in the extended royal household of the pharaoh. The household of the various pharaohs during this time could be quite large (e.g., Ramesses II [sometimes spelled Ramses or Rameses] had over 100 sons, as well as many daughters). Although there is disagreement over the date for Moses, both of the viable proposed options fall in the New Kingdom Period of Egyptian history (1550–1069 BC). Literary records from Egypt during this era indicate that while overall national literacy was low, the sons of the wealthier families, especially those of the pharaoh and the royal family, were educated in how to read and write. In addition, the large Egyptian governmental, military, and religious bureaucracy employed a large number of scribes educated in how to read and write.[15] Raised as the son of an Egyptian daughter of Pharaoh, it is highly probable that Moses was educated in one of the better schools in Egypt, probably the famous Royal Nursery, part of the royal court and harem that educated Egyptian royal youths as well as children of conquered kings and nobles.[16]

The New Kingdom period in Egypt produced a massive amount of literary documents, many of which have survived. Largely written on papyri, these include government records, military campaign accounts, national treaties, prayers, praises to the gods and to the pharaohs, other religious texts (especially the famous Book of the Dead describing death and the afterlife), love songs,

---

[15] On scribes and education in New Kingdom Egypt, see Edward R. Wente, "The Scribes of Ancient Egypt," in *Civilizations of the Ancient Near East*, vol. 4, ed. Jack M. Sasson (Peabody, MA: Hendrickson, 1995), 2214–17; and James P. Allen, "Language, Scripts, and Literacy," in *A Companion to Ancient Egypt*, ed. Alan B. Lloyd (Chichester, UK: Wiley Blackwell, 2014), 661–62.

[16] On the Royal Nursery see Silke Roth, "Harem," in *UCLA Encyclopedia of Egyptology*, ed. Elizabeth Frood and Willeke Wendrich (Los Angeles: UCLA, 2012), 6–7, http://digital2 .library.ucla.edu/viewItem.do?ark=21198/zz002bqmpp; and Betsy M. Bryan, *The Reign of Thutmose IV* (Baltimore: Johns Hopkins University Press, 1991), 261.

narrative stories, instruction guides, and personal letters.[17] It was a rich literary milieu in which to be educated.

Unlike during the earlier Middle Kingdom period, Egypt during the New Kingdom period was involved extensively in international affairs, both through military campaigns to the north (especially Syria-Palestine) and through international trade. This brought into the court of the pharaohs at this time not only tribute from abroad, but also international influences, literature, and ideas.[18] Likewise, since Egypt now played a large role as a significant international geopolitical power, many scribes were also trained to read and write in foreign languages and scripts.[19] Thus we can speculate with high probability that in his royal Egyptian education, Moses was taught, or at least exposed to, the three main writing systems of the ANE at that time. He would certainly have learned Egyptian hieroglyphics. But he was also probably taught Mesopotamian cuneiform, as well as the new, still-developing alphabetic system that is now called Canaanite Linear script, the forerunner of the Phoenician alphabet. We can probably credit Moses with putting the Hebrew language (still relatively new as a distinct language) into writing, and we can thank him for using the alphabetic system that had been developing in Syria-Palestine (Canaan) instead of Egyptian hieroglyphics, which is extremely complex and difficult to learn.

Indeed, the introduction of the alphabetic style of writing was a huge technological revolution in world history. A scribe writing with Egyptian hieroglyphics would be required to know over 700 signs and symbols. Similarly, one working with Babylonian cuneiform had to know around 300 signs and symbols.[20] Learning to read and write in these writing systems took years and years to learn, and thus typically only a small, highly educated, scribal class was able to do this. Writing with an alphabet, however, with its 22-plus signs, was easy to learn, and thus reading and writing became much more widespread, available to a much larger population.

---

[17] See, for example, the collections of Egyptian literature in William Kelly Simpson, ed., *The Literature of Ancient Egypt: An Anthology of Stories, Instructions, Stelae, Autobiographies, and Poetry*, 3rd ed. (New Haven, CT: Yale University Press, 2003); and William W. Hallo and K. Lawson Younger, *The Contexts of Scripture*, 3 vols. (Leiden: Brill, 1997–2003).

[18] Ian Shaw and Paul Nicholson, *The Dictionary of Ancient Egypt* (London: The British Museum, 1995), 202.

[19] Wente, "Scribes," 2214–17.

[20] A. R. Millard, "Writing," in *Dictionary of the Old Testament: Pentateuch*, 904.

The timing of this was no accident. God raised up Moses, delivered his people, and entered into a formal, written covenant relationship with Israel just as the alphabetic writing system developed. Stephen Dempster writes, "The beginnings of the Bible take place, then, in the midst of an epistemological and social revolution as well as a religious one—the God of the universe begins to make himself known in texts!"[21] This allowed for a certain degree of democratization in knowing God directly through written texts, such that God could state, "Write them [these commandments] on the doorframes of your houses and on your gates" (Deut 6:9).

The Primary Names for God in the Pentateuch

The Hebrew of the Pentateuch uses two major names for God. The first name, Elohim, along with closely related forms, occurs 812 times in the Pentateuch, out of 2,570 times total in the entire Hebrew Bible. Elohim is a generic term, like our English word *god*. It can refer to the all-powerful and true God who created the heavens and the earth (Gen 1:1) as well as to refer to the false gods of the nations (Exod 22:20). Grammatically, the term *Elohim* is plural (*El* and *Eloah* are the singular forms). When in this plural form and used of the false gods of the nations, it typically occurs with plural verb forms and plural pronoun referents. When used for the God of Israel, however, even though Elohim is itself a plural form, it is used with singular verb forms and singular pronoun references. In these cases the reference is clearly to one God. The plural form (Elohim) probably reflects a plural of majesty or intensification. Our English Bible translations translate Elohim regularly as "God" when referring to the God of Israel (with singular verbs) and as "gods" when referencing the pagan gods.

The other major name for God—indeed, the most frequent name for God in the Pentateuch (and in the Old Testament)—is Yahweh. This name occurs more than 1,700 times in the Pentateuch and 6,800 total in the Hebrew Bible. This term functions as God's personal name, and it carries strong connotations of God's personal, covenant relationship brought about by his close presence. The term *Yahweh* is a derivative of the verb "to be" and is closely related to God's self-description as "I AM WHO I AM" (Exod 3:14). Our English Bibles typically translate this word as "Lord," or "the Lord" using an initial cap and then small caps for the remaining three

---

[21] Dempster, "Production and Shaping," 1008.

letters, thus distinguishing it from the word *Lord*, which usually translates a Hebrew word that means "master, lord."

These two names often occur together in the sense that Yahweh (his personal name) is Israel's Elohim (God). For example, in the great *Shema* (*shema* is the Hebrew imperative for "hear!") declaration of Deut 6:4–5, God declares, "Hear, O Israel: Yahweh our Elohim, Yahweh is one. Love Yahweh your Elohim with all your heart and with all your soul and with all your strength" (author's translation).

Throughout the Pentateuch both names for God are used frequently. In Genesis, however, there is a slight preference for Elohim (213 occurrences of Elohim versus 161 occurrences of Yahweh). In the rest of the Pentateuch (Exodus through Deuteronomy), on the other hand, there is a strong preference for Yahweh (1,641 occurrences of Yahweh versus 584 occurrences of Elohim). Also keep in mind that often the two names are used together (Yahweh, your Elohim). Throughout the rest of this book, we will refer to our true, Christian God as "God" when discussing biblical, Gospel, and life connections, as well as throughout the chapter on Genesis (reflecting the majority usage of Elohim). In Exodus, Leviticus, Numbers, and Deuteronomy, however, when discussing the text in the Interpretive Overview sections, we will use the term *Yahweh* to refer to God, in keeping with the majority usage in those books.

Biblical Connections

When the Old Testament was translated into Greek (the Septuagint), the translators used the Greek generic word for god (*theos*) to translate the Hebrew word *Elohim*. However, they translated the Hebrew word *Yahweh* with the Greek word *kyrios*, which means "master" or "lord." This leads to some interesting interpretive and translation questions in the New Testament. When the New Testament writers, who are often quoting from the Septuagint, refer to Jesus as "Lord" (*kyrios*), do they mean he is their lord and master, or do they mean he is Yahweh, the God of Israel as revealed in the Old Testament Scriptures?[22] In actuality, they use "Lord" (*kyrios*) in both senses, and only context (or direct Old Testament quotation) identifies whether the term is referring to Jesus as "lord" and "master" or as Yahweh of the Old Testament.

---

[22] For a helpful study on this connection, see David B. Capes, *The Divine Christ: Paul, the Lord Jesus, and the Scriptures of Israel*, Acadia Studies in Bible and Theology (Grand Rapids: Baker, 2018).

1

Genesis

In the beginning God created the heavens and the earth.

—GENESIS 1:1

Outline

I.   Creation: God creates the world and blesses the first two people with his presence in the garden (1:1–2:25)

II. Human sin results in death, separation from God's presence, and scattering (3:1–11:32)

    A. Adam and Eve eat the forbidden fruit and are banished from the garden (3:1–24)

    B. Cain kills his brother, Abel, and is driven away (4:1–26)

    C. Worldwide wickedness brings on the flood as judgment (5:1–9:29)

    D. Arrogance at the tower of Babel results in scattering (10:1–11:32)

III. God responds to human sin by providing deliverance through the Abrahamic covenant (12:1–50:26)

    A. Abraham: the promise and obedience of faith (12:1–23:20)

        1. Abraham and the Promised Land (12:1–15:21)

    2.   Abraham and the Promised Seed (16:1–22:19)

    3.   Transition to Isaac; continuing the patriarchal promise (22:20–26:35)

  B. Jacob: struggles and the beginning of the twelve tribes of Israel (27:1–37:1)

    1.   Jacob, Esau, and family conflict (27:1–28:9)

    2.   Jacob chastened, yet still blessed, and the promise continues (28:10–30:43)

    3.   Jacob returns, followed by time of transition (31:1–37:1)

  C. Joseph: Faithfulness and God's sovereign deliverance (37:2–50:26)

    1.   Joseph is betrayed by his jealous brothers and sold into slavery (37:2–38:30)

    2.   Joseph rises to power in Egypt (39:1–41:57)

    3.   Joseph and his family are reconciled (42:1–46:27)

    4.   The patriarchal promise revived (46:28–50:26) [1]

The book of Genesis can also be organized around the repeated Hebrew introductory statement *'eleh toledoth*, which can be translated as "These are the records/these are the family records" (CSB), "this is the account" (NIV), or "these are the generations" (ESV). This phrase occurs as a heading ten times (Gen 2:4; 5:1; 6:9; 10:1; 11:10, 27; 25:12, 19; 36:1; and 37:2). Viewing Gen 1:1–2:3 as prologue, the outline of Genesis based on these headings would be as follows:

	1:1–2:3	Prologue
(1)	2:4–4:26	These are the records of the heavens and the earth.
(2)	5:1–6:8	These are the family records of Adam.
(3)	6:9–9:29	These are the family records of Noah.
(4)	10:1–11:9	These are the family records of Noah's sons.
(5)	11:10–26	These are the family records of Shem.
(6)	11:27–25:11	These are the family records of Terah.
(7)	25:12–18	These are the family records of Abraham's son Ishmael.

---

[1] Outline developed from J. Daniel Hays and J. Scott Duvall, *BIBH*, 42; and Bruce K. Waltke with Cathi J. Fredricks, *Genesis: A Commentary* (Grand Rapids: Zondervan, 2001), 7–10.

(8)	25:19–35:29	These are the family records of Isaac, son of Abraham.
(9)	36:1–37:1	These are the family records of Esau (that is, Edom).
(10)	37:2–50:26	These are the family records of Jacob.

Five of these headings introduce narrative stories (1—the creation story; 3—the flood story; 6—the Abraham story; 8—the Jacob story; and 10—the Joseph story). The other five headings introduce genealogies.

Author, Date, and Message

Author and Date

The view of this textbook is that Moses was the primary human author of the Pentateuch, including the book of Genesis (see the discussion on authorship and composition in the introduction). It is possible, even plausible, that Moses may have used some earlier written sources for the book of Genesis. However, the text itself says nothing about any earlier sources, so this assumption, although possible, is somewhat speculative.

If Moses is the author of Genesis, he probably wrote Genesis at some time during the forty years after the initial exodus out of Egypt and before his death, recorded at the end of Deuteronomy. Thus, determining the date for the composition of Genesis by Moses is linked to determining the date for the exodus event. As discussed in the next chapter, there is no consensus for the date of the exodus event. If the early date for the exodus is accepted, Moses wrote Genesis between 1446 BC and 1406 BC. If the later date for the exodus is accepted, Moses wrote Genesis between 1270/1260 and 1230/1220 BC.

In the Hebrew Bible the title for each book in the Pentateuch (Torah) is taken from the first few opening words of each respective book. Thus, the title for the first book of Moses in Hebrew translates as "in the beginning." When translated into Greek (the Septuagint), the translators used the Greek word *genesis* for the title, a word primarily meaning "origins." It occurs in Gen 2:4, and the title perhaps was drawn from that verse. A similar transliterated term was used for the later Latin Vulgate translation, and our English translations have followed in that tradition, titling this book "Genesis."

The Message of Genesis

GENESIS 1–11

In the beginning God creates the world and all that is in it, including people. That establishes right from the start who he is—the Creator . . . and who we are—the created beings. God creates a wonderful garden for his created people to live in, who are blessed especially by his presence there in the garden. Things are very good. However, we next read four stories of foolish human disobedience. Adam and Eve eat the forbidden fruit and are kicked out of the garden, away from the presence of God and the tree of life. Then Cain kills his brother, Abel. Next, the people become so bad that God has to destroy the world with a flood (reversing the creation) and, in essence, starting over. Then the next story shows people once again rebelling against God, building a tower to create a name for themselves, and thus they are scattered by God. In these four episodes we see that the human race is not off to a good start. This underscores the problem of humanity—sin and rebellion that separates them from God and results in death.

GENESIS 12–50

The rest of the Bible is about how God works to restore the relationship. Indeed, at the end of the story, we see God's people back in a garden enjoying the blessings of God's presence once again (Revelation 22). This story of redemption, of God working to bring people back into relationship with him (and especially the blessings of his close presence), begins in earnest with Abraham in Genesis 12. God calls Abraham and makes a covenant with him, promising him a land, numerous descendants, and blessing. (God even states that he would bless those who bless you [family of Abraham] and curse those who curse you.) He then adds that the people of the whole world would be blessed through Abraham. God also promises to be with Abraham, reestablishing, in part, the presence-based relationship lost in Genesis 2–3. Abraham has a son named Isaac, and Isaac has a son named Jacob. The promises God made to Abraham are repeated to each of these descendants of Abraham. Jacob then has twelve sons, one of whom is Joseph. These become the tribes of Israel, with Joseph producing two tribes (Manasseh and Ephraim). Joseph's brothers sell him into slavery and he is taken to Egypt, where under God's sovereign guidance he rises to power. A famine occurs, and Jacob and his sons eventually also travel to Egypt to escape the famine. Joseph graciously forgives his brothers and cares for them. As the book of Genesis ends, the family is in Egypt, awaiting their return to the land and the fulfillment of God's promises to Abraham.

In summary, Genesis lays out the human problem as well as the introduction to the solution that God provides. That is, the problem is that people sin and rebel against God, resulting in separation from him and thus bringing death. God, however, begins working through his covenant promises to Abraham to bring wayward humanity back into life-giving relationship with him.

Interpretive Overview

Creation: God Creates the World and Blesses the First Two People with His Presence in the Garden (1:1–2:25)

The opening verse, Gen 1:1, is a vital and foundational declaration that undergirds all of reality. God, in his sovereignty, created the universe. Standing at the beginning of Scripture, this proclamation and the implications of this statement echo throughout the rest of Scripture. Indeed, throughout the rest of the Bible the reality that God is the Creator of all things is constantly hovering in the background, continually underscoring and reminding us of his attributes that are demonstrated by the act of creation—his power, sovereignty, and authority.

Genesis 1:1 serves as an introductory summary or overview of the entire creation account described in the rest of Genesis 1 and Genesis 2.[2] That God created everything out of nothing is certainly implied but not stated directly in Genesis (yet see Exod 20:11; see also Acts 4:24; 14:15; and 17:24). That is, the details of the creation story start in 1:2 with a world covered with watery chaos. The creation account, therefore, is focused not so much on creation out of nothing as it is focused on bringing order and life to the chaotic and nonliving. In Gen 1:2 darkness covers the watery chaos, but, in contrast, the Spirit of God is also "hovering over the surface of the waters." There will be a close connection between the Spirit of God and his creative power throughout the rest of Scripture. Likewise, the spoken word of God drives the creation story, underscoring the close theological connection between God, his Spirit, his word, and his power to create.

---

[2] This is a widely held view, but it is not the only plausible interpretation. Indeed, there is no agreement among Old Testament scholars on how Gen 1:1 relates to v. 2 and the rest of the chapter. For two other defensible viewpoints, see John Goldingay, *Genesis*, BCOT (Grand Rapids: Baker Academic, 2020), 16, 25–27; and Gordon J. Wenham, *Genesis 1–15*, WBC (Waco, TX: Word, 1987), 11–13.

As mentioned in the discussion below regarding genre, Genesis 1 has a certain poetic or artistic character to it. For example, the sentence structure, "And there was evening, and there was morning—the *x* day" is repeated at the end of every one of the first six days (1:5, 8, 13, 19, 23, 31 NIV). Likewise, the phrase "and God saw that it was good" is repeated throughout the chapter.

Furthermore, observe that the first six days of creation are not so much a six-day linear account as it is two parallel three-day cycles. That is, on day 1 God separates light from darkness; and on day 4, the parallel day, he creates the sun, moon, and stars—those entities associated with the light and darkness. On day 2 he separates the sea from the sky; and on the parallel day 5 he creates fish and birds, those entities that dwell in the sea and the sky. This parallel is illustrated as follows:

Day 1 (1:3–5)	Day 4 (1:14–19)
Separates light from dark	*Creates the sun, moon, and stars to separate the day from the night*
Day 2 (1:6–8)	Day 5 (1:20–23)
Separates the sea from the sky	*Creates the fish and the birds*
Day 3 (1:9–13)	Day 6 (1:24–31)
Separates water from dry ground	*Creates livestock, crawling things,*
Creates vegetation	*wild animals, humankind*

Throughout the creation account, as God establishes domains or regions (days 1–3), he then not only creates but also assigns functions or roles to the entities that occupy those domains. Thus, he gives order and purpose to the creation.

On the sixth day, at the climax of creation, God creates people. He states, "Let us make man in our image, according to our likeness. They will rule over the fish of the sea" (1:26).[3] Then 1:27 explains, "So God created man in his own image; he created him in the image of God; he created them male and female." Note that the Hebrew word translated here as "man" (CSB) is *'adam*. Translating this word can be challenging, for it can mean "one man, the man," it can mean "mankind, people," or it can be a proper name (Adam). Throughout Gen 1:26–4:26 the various English translations (e.g., NIV, CSB, ESV) differ on how they translate *'adam*. In 1:26–27 *'adam* appears to refer to people in general, or at least to the first couple, both the male and the female. This is made clear in 5:2, which reads, "He created them male and female.

---

[3] These same two terms for image and likeness occur in Gen 5:3.

When they were created, he blessed them and called them mankind (*'adam*)." So, both men and women (all people) are created in the image of God.

Note, too, that these first people whom God creates are ethnically unidentified. He does not, for example, create "Hebrews" or "Israelites." This has strong theological implications about the value of human life. *All people* are created in the image of God and are thus special.

Yet what does it mean to be created in the image of God? Over the years scholars have proposed several possible meanings of the *imago Dei* (the image of God) as used in Genesis 1 and 5. Most Old Testament scholars today reject older views that understood the "image of God" as referring to spiritual, mental, or physical similarities. Arguing from ANE literary contexts, some advocate for a "royal/functional" understanding. Just as ancient kings would place small statues of themselves in their provinces to underscore their rule of that area, so God has placed people on earth to represent him and to stress his rule. Another, more recent view regarding ANE parallels notes the similarity between the image of God language in Genesis 1 and the language used for small "divine" statues placed in pagan temples in the ANE. This would stress the idea that people were designed to live in the presence of God (as those small statues did). Related to this, numerous scholars see the "image of God" as the ability to relate to God, to people, and to the creation. Finally, based on Gen 5:1–3, some scholars see implications of kinship. That is, God is presented as the Father of all mankind. These various views are not exclusive of each other; indeed, many scholars advocate for a combination of all these views.[4]

The creation story of Genesis 1 concludes in 2:1–3, when God rests on the seventh day. The text states, "God blessed the seventh day and declared it holy, for on it he rested from all his work of creation" (2:3). This event and declaration set the seven-day week as the major time cycle for human beings and will be connected to the Sabbath day of rest for Israel decreed in Exod 20:8–11.

While Gen 1:1–2:3 is an overview of the entire creation story, Gen 2:4 picks up on the creation of people and starts recounting the story going forward with the focus on people. God creates a plush, fruitful garden—a wonderful environment for

---

[4] For good discussions on the *imago Dei*, see J. Scott Duvall and J. Daniel Hays, *God's Relational Presence: The Cohesive Center of Biblical Theology* (Grand Rapids: Baker Academic, 2019), 17–19; Catherine L. McDowell, *The Image of God in the Garden of Eden* (Winona Lake, IN: Eisenbrauns, 2015); Gordon J. McConville, *Being Human in God's World: An Old Testament Theology of Humanity* (Grand Rapids: Baker Academic, 2016), 24–29; and J. Richard Middleton, *The Liberating Image: The Imago Dei in Genesis 1* (Grand Rapids: Brazos, 2005), 26–29.

people. He also states that it is not good (*tov*) for the man to be alone; thus, God creates woman and decrees the institution of marriage. The situation is great. Adam and Eve are living in the wonderful garden in the very presence of God (implied by 3:8) experiencing tremendous blessings. This is the consummation of God's creation activity in Genesis.

GENESIS 1–2: GENRE, ANE LITERATURE, AND SCIENCE

One of the first steps in the interpretative process is to identify the genre (the kind or type) of literature one is reading. Each genre has its own set of interpretive "rules of the game."[5] For example, regarding the genre of parable, most New Testament scholars would concur that when Jesus tells a parable, the lesson he conveys through the parable is absolutely true, but the characters in the parable are not historical characters but rather hypothetical characters used to illustrate the truth Jesus was teaching.[6] In Mark 4, for example, the genre of 4:1 is historical, theological narrative: "Again he [Jesus] began to teach by the sea." This sentence describes something that really happened as stated. But in 4:3 Jesus begins a parable: "Consider the sower who went out to sow." This parable, embedded in the narrative, is a different genre than the narrative. While the historical, theological narrative genre claims that Jesus, a historical figure, actually began teaching by the lake and telling parables, the parable genre lets us know that while the truth illustrated by the parable is absolutely true and without any error, the sower himself is hypothetical and not a historical character.

In interpreting Genesis 1–2 (or Genesis 1–11, for that matter) one of the critical first steps is to identify the genre. Identifying the genre for Genesis 1–2, however, has proven to be quite challenging, and there is no consensus today, even among evangelical Old Testament scholars. That is, among Bible-believing, inerrancy-affirming scholars who have done serious Hebrew exegesis in Genesis for decades, there is a lack of agreement regarding the identification of the genre in the opening chapters of Genesis. There is a strong consensus regarding the theological truth of the passage

---

[5] On the importance of genre in biblical interpretation, see J. Scott Duvall and J. Daniel Hays, *Grasping God's Word*, 4th ed. (Grand Rapids: Zondervan, 2020), 151–52. On specifically relating the importance of genre identification to our understanding of the early chapters of Genesis, see C. John Collins, *Reading Genesis Well: Navigating History, Poetry, Science, and Truth in Genesis 1–11* (Grand Rapids: Zondervan, 2018), 1–95.

[6] Tremper Longman III, "What Genesis 1–2 Teaches (and What It Doesn't Teach)," in *Reading Genesis 1–2: An Evangelical Conversation*, ed. J. Daryl Charles (Peabody, MA: Hendrickson, 2013), 103.

but considerable disagreement regarding the literal historicity (in the modern sense of historicity) of all the details. Thus, it is probably wise to proceed with caution and to be somewhat tentative (and humble), refraining from making quick, absolute judgments regarding the genre identification disagreements. At the same time, we should recognize that the central theological truths of Genesis 1–2 can be embraced with confidence: Yahweh, the God of Israel, created the heavens and the earth and all that is within them, especially people, with whom he has a special relationship. Also keep in mind one of the basic, foundational tenants that we as people of faith hold when interpreting the Old Testament: God has the power and authority to do whatever he wants.

At the heart of the disagreement is determining the role that should be assigned to corresponding ANE background literary material. Several ancient documents from Egypt, Ugarit (Syria), and Mesopotamia contain creation accounts and flood accounts.[7] Is this literature, as well as the general literary milieu of this period (the second millennium BC), relevant or irrelevant to the genre identification of Genesis 1–2? Likewise, even beyond genre identification, does the literary milieu of the ANE provide *any* historical or literary contextual background for our interpretation of Genesis? And, if so, in what way? Evangelical Old Testament scholars remain divided over these issues and have not reached any agreement on how to answer these two questions. Yet decisions regarding these two issues are critical starting hermeneutical points, especially for interpreting Genesis 1–2 (and in some cases, likewise impacting our understanding of Genesis 1–11).

Questions relating to geology and biology, such as the age of the earth, the origin and evolution of life, the fossil record, and so on, while very important to today's culture, are nonetheless secondary to the central theological truth of Genesis 1–2. Still, how our understanding of Genesis fits with the claims of science is an important issue that needs to be addressed for Christians living in our culture today. Defining what the tensions are between Genesis and science, however, and how one should respond to these tensions depends in large part on the genre identification of Genesis 1–2, thus underscoring, once again, the importance of genre.

Regarding their understandings of the genre for Genesis 1–2, respected, well-known evangelical Old Testament scholars fall into two general camps, and each camp, of course, also has some variations as well. Those in the first camp see the

---

[7] For most of the twentieth century scholarly attention regarding Genesis 1 and creation stories of the ANE focused on texts from Ugarit and Mesopotamia. More recently, several scholars have made a strong case for viewing Egyptian creation stories as playing the most important role in understanding Genesis 1. See, for example, Gordon H. Johnston, "Genesis 1 and Ancient Egyptian Creation Myths," *BSac* 165 (2008): 178–94.

genre of Genesis 1–11 as basic, historical theological narrative, the same genre as is found in the rest of Genesis as well as in other Old Testament historical books such as 1–2 Samuel and 1–2 Kings. Therefore, they would, for example, interpret the seven days of Genesis 1 as literal twenty-four-hour days and the sequence and process of creation described as being an exact description of what God did at creation. Most of these scholars tend to downplay the influence of the ANE literary milieu on how we should interpret Genesis.[8] Some, however, while arguing for a fairly literal reading of Genesis 1 (e.g., twenty-four-hour days) also maintain that one of the major purposes of the chapter was to refute the creation myths believed by the other peoples of the ANE.[9]

Some of the people in this first camp also propose a "young earth" view regarding the age of the earth. They attempt to answer the numerous tensions raised by the claims of science, particularly the field of geology, by emphasizing the important role that the universal flood in Genesis 6–9 played in the formation of the geological record found today.[10]

A variation of this view observes that at face value the story of creation in Genesis 1–2 depicts a created world that already has some apparent age to it. That is, Adam appears to have been created as an adult. In Gen 2:10 we already see a garden with full-grown trees and rivers. If we were able to take a scientific team back in time to Gen 2:10 and study the scene, would they describe Adam as "a healthy twenty-six-year-old male" (even though he had not lived that long yet)? If we cut down a tree, would it have rings, indicating years of life? Adherents of this "apparent age" view observe that all these features imply that the world may have been created by God to look much like it does now, with mountains, ocean shorelines, and river valleys. This means it was created with an apparent age at the moment of creation. Followers of the "apparent age" view suggest that perhaps the Grand Canyon, for example, was not formed by the great flood of Genesis 6–9, nor was it formed over millions and millions of years of time, but rather it was part of the initial creation. This would be true for the fossil record as well.

---

[8] For a good, recent defense of this view, see especially Vern S. Poythress, *Interpreting Eden: A Guide to Faithfully Reading and Understanding Genesis 1–3* (Wheaton, IL: Crossway, 2019), and Todd Beall, "Reading Genesis 1–2: A Literal Approach," in *Reading Genesis 1–2*, 45–59.

[9] Steinmann, *Genesis*, 18–21 (see intro., n. 7).

[10] See, for example, Ken Ham, "Young-Earth Creationism," in *Four Views on Creation, Evolution, and Intelligent Design*, ed. J. B. Stump and Stanley N. Gundry (Grand Rapids: Zondervan, 2017), 17–48.

The second general position, or "camp," one that has grown in popularity among evangelical Old Testament scholars over the last few decades, places a high degree of relevance on the written literary material from the ANE, both in identifying the genre and for describing the literary and historical context for understanding the early chapters of Genesis. Many of those with this view suggest that God employed a recognizable ancient genre, similar in some sense to that of the other ancient creation stories; but, while using similar language, style, and themes, God's creation story was radically different from the other ANE stories.[11] That is, the creation story in Genesis 1–2 did not evolve from the other ANE creation stories, nor did it borrow material or rely on material in those sources, but rather in the literary milieu context of those stories, and using an overlapping genre (with both similarities and differences), the Genesis 1–2 creation story presented a counter worldview. Tremper Longman III notes, "The main purpose of Gen 1–2 is to proclaim in the midst of contemporary counterclaims that Yahweh the God of Israel was the creator of everything and everyone." Thus, this text, Longman continues, is not interested in giving us details as to *how* God created the world, with which science can perhaps help us. But, he notes, "it is important for modern readers of Gen 1–2 to realize that this account of creation was not written against Darwinian but against Babylonian, Canaanite, and Egyptian claims."[12] That is, Genesis 1–2 is polemical against, or at least countering, the false religious beliefs of ancient Israel's neighbors.

Likewise, John Hilber points out that the ancients had a prescientific view of the world, one based on basic observational and phenomenological perceptions. Yet it is important, he notes, to realize that their perceptions of the world were integrally interconnected to their religious belief—the gods were responsible for sending the

---

[11] Kenneth Matthews discusses the difficulty in labeling exactly what this genre is. He notes that the creation account in Genesis 1–2 is tied into the historical framework of Genesis and has some narrative features. "It is not," Matthews clarifies, "the same kind of history writing as Genesis 12–50, or even chaps. 3–4, and it is quite different from Samuel and Kings. Neither is it like the creation hymns in the Psalms . . . it does not fit a traditional literary category." Kenneth A. Mathews, *Genesis 1–11:26*, NAC (Nashville: B&H, 1996), 109.

[12] Longman, "What Genesis 1–2 Teaches," 103–7. Recognizing that there is some variation in their understanding, works advocating this basic second view include: Richard E. Averbeck, "A Literary Day, Inter-Textual, and Contextual Reading of Genesis 1–2," in *Reading Genesis 1–2*, 7–34; Collins, *Reading Genesis Well*; Tremper Longman III, "Genesis," in *BIBBC*, 81–119; Tremper Longman III, *Genesis*, SGBC (Grand Rapids: Zondervan, 2016); Waltke and Fredricks, *Genesis*; Goldingay, *Genesis*; John W. Hilber, *Old Testament Cosmology and Divine Accommodation: A Relevance Theory Approach* (Eugene, OR: Cascade, 2020); and Johnston, "Genesis 1 and Ancient Egyptian Creation Myths," 178–94.

rain; the sun and the moon were gods to be worshipped; the agricultural seasons are determined by the gods, and so on. Thus, in Genesis 1–2, while using a similar recognizable genre for *his* creation story (the true story), God was countering the pagan view, stating that Israel's God created all things, even the sun, the moon, and the seasons. Hilber calls this use of ANE genre a "divine accommodation" and suggests that it would have been recognized easily by the ancient audience.[13]

Some scholars also observe an artistic element in the Genesis creation account.[14] That is, God seemed to be more interested in presenting the account with aesthetic concerns and with artistic flair than with any kind of modern scientific specificity. God, who in his sovereignty and power can do whatever he chooses, perhaps chose to describe the act of creation artistically rather than scientifically.

A strong advocate for the importance of interpreting the early chapters of Genesis in the context of ANE literature is John Walton. Within this framework, however, he argues that parallels with other ANE literature indicate that Genesis 1 is specifically about God establishing his *cosmic* temple here on earth in which he can dwell. These early chapters in Genesis, Walton argues, are not about creating matter (at all) but about assigning functions to the entities in the creation.[15] Yet while many scholars appreciate and agree with Walton's stress on the importance of ANE literary influences—and they frequently acknowledge that there are interconnected themes (such as the presence of God in his dwelling place) between the garden and the tabernacle or temple[16]—a number of them disagree with the extent to which Walton takes this thesis, especially his disavowal that Genesis 1–2 has anything to do with material creation.[17]

In general, those evangelical scholars who advocate for the second option, placing the interpretation of Genesis 1–2 into the context of the literary milieu of the ANE, posit that Genesis 1–2 does not speak to the specific manner of how God created the earth in regard to the geological age of the earth, the evolutionary development of

---

[13] Hilber, *Old Testament Cosmology*, 82–83.

[14] Waltke and Fredricks, *Genesis*, 78.

[15] John H. Walton, *Genesis 1 as Ancient Cosmology* (Winona Lake, IN: Eisenbrauns, 2011); *The Lost World of Genesis One: Ancient Cosmology and the Origins Debate* (Downers Grove, IL: InterVarsity, 2009); and *The Lost World of Adam and Eve: Genesis 2–3 and the Human Origins Debate* (Downers Grove, IL: InterVarsity, 2015).

[16] J. Daniel Hays, *The Temple and the Tabernacle* (Grand Rapids: Baker, 2016), 20–27, 36.

[17] See, for example, Richard E. Averbeck, "The Lost World of Adam and Eve: A Review Essay," *Themelios* 40, no. 2 (2015): 226–39; and Richard S. Hess, "Review: *The Lost World of Genesis One: Ancient Cosmology and the Origins Debate* by John H. Walton," *BBR* 20, no. 3 (2010): 433–36.

species, and so on. Yet while they would not interpret the days of creation in Genesis 1 as literal twenty-four-hour days, neither would they accept that the days can be interpreted subjectively or anachronistically as symbolic or otherwise representative of modern concepts (e.g., geological ages). Thus, the understanding of Genesis 1 among those evangelical Old Testament scholars in the second camp is quite different from the "day-age" theory or "old-earth" (progressive) creationism, which tries to demonstrate that the days of creation in Genesis 1 somehow symbolize or parallel the long ages and developmental stages of geological and biological history. These views ("day-age" theory and "old-earth" progressive creationism) are usually advocated by evangelical scientists and not evangelical Old Testament scholars.[18] They tend to suffer from weak biblical exegesis as well as seemingly stretched scientific connections.[19]

In conclusion, we see that among evangelical Old Testament scholars there are two major views regarding genre and how much relevance we give to background literature of the ANE. The current trend perhaps leans toward the view that recognizes more relevance of the ANE literary milieu and the use by God of a genre that implies that Genesis 1–2 should not be interpreted in a modern scientific sense nor in a historical narrative sense similar to 1 and 2 Kings. As a closing note to this discussion, remember that Christians face a similar interpretive challenge regarding genre (e.g., How much is literal?) in the parallel, closing two chapters of the Bible (Revelation 21–22), where we encounter the same themes in the closing climax of the biblical story that we found introduced in Genesis—the "new heaven and the new earth," along with a garden, the tree of life, and the presence of God.

ANCIENT CONNECTIONS SIDEBAR 1.1: CREATION ACCOUNTS IN ANCIENT LITERATURE

Throughout the various regions and religions of the ANE, numerous myths recounted the beginnings of things. These pagan myths circulated widely both as oral traditions and, occasionally, in written form. Moses, as well as his ancient

---

[18] See, for example, Hugh Ross, "Old Earth (Progressive) Creationism," in *Four Views on Creation, Evolution, and Intelligent Design*, 71–100.

[19] The argument that day 3 (creation of land vegetation), day 4 (creation of sun and moon), day 5 (creation of fish and birds), and day 6 (creation of land animals and people) are representative of long ages of time that parallel (accurately) the claims of scientific evolution is just not convincing, either from a hermeneutical point of view (this approach is quite foreign to biblical exegesis) or a scientific point of view (Vegetation before the sun? Birds before land animals?).

readers, would have been aware of a number of these myths; and, as discussed earlier, when Moses writes the true account of how the God of Abraham, Isaac, and Jacob created the world, he seems, perhaps, to have written it against the background of the challenging pagan myths—indeed, to rebut or refute these myths. Several of these ancient literary works have survived. Both the Babylonian account (*Enuma Elish*) and the Canaanite account (*The Baal Myth*) focus primarily on a huge battle that takes place among the gods, out of which the primary god of the region emerges victorious. The defeated god in each case is closely associated with the chaotic primordial waters of the sea. In *Enuma Elish*, for example, the god Marduk defeats the goddess Tiamat, splits her in two, and then forms the world from her carcass. A scene from this battle is described as follows:

> Tiamat and Marduk, sage of the gods, drew close for battle,
> They locked in single combat, joining for the fray.
> The Lord spread out his net, encircled her,
> The ill wind he had held behind him he released in her face.
> Tiamat opened her mouth to swallow,
> He thrust in the ill wind so she could not close her lips. . . .
> He shot off the arrow, it broke open her belly,
> It cut to her innards, it pierced the heart. . . .
> He split her in two, like a fish for drying,
> Half of her he set up and made as a cover, heaven.[20]

Although some scholars question whether *The Baal Myth* is a creation story versus a "battle with chaos" story, the distinction is probably moot. In the Baal Myth, the god of the primordial sea is Yam (*yam* is also the word for "sea" in most Semitic languages, including Hebrew). Yam is defeated by Baal. The text probably then alluded to the creation of the world from her body, as in *Enuma Elish*, but this part of the text in *The Baal Myth* is damaged and unreadable. In the ancient Egyptian texts, the story focuses on how the top gods emerged out of the primordial waters and then procreated to produce the other gods of the pantheon.[21]

---

[20] "Epic of Creation, *Enūma Elish*," trans. Benjamin R. Foster, *COS* 1.111:90–102, 137–38.
[21] Longman, *Genesis*, 29–34. For English translations of these other ANE creation accounts, see: "Epic of Creation, *Enūma Elish*," *COS* 1.111:390–402; "The Baʿlu Myth," trans.

The differences between the biblical account in Genesis 1 and these ancient myths of creation are rather stark. In Genesis 1 there is no battle or struggle with the waters to determine which god will emerge as the most powerful god. Rather, the God of Genesis (later identified as Yahweh, the God of Abraham, Isaac, and Jacob—the God who will one day bring the Israelites out of Egypt) is already there as supreme when the story opens. He does not struggle or fight with the primordial waters, but with his Spirit hovering over the waters, he speaks the heavens, earth, and all life into ordered existence.

WORD STUDY
GOOD (*TOV*) AND "EVIL/BAD" (*RA'*) IN GENESIS 1–3 AND IN BIBLICAL CONTEXT

Numerous times in Genesis 1 the text states that "God saw that it was good" (Hebrew, *tov*). After day 6, he saw that the creation was "very good." Genesis 2:9 explains that God put trees in the garden that were "good [*tov*] for food, including the tree of life . . . as well as the tree of the knowledge of good [*tov*] and evil [*ra'*]."

There is no agreement at all among scholars regarding what the phrase "the knowledge of good and evil" means. Yet we can perhaps capture a feel for the implications of the phrase by undertaking a brief word study of the major terms. The Hebrew words *tov* (good) and *ra'* (evil or bad), along with various other forms of the word *ra'* (e.g., *ra'ah*), are common yet highly significant terms used extensively throughout the Old Testament. Indeed, *tov* occurs 580 times, and *ra'* and related forms occur over 750 times. They are antonyms, and they appear frequently together as contrasts. The English word *good* captures the Hebrew nuance of *tov* quite well, but the English word *evil* is perhaps a bit misleading and too narrow as a translation for *ra'*. The foundational meaning of this word relates to "an action or state that is detrimental to life or its fullness."[22] Throughout the Old Testament the Hebrew word *ra'* frequently refers to (1) bad "things" in general; (2) bad, sinful actions of people; (3) the bad consequences of those actions; or (4) the actions of God in judgment. When it is used of God, it is often translated into English as "disaster" (Jer 4:6; 6:1, 19; 18:11 [ESV]; etc.). For example, in Jer 18:8 God states, "If that nation about which I have made the announcement turns from its *evil* [*ra'*], I will relent concerning the *disaster* [*ra'*] I had planned to

Dennis Pardee, *COS* 1.86:241–73; and "Egyptian Coffin Texts Spells," trans. James P. Allen and Robert K. Ritner, *COS* 1.1–1.19:5–31.

[22] David W. Baker, "רעע," *NIDOTTE* 3:1154.

do to it" (emphasis added). We see that *ra'* can be used of people as well as of God; thus the concept of evil is often inappropriate as a meaning. A good informal translation for this word would be "bad stuff." In Jer 18:8, if the people turn from their bad stuff (sin), God will relent from bringing bad stuff (judgment) on them.

Furthermore, *tov* (the good) is often associated with life, while *ra'* (the bad) is often associated with death. Deuteronomy 30:15, for example, highlights this association, stating, "See, today I have set before you *life* and *prosperity* [*tov*], *death* and *adversity* [*ra'*]" (emphasis added). This close association (life with *tov* and death with *ra'*) is also apparent in Genesis 2–3. In 2:9 God mentions the tree of *life* right before mentioning the tree of the knowledge of *good* and *evil* (*bad stuff*). Then in 2:17 he declares that if Adam and Eve eat of the tree of the knowledge of *good* and *evil* (*bad stuff*), they will certainly *die*. Up until Genesis 3, everything Adam and Eve experienced was *tov* (good). After eating the forbidden fruit, they also begin to learn about and experience things that are *ra'* (bad). As God explains, "The ground is cursed because of you. . . . You will eat bread by the sweat of your brow until you return to the ground, since you were taken from it" (3:17–19). Then they are driven away from the presence of God without access to the tree of life as they had before (3:23–24).

In contrast to the *tov* throughout Genesis 1–3, in the chapters that follow, the human race now starts to know *ra'*. In Genesis 4 Cain murders Abel, bringing about the first human death. By Gen 6:5 *ra'* is dominating the human race: "The LORD saw that human *wickedness* [*ra'ah*; a related form of *ra'*] was widespread on the earth and that every inclination of the human mind was nothing but *evil* [*ra'*] all the time" (emphasis added; see also 8:21). Yet, at the very end of Genesis, included in the salvation story we see God counteracting the bad stuff and bringing about good (life and deliverance). At the very end of Genesis, perhaps serving as an *inclusio* to 2:17, in 50:20 Joseph declares to his brothers, "You planned *evil* [*ra'ah*] against me; God planned it for *good* [*tov*] to bring about the present result—the survival of many people [lit., "to give *life* to many people"] (emphasis added).

Human Sin Results in Death, Separation from God's Presence, and Scattering (3:1–11:32)

Genesis 3–11 provides an overview recounting the ways people rebel against God and thus experience death, separation from God's presence, and a scattering across the ancient world. First, Adam and Eve eat of the forbidden fruit (3:1–24). Then Cain kills Abel—that is, from the two sons of the next generation, one will kill the other (4:1–26). Next, the people who then populate the world become so bad that God decides to destroy them in the flood (5:1–9:29). After that, the people at the Tower of Babel arrogantly rebel against God and thus are scattered (10:1–11:32). Indeed, humanity is off to a bad start.

Adam and Eve Eat the Forbidden Fruit and Are Banished from the Garden (3:1–24)

Genesis 3 introduces several events and themes that will affect the rest of the biblical story. An antagonist (the serpent, representing Satan) challenges God's established order, seeking to tempt God's created people to doubt and to disobey their Creator. The following disobedience of Adam and Eve will result in judgment—they are driven out of the garden and separated from the presence of God and from the tree of life, thus losing eternal life. Indeed, the rest of the biblical story is about how God works in human history to restore this broken relationship, to bring his people back into the blessings of his life-giving presence, and to restore eternal life to them. As mentioned earlier, this is the culminating picture we see at the end of the biblical story in Revelation 21–22 when God's people are back in the garden with God's presence and the tree of life.

ANCIENT CONNECTIONS SIDEBAR 1.2: CHAOS AND THE SERPENT

The serpent in Genesis 3 appears out of nowhere without any explanation. While to modern readers the appearance of a talking (perhaps even "walking"; see Gen 3:14) serpent is quite bizarre, ancient readers would have recognized the serpent immediately as representing evil, one who challenges the ordered good in the world. Throughout the religious literature of the ANE, in both Mesopotamia and in Egypt, serpents were negative and disruptive characters. For example, in the Gilgamesh epic, the main character, Gilgamesh, is searching for the way to eternal life. He is told that there is a plant in the depths of the sea that he can eat to obtain life. Gilgamesh goes deep into the sea and retrieves the plant, but before he can eat it, a serpent takes it from him. The text reads:

I will disclose, O Gilgamesh, a hidden thing,

And [*a secret of the gods* I will] tell thee. . . .

If thy hands obtain the plant, [thou wilt find new life]. . . .

Gilgamesh . . . took the plant. . . .

Gilgamesh says to him, to Urshanabi, the boatman:

"Urshanabi, this plant is a plant apart,

Whereby a man may regain his life's breath. . . .

Its name shall be 'Man Becomes Young in Old Age'". . . .

A serpent snuffed the fragrance of the plant;

It came up [from the water] and carried off the plant. . . .

Thereupon Gilgamesh sits down and weeps. . . .[23]

In addition, Longman notes, "In the Enuma Elish . . . Tiamat, the goddess of chaos that resists the forces of creation . . . seems to be depicted as a walking serpent. . . . She certainly gives birth to serpentine demonic figures."[24] In Egypt mythology the serpent-god of the underworld was Apophis. He was not a god to be worshipped but rather a demon to be protected against. Symbolizing chaos and evil, each morning and evening Apophis challenged the sun-god (and the rising of the sun), thus threatening world stability.[25]

Cain Kills His Brother, Abel, and Is Driven Away (4:1–26)

Although driven from God's presence in the garden, and destined now to experience death, the first couple is nonetheless blessed and empowered by God (in his grace) to reproduce and thus to continue human life (4:1–2). The irony is that Cain, one of their first two sons, murders Abel, the other son (4:8), even though God has directly tried to talk him out of it (4:6–7). Cain is driven even further away from God's presence (4:16). One of Cain descendants, Lamech, is even more violent and bloodthirsty than Cain (4:24), perhaps indicating the spread and growth of sin from the family into the society.

Adam and Eve, however, have another son, Seth, and in contrast to Cain's violent descendants, Seth's descendants begin to "call on the name of the LORD" (4:26). This phrase will be used frequently of the patriarchs (12:8; 13:4; 21:33; and 26:25),

---

[23] *The Epic of Gilgamesh*, trans. E. A. Speiser, *ANET*, XI:267–88.

[24] Longman, "Genesis," 86.

[25] Richard Wilkinson, *The Complete Gods and Goddesses of Ancient Egypt* (New York: Thames & Hudson, 2003), 221–23; Ian Shaw and Paul Nicholson, "Apophis," *The Princeton Dictionary of Ancient Egypt* (Princeton, NJ: Princeton University Press, 2008), 38.

and it probably included "proclamation" in addition to worship (including prayer and sacrifice).[26]

WORLDWIDE WICKEDNESS BRINGS ON THE FLOOD AS JUDGMENT (5:1–9:29)

The genealogy in Genesis 5 connects the first founder, Adam, with the new founder, Noah.

In this genealogy, however, "death" is mentioned eight times, a reminder of the consequences of Genesis 3. Yet there are glimpses of hope and life in the midst of the curse of death. Enoch walks faithfully and is taken away by God, apparently avoiding death (5:24). Procreation itself is a divine blessing as the divine image is transmitted and life is created. In this context of hope and life, Gen 6:1–8 comes as a shock, where even this blessing (human procreation) is abused and perverted.

In Gen 6:1–2, after "mankind began to multiply on the earth and daughters were born to them, the sons of God saw that the daughters of mankind were beautiful, and they took any they chose as wives." Identifying the "sons of God" in Gen 6:2 is difficult. Plausible options include (1) angels or similar lower-level divine beings; (2) dynastic rulers, reflecting an early aristocracy; and (3) righteous descendants of Seth.[27] Whoever they were, the sin was great. Genesis 6:5–8 declares, "When the LORD saw that human wickedness [*ra'ah*] was widespread on the earth and that every inclination of the human mind was nothing but evil [*ra'*] all the time, the LORD regretted that he had made man on the earth, and he was deeply grieved. Then the LORD said, 'I will wipe mankind, whom I created, off the face of the earth.'"

In contrast, however, Noah, a "righteous man" who "walked with God," "found favor" (or "grace"—that is, unmerited favor) with God (6:8–9). In essence Noah will serve as a one-man remnant, although, of course, his entire family will be spared. The widespread *ra'ah* (evil, wickedness, bad stuff) practiced by people will bring God's terrible judgment. Only grace will deliver the remnant.

Instead of continuing the separation between God and those guilty of overt sin and rebellion as in the previous episodes in Genesis, now God decides to destroy the world with a flood and, in essence, to start over. Genesis 6:1–9:29 describes the flood and its aftermath. Remarkably (and ironically) many of the same terms that were used of creation in Genesis 1–2 are repeated here, only in reverse. In Genesis 1 God

---

[26] Allen P. Ross, *Creation and Blessing: A Guide to the Study and Exposition of Genesis* (Grand Rapids: Baker, 1988), 169; Wenham, *Genesis 1–15*, 116.

[27] See the discussion in Goldingay, *Genesis*, 121–22, who argues for option 1 above.

saw that things were "good" (*tov*), while in 6:5 he sees that things are "bad" (*ra'ah*). In 1:6–7 God separates the waters above and waters below while in 7:11 this separation collapses into a mighty flood. The dry ground that appeared in 1:9 now disappears beneath the waters (7:17–20).

In Genesis 8 God starts the "re-creation." At the original creation, in Gen 1:2 the "Spirit of God" was hovering over the waters. The Hebrew word translated as "Spirit" in 1:2 is *ruah*. This word can mean "Spirit" (i.e., the Holy Spirit), "spirit" (i.e., a spirit related to people), or even "wind." Now in the "re-creation" of Genesis 8, and in parallel with Gen 1:2, the *ruah* appears again over the waters (8:1), but here it is usually translated as "wind." The waters recede, the dry land appears, and the animals emerge out of the ark (8:1–22). In Genesis 9, after the flood is over, God makes a covenant promise not to destroy the world again by floodwaters (9:8–11).

The narrative story about Noah ends in a rather peculiar fashion. While Noah is drunk, his son Ham does something very offensive. Noah then curses Ham's son Canaan (9:18–27). Although the exact nature of the sin that Ham committed is not clear, it does seem to have sexual connotations. Sexual immorality will be closely connected to Baal worship, and the Canaanite inhabitants of the future Promised Land will likewise be associated with a range of aberrant sexual behavior. Note that Leviticus 18, which addresses such aberrant behavior, opens and closes by attributing this immorality to the inhabitants of the land (i.e., the Canaanites). Therefore, this curse seems to have some kind of future, prophetic nuance; the implication is that the Canaanites will descend from Ham's son Canaan. The Canaanites will become one of the major enemies of Israel. These Canaanites, who worship Baal and who cause numerous theological and sexual or moral problems for Israel, will become a paradigmatic enemy of Israel.[28] Thus a curse on them seems appropriate. Note that the names of Noah's sons (Ham, Shem, and Japheth) have nothing to do with racial groups or ethnic categories, and the curse on Ham has absolutely nothing to do with any specific ethnicity. In American history this verse was often used to claim biblical support for the brutal enslavement of Black Africans by White Caucasians. That usage reflected a serious misinterpretation of this passage and an evil and totally incorrect application of this text.

ARROGANCE AT THE TOWER OF BABEL RESULTS IN SCATTERING (10:1–11:32)

In Gen 8:20 Noah builds an altar to the LORD (Yahweh). Later, in Gen 12:8, Abraham also will build an altar to the LORD (Yahweh), and then he will call on the name of

---

[28] See the discussion by Goldingay, *Genesis*, 168–69.

the LORD (Yahweh). In contrast, here in Gen 11:4 the people on earth say, "Come, let's build ourselves a *city* and a *tower* with its top in the sky. Let's make a *name* for ourselves; otherwise we will be scattered throughout the earth" (emphasis added). They are not concerned with the name of Yahweh but only their own name. Genesis 11:1–9, the Tower of Babel rebellion, is the fourth (and final) story of human rebellion presented in these early chapters of Genesis. The situation regarding peoples and nations described in Genesis 10 is likely the consequence of what happens at the Tower of Babel in Genesis 11. That is, at the beginning of Genesis 11 there is one people group speaking one primary language. In Gen 11:8–9 God scatters them across the earth and confuses their language; thus, a variety of languages (and peoples) develops. This is the world described in Genesis 10.

Genesis 10 is fraught with hermeneutical challenges, and we should approach it with a certain amount of interpretive caution and humility. The seventy nations listed (note the symbolic number) are grouped into genealogies connected to the three sons of Noah. Although a popular view in the past was to view these three groupings as racial groups, this view has been overwhelmingly rejected by Old Testaments scholars today.[29] Genealogies in the ANE were often not strictly father-son lists. The names and the way they were grouped in these ancient genealogies usually fell into one or more of three grouping criteria: (1) one of kinship relationships based on not only biological ties but also economic and geographical ties; (2) political alliances; and (3) shared religious practice and belief.[30] Indeed, the lists in Genesis 10 include names of individuals, peoples, tribes, countries, and cities. The basis for the grouping seems to be a combination of anthropological, linguistic, political, and geographical elements.[31]

One of the most significant aspects of Genesis 10 is the repetition of the same four words to summarize the groupings—according to their clans [*mishpachah*], languages [*lashon*], lands [*eretz*], and nations [*goy*]. These same four terms occur in Gen

---

[29] See, for example, Goldingay, *Genesis*, 179–80; and Longman, *Genesis*, 142.

[30] Robert R. Wilson, "The Old Testament Genealogies in Recent Research," in *I Studied Inscriptions from before the Flood*, ed. Richard S. Hess and David Toshio Tsumura (Winona Lake, IN: Eisenbrauns, 1994), 213–14.

[31] Note for example, that Gen 10:6 groups together (as descendants of Ham) Cush, Egypt, Put (Libya), and Canaan. These four groups do not seem to be related racially, religiously, or linguistically. They were, however, all under Egyptian political control for most of the patriarchal period. See the discussion in J. Daniel Hays, *From Every People and Nation: A Biblical Theology of Race*, NSBT (Downers Grove, IL: IVP, 2003), 56–60; and Nahum M. Sarna, *Genesis*, JPS Commentary (Philadelphia: JPS, 1989), 68.

10:5, 10:20, and 10:31, and they summarize the scattering of people away from the presence of God that started in Genesis 3.

Yet as the story of salvation is introduced in Gen 12:1–3, three of these same terms will be used by God in his call and promise to Abraham: "Go . . . to the land [*eretz*] that I will show you. I will make you into a great nation [*goy*] . . . and all peoples [*mishpachah*] on earth will be blessed through you."

The four corresponding words in the LXX Greek translation of Genesis 10 are *phyle* (clans), *glossa* (language), *chora* (land), and *ethne* (nation). In the New Testament the scattering and separation due to the confusion of language in Gen 11:1–9 will be reversed by the pouring out of God's Spirit at Pentecost in Acts 2, where the term *glossa* (language) is used repeatedly as the confusion associated with language is removed. Then in the book of Revelation, at the concluding climax of the salvation story, the text declares that the Lamb (Christ) has "purchased for God persons from every tribe [*phyle*] and language [*glossa*] and people [*laos*] and nation (*ethne*)" (Rev 5:9 NIV; the same four words are repeated in Rev 11:9 and 14:6), apparently connecting back to the story of scattering and separation in Genesis 3–11 and declaring how Christ has reversed that, bringing all of these various groups together to worship him.[32]

Indeed, throughout Genesis 3–11 we have seen repeated sin and rebellion by the people God created, resulting in scattering across the world along with separation from God, the garden, and the tree of life. The stage is set for the salvation story to begin in Genesis 12 with the calling of Abraham and the formation of Israel.

Note, however, that Genesis 3–11 has already introduced the two major enemies that future Israel will confront. The Canaanites, introduced in Gen 9:25 ("Cursed be Canaan," NIV) will be their primary hostile opponent at their beginning (the conquest). The Babylonians, introduced in Gen 11:1–9, and clearly identified by the reference to "the land of Shinar" (11:2) and by the name "Babel" (11:9 NIV), will be their primary hostile opponent at the end (the destruction of Jerusalem and the exile). Indeed, Babylon is a symbol of opposition to God throughout the Bible.[33]

---

[32] Notice that the Revelation texts follow the same exact order as the Genesis 10 texts, with the exception that the Revelation texts drop the land terminology and substitute an additional term for people (*laos*).

[33] For example, see the long oracle of judgment against Babylon in Jeremiah 50–51, and note Babylon's role as a paradigmatic evil and hostile force against God in the book of Revelation (14:8; 16:19; 17:5; 18:2, 10, 21).

God Responds to Human Sin by Providing Deliverance through the Abrahamic Covenant (12:1–50:26)

ABRAHAM: THE PROMISE AND OBEDIENCE OF FAITH (12:1–23:20)

Abraham and the Promised Land (12:1–15:21)

The Abraham narrative (Gen 12:1–23:20) is one of the most important texts in the Old Testament. In response to the widespread human sin and rebellion described in Genesis 3–11, God now begins to unfold his master plan of restoration, a plan that zeroes in on one man (Abraham), his family, and his descendants (the Israelites) as the means to bless the rest of humankind and to restore their relationship with God. This story of salvation begins in Genesis 12 and culminates with the death, resurrection, and return of Jesus Christ.

Starting in Gen 11:27 and continuing until 17:2, the main character is known throughout the narrative as Abram, whose name means "exalted father." In 17:3–5 God changes his name to Abraham, which means "father of many nations," in keeping with the promise in 17:5–7. Since the New Testament and Christianity in general knows this famous patriarch as Abraham, we will use the name Abraham throughout, even in the early chapters that call him Abram.

Abraham, probably speaking a Northwest Semitic dialect (Hebrew has not developed yet), is living in Mesopotamia when God calls him. God tells him to leave his land, his people, and his father's house and to travel to a new land that God will show him (12:1). Indeed, this theme of separating from others for special service to God is a theme that runs throughout the Pentateuch.

God then makes an incredible promise to Abraham (12:2–3, 7): he promises to bless Abraham, to make him into a great nation, to make his name great, to bless those who bless Abraham, and to curse those who curse him, and through Abraham to bless all the people of the world. Note the contrast with the people who tried to construct the Tower of Babylon in Gen 11:1–9, who sought to make a name for themselves. Here God promises to make Abraham's name great. Then in Gen 12:8 Abraham builds an altar to the LORD (Yahweh) and calls on his name.

Due to poor decision-making and perhaps a lack of trust, however, Abraham ends up in Egypt, about to lose his wife (12:10–16). Yet, in accordance with God's earlier promises, God rescues Abraham and his wife, Sarah. In Genesis 13–14 the narrative demonstrates how God's blessings on Abraham will spill out on those around him, illustrating the tight connection between God's grace and his promises to Abraham.

In Genesis 13–14, Abraham's nephew Lot, who has separated from Abraham to live in the sinful city of Sodom, is captured and taken captive by an invading army. Abraham rallies the men in his entourage, defeats the invading army, and rescues Lot, recapturing all of Lot's possessions, and numerous other people. At this point Abraham is met by a rather enigmatic character, Melchizedek, king of Salem, who greets Abraham and blesses him (14:18–20). Abraham then gives Melchizedek a tenth of everything he has recaptured.

Along with Genesis 12, chapters 15 and 17 stand out as critical chapters in the overall story of Scripture, and they will feature prominently in our later discussion of Biblical and Gospel Connections. In Genesis 15 and 17 God appears to Abraham again and formalizes his promises from Genesis 12 into a covenant. As Genesis 15 opens, Abraham worries that he has no heirs. God takes Abraham outside and tells him to look at the stars, declaring that his descendants (Hebrew, *zera'*; lit., "seed") will be as numerous as the stars. According to v. 6, Abraham "believed the LORD, and he credited it to him as righteousness." In the New Testament this verse, which connects righteousness to faith, is foundational for Paul's theology of justification by faith.

God next leads Abraham through a formal covenant-making ceremony. He directs Abraham to cut several animals in half (15:9–10). Normally in this kind of ceremony both parties would pass between the animal halves, probably suggesting symbolically "may this happen to us if we break the covenant" (cf. Jer 34:18–20). Yet, in this instance, God passes through the cut halves alone (Gen 15:17–18), implying that he binds himself unilaterally to establishing and fulfilling this covenant, the Abrahamic covenant. This unearned favor and unilateral blessing from God is the Old Testament picture of grace.

Abraham and the Promised Seed (16:1–22:19)

In Genesis 17 God appears to Abraham again, telling him, "I am God Almighty. Live in my presence [lit., "walk before me"] and be blameless. I will set up [or "establish"] my covenant between me and you, and I will multiply you greatly" (17:1–2). God then restates several of his earlier promises to Abraham as ongoing components of this covenant. He explains that this will be a "permanent covenant" (17:7) and will continue with Abraham's offspring (descendants; lit., "seed") as the LORD (Yahweh) promises to be their God and to give them the land of Canaan. Finally, God tells Abraham that all his male descendants must be circumcised as a sign that they are part of the covenant (17:10–14).

In accordance with the establishment of this covenant, God also changes the names of Abraham and his wife. Up to this point, the patriarch's name was Abram, which meant "exalted father." God changes his name to Abraham, which means "father of a multitude" (17:3–5), reflecting the reality of the covenant promise that God has made him "the father of many nations" (17:5). The covenant itself is enshrined in the new name of the patriarch, Abraham. God had also included Abraham's wife, Sarai, in the covenant promises, stating that she will be blessed and that nations and kings will come "from her" (17:16), regardless of her advanced age and her life of barrenness, which is mentioned several times (15:2; 16:1; 17:17; 18:11; 21:1–7).[34] God also changes her name from Sarai to Sarah. In contrast to Abraham's name change, however, no meaning of either name is provided in the text. The two names are probably variant spellings and pronunciations of the same word meaning "princess," an appropriate name since God declares that nations and kings will come from her. The point of the name change is not in the meaning change in her name (which did not really change), but simply in the fact that God changed her name, an event that indicates she is also included in this centrally important covenant he has just established.[35]

Both Abraham (17:17) and Sarah (18:11–12) "laugh" with incredulity at the promise that she will bear a son in their old age. Yet God restates this promise firmly (17:19; 18:13–14), also indicating that this son will be named Isaac, a name that appropriately means "he laughs." Furthermore, God reminds them, "Is anything impossible for the LORD?"

In Genesis 18 God appears to Abraham to reiterate the promise of a son, but also to inform him of the upcoming judgment on Sodom and Gomorrah due to their serious sin (18:20). Remember our earlier study of the Hebrew word *ra'/ra'ah* ("bad stuff"). When the city of Sodom was first introduced in Gen 13:13, this word was used to describe the people of Sodom: "Now the men of Sodom were evil [*ra'ah*], sinning immensely against the LORD." Abraham's nephew Lot was living in Sodom at this time, and Abraham was worried about the upcoming judgment. He argues with God, asking, "Will you really sweep away the righteous with the wicked?" (18:23). Eventually, God agrees that if there are only ten righteous people in Sodom, he will not destroy it (18:32). But, alas, as Genesis 18 explains, there are not ten righteous people in Sodom. The only candidates are Lot, his wife, and his two daughters, and the righteousness of all of them is questionable.

---

[34] See also the New Testament reference in Heb 11:11–12.

[35] Goldingay, *Genesis*, 281; Gordon Wenham, *Genesis 16–50*, WBC 25.

In essence, all the men of the city of Sodom gather with the intention of gang-raping the two visitors (angels from God sent, ironically, to check out how sinful the city actually was; 18:20–21; 19:1–5).[36] The angels strike the people in this crowd with blindness and then force Lot and his family to leave, just before the destruction of both Sodom and Gomorrah. Throughout the rest of Scripture, the sin of Sodom and Gomorrah, along with the destruction of those cities, will be referenced frequently (twenty times) as a paradigm of serious sin and as an example of God's consequential righteous judgment, often as a warning.[37]

At last Sarah gives birth to the promised son, Isaac, in fulfillment of God's promise (21:1–7). Likewise, God confirms that it will be through Isaac that the promise of numerous offspring will be fulfilled (21:12). This sets up the dramatic and emotional events of Genesis 22, in which God tells Abraham to do the unthinkable: "Take your son . . . your only son Isaac, whom you love, go to the land of Moriah, and offer him there as a burnt offering on one of the mountains I will tell you about" (22:2). By faith Abraham obeys, and at the very last minute, God provides a substitute sacrifice for Isaac (22:11–13). God then restates two central aspects of his covenant promises to Abraham: (1) Abraham's descendants will be numerous, and (2) "through your offspring ['seed'] all nations on earth will be blessed" (22:18 NIV).

Transition to Isaac: Continuing the Patriarchal Promise (22:20–26:35)

Sarah's death is described in Genesis 23, along with the details of her burial by her husband, Abraham. Attention will now focus on the child of the promise, Isaac. As the story unfolds, however, Isaac plays a passive role (both with his father, Abraham, and in the dispute between his sons Jacob and Esau). His importance to the overall story, however, lies in the fact that God restates the covenant promise to him (Gen 26:1–5), indicating that it is through Isaac that the covenant will be continued. Thus he is the link that transmits the covenant promises from Abraham to Jacob and the twelve tribes of Israel.

---

[36] Goldingay, 303–4, notes that the stress of Gen 19:4 is on the culpability of the entire city.

[37] Deut 29:23; Judg 19:1–30; Isa 1:9–10; 3:9; 13:19; Jer 23:14; 49:18; 50:40; Lam 4:6; Ezek 16:44–58; Amos 4:11; Zeph 2:9; Matt 10:15; 11:23–24; Luke 10:12; 17:29; Rom 9:29; 2 Pet 2:6; Jude 1:7; Rev 11:8.

JACOB: STRUGGLES AND THE BEGINNING OF THE TWELVE TRIBES OF ISRAEL (27:1–37:1)

Jacob, Esau, and Family Conflict (27:1–28:9)

In contrast to his father, Isaac's, passive role, Jacob takes things into his own hands, scheming and struggling to get his inheritance and the accompanying promises. Like his grandmother Sarah, who had tried to help bring about the promised son by giving Abraham her servant Hagar (Gen 16:1–16), Jacob and his mother, Rebekah, seem intent on helping bring about what God has promised. God enables Rebekah, barren at first, to get pregnant—with twins, no less. The twins begin their fight even while in the womb (Gen 25:22), a struggle that will foreshadow an ongoing conflict between Jacob and Esau that will drive the story all the way to Genesis 36. Yet during the pregnancy God tells Rebekah that "the older will serve the younger" (25:23). This lays the groundwork for an ongoing narrative tension between how God moves to fulfill his divine promise and how the central people in his plan employ human efforts—trickery and deceit—to try to bring about the fulfillment of this plan.

Jacob's twin brother, Esau, was born first, giving Esau the firstborn rights of inheritance, but Jacob, with Rebekah's help, tricks his blind father, Isaac, into giving him the family blessing (the inheritance) instead. The infuriated Esau seeks to kill Jacob, so Rebekah proposes to Isaac that Jacob go back to Paddan-aram (in Mesopotamia) to live with her relatives and to find a proper wife there. This was in contrast to Esau, who had first married a local Hethite woman,[38] a Canaanite (26:34–35), and then made things even worse by marrying an Ishmaelite (28:9). Isaac agrees to Rebekah's proposal.

Jacob Chastened, Yet Still Blessed, and the Promise Continues (28:10–30:43)

On Jacob's trip to Paddan-aram, God appears to him in a dream, identifying himself as "the LORD, the God of your father Abraham and the God of Isaac" (28:13). God then restates the patriarchal promise of land and descendants and that "all the peoples on earth will be blessed through you and your offspring" (28:14). God likewise promises "I am with you" (28:15).

---

[38] While many English translations still translate this word *Hethite* as "Hittite" (e.g., NIV, ESV, NRSVue), recent scholarship is trending toward translating it "Hethite." The Hethites were a subgroup of the Canaanites. See Longman, "Genesis," 102, 105.

Jacob arrives in Paddan-aram and falls in love with Rachel, the beautiful daughter of Laban, a relative of his mother, Rebekah. Jacob agrees to live with Laban and to work for him for seven years so he can marry Rachel. However, just as Jacob deceived his father, Isaac, to reverse the firstborn/second-born blessings, Laban deceives Jacob into following the normal firstborn/second-born order in marrying off his daughters. Jacob is tricked into marrying Leah, the firstborn daughter, first. To marry Rachel, Jacob must agree to work for Laban another seven years (29:1–30). The trickster has himself been tricked, but despite this family discord and deceit, the plan of God and his promise to these patriarchs continues to move forward.

These two wives (Leah and Rachel), along with their maidservants (who become Jacob's concubines, a sort of secondary wife with rights for support but not inheritance), will give birth to twelve sons, whose descendants will develop into the twelve tribes of Israel. These sons are Reuben, Simeon, Levi, Judah, Zebulun, Issachar, Dan, Gad, Asher, Naphtali, Joseph, and Benjamin. All these sons will develop into a tribe except Joseph, who will have two sons (Manasseh and Ephraim), each of whom develops into a tribe. Levi will become a special tribe, the tribe of priests (the Levites). Someday, after the conquest of the Promised Land in the book of Joshua, specific territory will be allocated to each of the other twelve tribes, including Manasseh and Ephraim. The Levites, as priests, however, were to be scattered throughout the land, and thus they were not allocated any specific tribal territory. Instead, they are allocated several cities within the other tribal regions (Joshua 21). When referring to the territorial breakdown of early Israel, there are twelve tribes, while in actuality, including the Levites, there were thirteen. Not only was Jacob blessed to have twelve sons, but God also blessed him with large flocks and herds as well as numerous servants (30:43).

Jacob Returns, Followed by Time of Transition (31:1–37:1)

Eventually Jacob returns to Canaan and repairs his relationship with his brother, Esau. Yet the theme of deceit continues to play an ironic role in the story. The Hebrew word *ganab* can mean "to steal" or "to deceive" (i.e., "to steal the heart of"). In a wordplay it is used with both meanings in Gen 31:19–20, as Jacob sneaks away from Laban. The text says, "When Laban had gone to shear his sheep, Rachel *stole* [*ganab*] her father's household idols. And Jacob *deceived* [*ganab*] Laban the Aramean, not telling him that he was fleeing" (emphasis added). This word *ganab* is used four more times in the following verses (31:26, 27, 30, 32). When Laban catches up to Jacob and accuses him of stealing his household gods, Jacob, not knowing that Rachel was the thief, declares in a vow that anyone who has Laban's gods "will not live" (31:32). Ironically, his vow apparently comes true when his beloved Rachel dies giving birth to Benjamin (35:16–19).

While on that trip, Jacob has another dramatic encounter with God (Gen 32:22–32), after which Jacob is renamed Israel (which probably means "he struggles with God"). Although Jacob's character and behavior are often questionable, not to mention the terrible behavior of his sons (34:1–31; 35:22), God in his grace blesses him anyway (32:29) and continues the Abrahamic covenant promises with him (35:9–15).

This unit ends with the death and burial of Rachel and Isaac (35:16–29), followed by a genealogy of Esau's descendants in Genesis 36. He will be the "father" of the Edomites, and a list of Edomite kings is added here as well (36:31–43). The Edomites, living to the southeast of the Israelites, will be a perennial enemy of Israel's (and Judah's) for much of the rest of the Old Testament (Jer 49:7–22; Obadiah vv. 1–6).

Joseph: Faithfulness and God's Sovereign Deliverance (37:2–50:26)

Joseph Is Betrayed by His Jealous Brothers and Sold into Slavery (37:2–38:30)

Paralleling the conflict between Jacob and Esau, a similar conflict between Joseph and his ten older brothers will drive the story for the rest of Genesis. What is shocking in this narrative story is the terrible immoral behavior of the older brothers, who at first plan to kill Joseph and then decided instead to make money by selling him into slavery (37:2–36). The theme of deceit continues, as the older brothers then dip Joseph's robe in goat blood to deceive their father Jacob into thinking that a vicious animal had killed his favorite son (37:31–35). Once again, the trickster gets tricked.

In addition, an entire chapter (38) is devoted to presenting the immoral lifestyle and behavior of Judah, one of Joseph's older brothers. In this context, the strong moral character of Joseph will be a huge contrast to that of Judah. For example, Judah sleeps with his daughter-in-law, thinking she is a prostitute. Later, after he finds out that she is pregnant—but not knowing yet that he is the father—he proclaims that she should die, which he later retracts (38:6–26). Joseph, on the other hand, refuses the advances of his master, Potiphar's, wife, telling her, "How could I do this immense evil, and how could I sin against God?" (39:9). Indeed, Joseph is one of the few people in this family who trusts in God and seeks to live a righteous and moral life.

Joseph Rises to Power in Egypt (39:1–41:57)

In stark contrast to the story of Judah's immoral behavior in Genesis 38, Joseph, when confronted with an immoral sexual temptation, responds virtuously (39:1–23). As a result, however, he ends up in prison. Throughout this story, the text notes that "the LORD was with Joseph" (39:2, 21, 23), giving him success in all that he did, even as a prisoner or slave.

One of the blessings that God gave to Joseph in Egypt was the ability to interpret dreams. This leads to a favorable relationship with the Egyptian pharaoh, who, ironically, soon promotes Joseph from imprisoned slave to the second-highest position in Egypt. While in this position, Joseph initiates a national food gathering and storage program that will save Egypt from a famine (40:1–41:57), thus fulfilling what God had promised Abraham in Gen 12:3: "I will bless those who bless you."

Joseph and His Family Are Reconciled (42:1–46:27)

This famine, however, also strikes the land of Canaan, sending Joseph's family to Egypt to try to buy food. Joseph, unrecognized by his brothers at first, now has the power of life and death over them. The ironic trickery continues when Joseph chooses not to reveal who he is (42:7–9), connives to get the brothers to bring Benjamin to Egypt (42:14–20), and then plants a silver cup (used for divination; 44:5) in Benjamin's sack to indict him (44:1–13). (Recall that Benjamin's mother, Rachel, had hidden the household gods in her camel's saddlebag; 31:34.) Yet, in contrast to his earlier treacherous and immoral behavior, Judah, one of Joseph's older brothers, exhibits an attitude of selflessness, willing to offer himself as a ransom instead of Benjamin (44:33). Likewise, although his treacherous brothers had sold him into slavery, Joseph now reveals his identity to them, forgives them, and restores the relationship, caring and providing for them. With Pharaoh's full financial support, Joseph invites his father, Jacob, and his entire family to come live in Egypt (45:16–20). The trickery and deceit have ended.

The Patriarchal Promise Revived (46:28–50:26)

Pharaoh invites the family of Joseph to settle in "the best part of the land" (47:6). Jacob, in his old age, is able to come to Egypt as well, blessing Pharaoh as he arrives (47:7–10). Because of Joseph's planning, even though the famine hits the entire area, Egypt has plenty of food. His family settles in the region of Goshen, where they become "fruitful and very numerous" (47:27), a further fulfillment of God's promise to Abraham.

Before Jacob dies, he gives a blessing to Joseph's two sons, Manasseh and Ephraim (48:1–22), in addition to giving a final blessing on his eleven other sons (49:1–28). Jacob then dies and is buried back in the land of Canaan (49:29–50:14), although the rest of the family remains in Egypt. Joseph reassures his brothers that he will still look out for them. Using the familiar contrasting terms *good* (*tov*) and *bad* (*ra'ah*), Joseph interprets the events that have transpired in light of God's plan: "You intended to harm me [*ra'ah*], but God intended it for good [*tov*]" (50:20 NIV). Right before Joseph dies he reminds his brothers of the important promise that God had made with their forefathers, stating, "I am about to die, but God will certainly come to your aid and bring you up from this land to the land he swore to give to Abraham, Isaac, and Jacob" (50:24). Indeed, fulfilling this promise will drive the story from Exodus to Joshua.

Biblical Connections

Serving as the opening book of the canon, and introducing several major biblical themes, Genesis unsurprisingly connects to the rest of the Bible in numerous ways. For example, the theme of creation introduced in Genesis is developed into an eschatological hope of a "new creation" in the prophets (see esp. Isa 65:17), a hope brought to consummation in Revelation 21–22.[39]

Likewise, several parallels can be found between Genesis 1–3 and Revelation 19–22 (see table 1.1). This creates an *inclusio*, or "bookends," type of canonical opening and closing. Besides the theme of God as Creator, one of the other most critical theological features of this *inclusio* is the presence of God among his people. That is, the Bible opens with the presence of God in the garden interacting with his people, and it closes with the same picture—a restored presence of God with his people (and a restored relationship) in the garden again. This is the culmination of the theological theme of God's relational presence that starts in Genesis and drives the story of Scripture all the way to Revelation.[40]

---

[39] Frank Thielman, *The New Creation and the Storyline of Scripture*, SSBT (Wheaton, IL: Crossway, 2021).

[40] Duvall and Hays, *God's Relational Presence*, 335–36.

Table 1.1: Parallels between Genesis 1–3 and Revelation 19–22[41]

Genesis 1–3	Revelation 19–22
"In the beginning . . ." (1:1)	"I am . . . the beginning and the end." (21:6; 22:13)
"In the beginning God created the heavens and the earth . . . darkness covered the surface of the watery depths." (1:1–2)	"Then I saw a new heaven and a new earth; for the first heaven and the first earth had passed away, and the sea was no more." (21:1)
"God made the two great lights—the greater light to rule over the day and the lesser light to rule over the night." (1:16)	"The city does not need the sun or the moon to shine on it, because the glory of God illuminates it. . . . Night will be no more; people will not need . . . the light of the sun, because the Lord God will give them light." (21:23; 22:5)
"A river went out from Eden to water the garden." (2:10)	"Then he showed me the river . . . flowing from the throne of God." (22:1)
"The LORD God planted a garden . . . and . . . caused to grow out of the ground every tree pleasing in appearance and good for food, including the tree of life in the middle of the garden." (2:8–9)	"Then he showed me the river of the water of life. . . . The tree of life was on each side of the river, bearing twelve kinds of fruit." (22:1–2)
"The ground is cursed because of you. . . . You will eat bread by the sweat of your brow until you return to the ground, since you were taken from it." (3:17, 19)	"There will no longer be any curse." (22:3)
"Now the serpent was the most cunning of all the wild animals. . . . He said to the woman, 'Did God really say . . . ?'" (3:1)	"He seized the dragon, that ancient serpent who is the devil and Satan, and bound him for a thousand years. . . . The devil who deceived them was thrown into the lake of fire and sulfur." (20:2, 10)
"Then the LORD God . . . brought her to the man. . . . This is why a man leaves his father and mother and bonds with his wife, and they become one flesh." (2:22, 24)	"The marriage of the Lamb has come, and his bride has prepared herself. . . . 'Come, I will show you the bride, the wife of the Lamb.'" (19:7; 21:9)

---

[41] Taken from J. Scott Duvall, "Revelation," *BIBH*, 991.

Genesis 1–3	Revelation 19–22
"Then the man and his wife heard the sound of the LORD God walking in the garden at the time of the evening breeze." (3:8)	"Look, God's dwelling is with humanity, and he will live with them." (21:3)

Related to this is the important theological truth echoing from Genesis throughout Scripture that God is the Creator, the one who created all things. As Creator, God is worthy of praise (see especially Psalms), and he also thus has the sovereign, authoritative right to rule and to decree both judgment and deliverance (see especially Isaiah and Job),[42] themes that likewise continue to be stressed in the New Testament (e.g., Rom 1:25; Eph 3:9; Col 1:15–20; 1 Pet 4:19; Rev 4:11). Not only does the creation story in Genesis 1–3 play a critical role in our theology of God, but Genesis 1–3 also is crucial in other doctrines as well, including anthropology (e.g., the nature or composition of human beings, sin, fallenness, marriage, sexuality) and our understanding of Satan.[43]

Twice Paul pulls Adam into his Christological/soteriological explanations, contrasting him with Christ. In Rom 5:12–21 Paul contrasts the consequences brought about by the "one man" Adam with the consequences brought about by the "one man" Christ. At the heart of the discussion, Paul states, "If by the one man's [Adam's] trespass, death reigned through that one man, how much more will those who receive the overflow of grace and the gift of righteousness reign in life through the one man, Jesus Christ" (5:17).

In 1 Cor 15:42–49 Paul uses the contrast between Adam and Christ to help explain the resurrection. He writes, "The first man [Adam] was of the dust of the earth; the second man [Christ] is of heaven. As was the earthly man, so are those who are of the earth; and as is the heavenly man, so also are those who are of heaven" (15:47–48 NIV).

---

[42] Terence E. Fretheim, *God and World in the Old Testament: A Relational Theology of Creation* (Nashville: Abingdon, 2005). Fretheim argues that God's role as Creator in Scripture stresses his relationship to the creation. See also David P. Nelson, "The Work of God: Creation and Providence," in Daniel L. Akin, ed., *A Theology for the Church* (Nashville: B&H Academic, 2007), 242–92.

[43] John Goldingay, *Biblical Theology: The God of the Christian Scriptures* (Downers Grove, IL: IVP, 2016), 134–214; John S. Hammett, "Human Nature," in *A Theology for the Church*, 340–408.

Another character introduced in Genesis that echoes across Scripture is the serpent (Hebrew, *nahash*; LXX Greek, *ophis*), typically understood to represent Satan. The depiction of Satan as a serpent, snake, or dragon, and thus as a hostile enemy of God, appears in several places, usually with a focus on God's defeat of the serpent. Isaiah 27:1 equates the serpent with Leviathan: "On that day the LORD . . . will bring judgment on Leviathan, the fleeing serpent" (Hebrew, *nahash*; LXX Greek, *ophis*). The references to Leviathan in Job 41 are perhaps a reference to Satan the serpent as well. Then in Revelation, the serpent (*ophis*) is mentioned again, identified twice clearly as Satan (Rev 12:9; 20:2).[44]

Another central theme introduced in Genesis that helps to drive the overall biblical story is God's promise and covenant with Abraham, Isaac, and Jacob. The fulfillment of God's promise of land, descendants, and blessings, as well as his promise that in Abraham all the nations of the world would be blessed, drives the story from Exodus all the way into the New Testament. Note especially the following Old Testament texts:

> God heard their groaning, and God remembered his covenant with Abraham, with Isaac, and with Jacob. God saw the Israelites, and God knew. (Exod 2:24–25)

> "Enter and take possession of the land the LORD swore to give to your ancestors Abraham, Isaac, and Jacob and their future descendants." (Deut 1:8)

> So the LORD gave Israel all the land he had sworn to give their ancestors, and they took possession of it and settled there. (Josh 21:43)

> But the LORD was gracious to them, had compassion on them, and turned toward them because of his covenant with Abraham, Isaac, and Jacob. He was not willing to destroy them. Even now he has not banished them from his presence. (2 Kgs 13:23)

> He remembers his covenant forever, the promise he ordained for a thousand generations—the covenant he made with Abraham, swore to Isaac, and confirmed to Jacob as a decree and to Israel as a permanent covenant: "I will give the land of Canaan to you as your inherited portion." (Ps 105:8–11)

---

[44] For a development of this theme across Scripture see Andrew David Naselli, *The Serpent and the Serpent Slayer*, SSBT (Wheaton, IL: Crossway, 2020); and L. Michael Morales, *Exodus Old and New: A Biblical Theology of Redemption*, ESBT (Downers Grove, IL: IVP, 2020), 54–65.

Likewise, in Matt 1:1 the New Testament opens with, "An account of the genealogy [Greek, *genesis*] of Jesus Christ, the Son of David, the Son of Abraham." This is probably an allusion back to God's Old Testament covenants with David (2 Samuel 7) and with Abraham (Genesis 12, 15, 17, 22), presenting Jesus Christ as the fulfillment of these two covenants.[45] Furthermore, as discussed later, in Romans 4 and Galatians 3 Paul explains in depth the multifaceted ways in which the Abrahamic covenant is fulfilled in Christ and how it underpins the doctrine of justification by faith.

In Genesis 14 Abraham encounters the priestly-king Melchizedek, king of Salem. In Psalm 110, a Messianic-Davidic psalm, God declares to the coming messianic king, "You are a priest forever according to the pattern of Melchizedek" (Ps 110:4). In the New Testament, the book of Hebrews draws numerous connections in pattern between Melchizedek and Jesus Christ. Speaking of Melchizedek, Heb 7:2–3 explains, "First, his name means king of righteousness, then also, king of Salem, meaning king of peace. Without father, mother, or genealogy, having neither beginning of days nor end of life, but resembling the Son of God, he remains a priest forever."

The thirteen tribes (twelve tribes who receive settlement land in Joshua, plus the Levites, who are not assigned a specific region) introduced in Genesis 37–50 will continue to define the organizational structure and regional living situation throughout the rest the Old Testament.

The terrible behavior of Joseph's older brothers in Genesis seems to foreshadow difficulties and bad behavior in the future. Numerous scholars note the implied intertextual parallels between the immoral behavior of Jacob's four oldest sons (Reuben, Simeon, Levi, and Judah) and the struggle for power and behavior of David's four sons (Amnon, Absalom, Adonijah, and Solomon) in the unraveling of David's kingdom in 2 Sam 13:1–20:26.[46]

---

[45] W. D. Davies and Dale C. Allison Jr., *The Gospel According to Saint Matthew*, ICC, 3 vols. (Edinburgh: T&T Clark, 1988–97), 1:149–59. Davies and Allison, 149–54, also argue that the use of the term *genesis*, although usually translated as "genealogy," nonetheless suggests a connection to the book of Genesis (esp. Gen 1:1; 2; and 5:1) and implies the "new creation" concept. They suggest the translation "Book of the New Genesis wrought by Jesus Christ, son of David, son of Abraham." Similarly, see also Thielman, *The New Creation*, 59–60.

[46] For example, in Genesis 35 Reuben sleeps with his father's concubine, and in 2 Samuel 16 Absalom sleeps with several of his father's concubines. See the discussion in J. Daniel Hays, "1 and 2 Samuel, Books of," in *The Dictionary of the New Testament Use of the Old Testament*, ed. Gregory K. Beale et al. (Grand Rapids: Baker Academic, 2023); and Gary Edward Schnittjer, *The Torah Story: An Apprenticeship on the Pentateuch* (Grand Rapids: Zondervan, 2006), 151–52.

Gospel Connections

In Romans 4 and Galatians 3 the apostle Paul provides an extensive explanation of the critical theological relationship between God's promises to Abraham in Genesis 12, 15, 17, and 22, and the fulfillment of these promises in Christ. In Rom 4:3 and 4:22–23, Paul quotes Gen 15:6 as foundational to his explanation of the doctrine of justification by faith. He likewise argues that if the promise comes by faith to Abraham (and not through the law), then the promise comes by faith to Abraham's descendants, including the Gentiles, who come by faith. Paul concludes, "This is why the promise is by faith, so that it may be according to grace, to guarantee it to all the descendants—not only to the one who is of the law but also to the one who is of Abraham's faith. He is the father of us all" (Rom 4:16).

In Galatians 3, Paul is even more explicit, explaining the importance and centrality of faith as well as the fact that Gentiles who come to Christ by faith are the heirs of the promise to Abraham. For example, after quoting Gen 15:6, Paul declares, "You know, then, that *those who have faith, these are Abraham's sons*. Now the Scripture saw in advance that God would justify the Gentiles by faith and proclaimed the gospel ahead of time to Abraham, saying, **All the nations will be blessed through you**. Consequently, those who have faith are blessed with Abraham, who had faith" (Gal 3:7–9, emphasis added). A few verses later Paul states, "The purpose was that the blessing of Abraham would come to the Gentiles by Christ Jesus, so that we could receive the promised Spirit through faith" (3:14).

Similarly, Paul expounds the theological ramifications brought about by Christ regarding the Abrahamic promises concerning Abraham's "seed" (descendants or offspring). Two themes are central in the Abraham promises regarding his "seed": (1) God promises that Abraham's "seed" will be too numerous to count (Gen 22:17 KJV), and (2) God promises that through Abraham's "seed" all nations on earth [will] be blessed (22:18 KJV). Paul will stress that it is through faith that people, including Gentiles, become the "seed" of Abraham, not through physical descent (Rom 4:16–17; 9:6–8; Gal 3:7–9 KJV). Paul also indicates that in a sense the "seed" promise was fulfilled by Christ. Noting the use of the singular word *seed*, Paul points out that the promise about the "seed" is ultimately fulfilled in Christ, who is "the Seed" (Gal 3:16–19). Paul then explains that if people are baptized into Christ by faith, they belong to Christ and are Abraham's "seed" and thus become the heirs of the covenant promises (3:26–29 KJV).

Finally, although there is no consensus about this, it is very probable that Genesis 22 (Abraham about to sacrifice his son Isaac) functions as a typology (or foreshadowing) for the sacrifice of Jesus Christ. A number of similarities in the two stories suggest this: (1) a father and the sacrifice or threatened sacrifice of the son, (2) the mention of the father's son and the father's love for the son, (3) the proximity of the two locations (that could be identical—a mountain near Moriah [probably the Temple Mount] versus Calvary), and (4) the son carrying wood. Likewise, a few instances in the New Testament use nearly identical phrases:

"Take your son, your only son, whom you love . . ." (Gen 22:2 NIV)

"This is my Son, whom I love." (Matt 3:17 NIV; cf. Luke 3:22)

". . . because you have *not withheld* [LXX Greek, *ouk epheisō*] from me your son, your only son." (Gen 22:12 NIV, emphasis added)

He who did not spare [Greek, *ouk epheisato*] his own Son, but gave him up for us all . . . (Rom 8:32 NIV)

The point of the typology would be that the Genesis 22 account is presenting the sacrifice of the son from the father's agonizing perspective, underscoring how painful and difficult such a sacrifice would be. Of course, the huge contrast between the two events is that Abraham the father is allowed a reprieve and is not actually required to sacrifice his son. A substitute is provided. For God the Father, however, no substitute can be provided because his Son is the substitute. Thus, he has to go through with the sacrifice. Ironically, the sacrifice of God's Son becomes the means of fulfilling the promises God makes to Abraham.

Life Connections

One of the most foundational, underlying theological and relational realities of life that we can learn as Christians comes from Genesis 1—God is the Creator, and we are the creatures. If we get this basic relationship straight and live accordingly, a lot of life's complications dissipate and disappear. The implications are equally important. If God is the Creator, then he is sovereign over all, and thus he is the one who determines what is right and what is wrong, what is true and what is false. Our role as "the creatures" is to obey him.

Likewise, the understanding that everyone is created in the image of God is foundational for how we view and treat people. All people thus have this special dignity of being in God's image, and there is no place for racial, ethnic, or socioeconomic prejudices among the people of God.

From the Abraham narratives we learn that salvation is by grace through faith, one of the most important and foundational theological truths in Christianity. The apostle Paul points out that not only did God credit Abraham's faith to him as righteousness (Gen 15:6) but that this occurred before the law was even given (Romans 4; Galatians 3). Thus, we learn the critical truth that we are not saved by the law but by grace through faith. In addition, we learn from Abraham how true faith produces faithful obedience.

How we as Christians see the world and how we view human history should be driven by God's promise to Abraham that all peoples and nations on earth will be blessed through him, or through his "seed" (i.e., Jesus Christ; Gen 12:3; 22:18). Jesus Christ is the means by which the nations of the world will be blessed (and find salvation). This reality underlies our theology of missions. Indeed, all of human history flows toward this goal.

Interactive Questions

1-1. Explain the implications of Genesis 1 with regard to the philosophical question of how right and wrong is determined.

1-2. In your view, how does Genesis 1–2 relate to scientific theories regarding the origin of the universe and the origin of life? What is the genre of Genesis 1–2, and how much relevance should be given to the ANE literary background?

1-3. What can we learn from Genesis 3 about marriage?

1-4. Why are God's promises to Abraham so important? How does the New Testament interact with these promises?

1-5. Using a concordance, track the theme of "the seed of Abraham" throughout the Old Testament and the New Testament. Why is this phrase significant?

1-6. In what ways does Abraham demonstrate faith in God? When does he seem to be doubting or not trusting?

1-7. Explain the roles of the matriarchs (Sarah, Rebekah, Leah, and Rachel) in the story of the patriarchs.

1-8. Jacob has sometimes been called "the trickster." Trace out the theme of deceit or trickery in the life of Jacob.

1-9. In what ways does the character of Joseph stand in contrast to the character of his brothers, especially Reuben, Simeon, Levi, and Judah?

1-10. Discuss how Joseph went from slave to the second most powerful man in Egypt. How did he deal with despairing circumstances, and how actively was God involved?

Recommended Resources

Charles, J. Daryl, ed. *Reading Genesis 1–2: An Evangelical Conversation*. Peabody, MA: Hendrickson, 2013.

Collins, C. John. *Reading Genesis Well: Navigating History, Poetry, Science, and Truth in Genesis 1–11*. Grand Rapids: Zondervan, 2018.

Dozeman, Thomas B. *The Pentateuch: Introducing the Torah*. Minneapolis: Fortress, 2017.

Goldingay, John. *Genesis*. BCOT: Pentateuch. Edited by Bill T. Arnold. Grand Rapids: Baker Academic, 2020.

Longman, Tremper, III. *Genesis*. SGBC. Grand Rapids: Zondervan, 2016.

———. "Genesis." In *BIBBC*, edited by J. Scott Duvall and J. Daniel Hays, 80–119. Grand Rapids: Baker, 2020.

Walton, John H. *Genesis*. NIVAC. Grand Rapids: Zondervan, 2001.

Wenham, Gordon J. *Genesis 1–15*. WBC. Waco, TX: Word, 1987.

———. *Genesis 16–50*. WBC. Waco, TX: Word, 1994.

2

Exodus

"And they will know that I am the Lord *their God, who*
brought them out of the land of Egypt, so that I might
dwell among them. I am the Lord *their God."*

—Exodus 29:46

Outline

I.   Deliverance and covenant (1:1–24:18)[1]
    A. Yahweh delivers Israel from Egypt (1:1–15:21)
        1. Pharaoh oppresses the Israelites (1:1–22)
        2. Holiness, presence, and power: Yahweh calls Moses from within the burning bush (2:1–4:17)

---

[1] As explained in the introduction, while discussing the books of Exodus, Leviticus, Numbers, and Deuteronomy, the transliterated term *Yahweh* will be the primary name used when referring to God.

61

   3.   Who is Yahweh? The initial confrontation with Pharaoh
        (4:18–7:7)
   4.   Yahweh versus Pharaoh: the first nine plagues (7:8–10:29)
   5.   The tenth plague, the exodus, and deliverance at the Red Sea
        (11:1–15:21)
   B. Yahweh establishes a covenant with Israel at Mount Sinai
       (15:22–24:18)
       1.   Yahweh leads Israel from the Red Sea to Mount Sinai
            (15:22–18:27)
       2.   Holiness, presence, and power: Yahweh calls Israel from Mount
            Sinai (19:1–25)
       3.   Yahweh gives the heart of the covenant: the Ten
            Commandments (20:1–21)
       4.   The book of the covenant: revealed, written, and ratified
            (20:22–24:18)
II.   Yahweh guides the Israelites in constructing the tabernacle, the dwelling
      place for his presence (25:1–40:38)
      A. Yahweh gives instructions for building the tabernacle (25:1–31:18)
          1.   Yahweh gives instructions for constructing the tabernacle and
               the items inside and outside of the tabernacle (25:1–27:19)
          2.   Yahweh gives instructions for the priests and for operating the
               tabernacle (27:20–30:38)
          3.   Yahweh selects the lead workers and restates the importance of
               Sabbath observance (31:1–18)
      B. An unexpected interruption: sinful rebellion and covenant
          restoration (32:1–34:35)
          1.   The golden calf episode jeopardizes the people of Israel's
               covenant relationship with Yahweh, and his indwelling presence
               with them (32:1–10)
          2.   Moses intercedes and Yahweh reestablishes his covenant
               relationship and presence with Israel (33:7–34:35)
      C. Moses and Israel complete the tabernacle according to Yahweh's
          instructions and Yahweh comes to reside there (32:11–40:38)
          1.   The tabernacle is built exactly as Yahweh instructed
               (35:1–40:33)
          2.   The glory of Yahweh fills the tabernacle (40:34–38)

Author, Date, and Message

Author and Date

As discussed in the introduction, the view of this book is that Moses wrote the book of Exodus, with perhaps a small degree of grammatical and place-name updating occurring later. As underscored in that discussion, recall that several texts in Exodus mention the process of transcribing material into writing, whether by Moses or by Yahweh himself (Exod 24:4, 12; 31:18; 34:1, 27–28). Likewise, Exodus includes references to these written documents, such as "the covenant scroll" (24:7), "the stone tablets," the "tablets," and the "tablets of the testimony" (24:12; 31:18; 32:15–19; 34:1–4, 28–29).

The writing events of Exodus 24 take place three months after Yahweh led the Israelites out of Egypt. Because the book of Exodus does not provide the name of either pharaoh in the story, and due to the ambiguity of the archaeological data, there is some uncertainty about the date of the exodus event. In fact, there is no agreement even among evangelical scholars. Two primary options have been identified: an early date (1446 BC) and a later date (around 1270–1260 BC).[2] The early date is derived from 1 Kgs 6:1, which states that the fourth year of Solomon's reign (the start of the temple construction) was 480 years after the exodus. Solomon's fourth year can be placed accurately at 996 BC. If the 480 years is to be taken literally, the exodus occurred in 1446 BC. The second view relies on Exod 1:11, which mentions that the Israelites built a supply city or store city named Rameses. This suggests a reference to Pharaoh Ramesses II, who built this store city in 1270 BC. In addition, those advocating a later date argue that the archeological evidence in several Canaanite cities indicates that the conquest took place in the thirteenth century. Yet both sides have produced counterarguments. Are the 480 years to be taken literally, or is it a symbolic number for an idealized amount of time—40 × 12 (both 40 and 12 are special biblical numbers; i.e., 40 years of wandering, 12 tribes)? Was the store city of Rameses called "Rameses" when the Israelites built it, or was it renamed that later, after Ramesses II came to the throne? Likewise, the

---

[2] Cautiously favoring the early date is Longman and Dillard, *An Introduction to the Old Testament*, 65–69 (see intro., n. 14). For a defense of the late date (while primarily arguing for general historicity) see James K. Hoffmeier, "The Thirteenth-Century (Late-Date) Exodus View," in *Five Views on the Exodus: Historicity, Chronology, and Theological Implications*, ed. Mark D. Janzen (Grand Rapids: Zondervan, 2021), 81–108.

archaeological evidence used to support the late date for the conquest is often rather ambiguous.[3]

It is perhaps good to keep in mind that the range between the two dates is not large, only 186–87 years, more or less. For determining historical and cultural background, both dates fall in the New Kingdom period of Egypt (1550–1069 BC). The historical and cultural background would be similar for both dates. Determining the date would help us in identifying the two pharaohs, but the text itself seems to deliberately omit those names (see below). Thus, deciding on the early date or the late date is not a critical factor in interpreting the book.

What is critical for interpreting the book of Exodus is whether or not one views it as historical. Some nonevangelical scholars maintain that the exodus event is largely myth and did not really happen, or that it did not happen on the scale described in the book of Exodus.[4] Among evangelical scholars, however, there is a consensus that the exodus event did happen. Yahweh did really bring the Israelites out of Egypt in miraculous fashion and enter into a covenant with them. This is the testimony, not only of Exodus, but also the rest of the Bible. Furthermore, the exodus is not a marginal event; it is the central paradigm for salvation and deliverance in the Old Testament, and it is central to the self-identity by which God reveals himself ("I am Yahweh who brought you up out of Egypt"). It is central to the message of the Old Testament. Thus, while the arguments over the early date versus the late date might not be all that important, the argument over the historicity of the exodus event is extremely important.[5]

---

[3] For example, Bimson challenges the way the archaeological data in Canaan have been used to defend the late date. See John J. Bimson, *Redating the Exodus and Conquest*, JSOTSS 5 (Sheffield, UK: University of Sheffield, 1981).

[4] Hendel, for example, argues that the biblical account of the exodus is "cultural memory," which he defines as "a representation of the past with present relevance. . . . To make the past relevant for the present, cultural memory distorts, omits, and fictionalizes aspects of the past." See Ronald Hendel, "The Exodus as Cultural Memory View," in Janzen, *Five Views on the Exodus*, 235–55.

[5] For a good defense of the historicity of Exodus from an academic evangelical viewpoint, see James K. Hoffmeier, *Israel in Egypt: The Evidence for the Authenticity of the Exodus Tradition* (Oxford: Oxford University Press, 1996); James K. Hoffmeier, *Ancient Israel in Sinai: The Evidence for the Authenticity of the Wilderness Tradition* (Oxford: Oxford University Press, 2005); James K. Hoffmeier, Alan R. Millard, and Gary A. Rendsburg, eds., *"Did I Not Bring Israel Out of Egypt?": Biblical, Archaeological, and Egyptological Perspectives on the Exodus Narratives*, BBRSup 13 (Winona Lake, IN: Eisenbrauns, 2016); and K. A. Kitchen, *On the Reliability of the Old Testament* (Grand Rapids: Eerdmans, 2003), 241–312.

In the Hebrew Bible, in keeping with the rest of the Pentateuch, the Hebrew title of this book comes from the opening phrase in the book and translates as "These are the names." The Septuagint (the Greek translation of the Old Testament) titled this book as *Exodos*, a Greek word that means "going out," or simply "exit." Indeed, even today throughout modern Greece one will see the Greek word *exodos* on exit signs in buildings and for off-ramps from highways. The Latin Vulgate "latinized" the spelling as *exodus*, and our English translations follow that spelling.

The Message of Exodus

The story of Exodus breaks into two halves and yet centers around three focal events: In the first half, (1) Yahweh delivers the Israelites from Egypt, and (2) Yahweh then enters into a covenant agreement with Israel at Mount Sinai. As part of that covenant agreement, Yahweh promises to dwell in Israel's midst. Then, in the second half, (3) Yahweh gives the details for constructing the tabernacle (the place where he will dwell) and the Israelites build the tabernacle, followed by Yahweh's descent to indwell the tabernacle. Likewise, three major interrelated theological themes run throughout the book and drive the story: deliverance by Yahweh, knowing Yahweh, and the presence of Yahweh.

Interpretive Overview

Deliverance and Covenant (1:1–24:18)

Yahweh Delivers Israel from Egypt (1:1–15:21)

Pharaoh Oppresses the Israelites (1:1–22)

The book of Genesis ended with the family of Jacob (renamed Israel) living in Egypt. Exodus 1 connects to the ending of Genesis and continues the story. Exodus 1:1–7 indicates that time has passed (Gen 15:13 predicted a time in Egypt of 400 years); Joseph and his brothers have died. Perhaps the main point stressed in this opening is that the descendants of Jacob/Israel numbered only seventy when they went into Egypt but that now "the Israelites [lit., 'the sons of Israel'] were fruitful, increased rapidly, multiplied, and became extremely numerous so that the land was filled with them" (1:7). Recall that one of the central promises Yahweh repeatedly made to Abraham in Genesis 12–22 was that his descendants would proliferate. Thus, the opening in Exodus is explicitly reminding the reader of Yahweh's covenant with Abraham. A short synthesis of the three basic components of the promises in this covenant are (1) land, (2) numerous descendants, and (3) blessings. The opening of Exodus declares that Yahweh is fulfilling the promise of numerous descendants. The implied suggested question for readers to ask is, "What about the promise of land and blessings?" Indeed, Yahweh's fulfillment of the Abrahamic covenant, especially concerning those two questions, will drive the story from Exodus 1 to the end of Deuteronomy.

WHY IS THE NAME OF THE PHARAOH OF EGYPT NOT MENTIONED?

One of the peculiarities of Exodus 1–15 is that the name of the pharaoh is never mentioned. This is quite unusual. Throughout the rest of the Old Testament the names of numerous foreign kings, including other pharaohs of Egypt, are frequently included in the story. Undoubtedly, Moses knew the pharaoh's name and could have included it. Yet notice the irony in Exodus 1–2. The book opens with the statement, "These are the *names* of the sons of Israel" (emphasis added) and then all the sons' names are listed. Likewise, the two Hebrew midwives (Shiphrah and Puah) are named (1:15), and the name for Moses is also given and explained (2:10). But there is nothing about the name of the pharaoh. Note also that there are two different pharaohs in the story— the pharaoh of the oppression in Exodus 1 and the pharaoh of the plagues and the exodus (see Exod 2:23). They are both called "king" and "pharaoh," but no names are given. Without the names, the two individuals almost blur into one antagonist, "Pharaoh," at least literarily. The reason for this silence regarding Pharaoh's name is perhaps related to Yahweh's sense of poetic justice, which surfaces several times in Exodus 1–15. At one of the most climactic moments in Pharaoh's encounter with Moses, a moment that sets the stage for the coming plagues and the destruction of Egypt, Pharaoh arrogantly says, "Who is the Lord [Yahweh] that I should obey him . . . ? I don't know the Lord [Yahweh] . . ." (5:2). In Exod 7:5 Yahweh counters this by declaring, "The Egyptians will know that I am the Lord [Yahweh] when I stretch out my hand against Egypt and bring out the Israelites from among them." By the end of Exodus 15 everyone knows who Yahweh is—the Israelites know him as great deliverer and protector, and the Egyptians know him as terrifying judge and powerful enemy who has destroyed them. Thus, everyone knows the name of Yahweh. Pharaoh, on the other hand, remains unnamed, and to this day we are uncertain about the name of the pharaoh who dared to mock Yahweh by saying, "Who is the LORD [Yahweh]?"[6]

In Exod 1:8 a new king (pharaoh) comes to power who has no memory of all that Joseph had done for Egypt. He becomes alarmed at the rapid population growth of the Israelites and determines to stop that expansion (putting him at odds with Yahweh's fulfillment of the Abrahamic promises). Pharaoh tries three different strategies. Plan A was to work the Israelites so hard that their population would decrease. This failed. Plan B was to order the midwives to kill the male babies at birth. This also failed. Plan C was the order to execute every male Hebrew baby by throwing them into the Nile River (1:9–22). This plan, as the story unfolds in Exodus 2, puts the deliverer Moses right into the household of Pharaoh.

Keep in mind that part of Yahweh's promise to Abraham was that "I will bless those who bless you, and whoever curses you I will curse" (Gen 12:3 NIV). Pharaoh, who is killing the baby boys of Yahweh's people, the descendants of Abraham, has moved Egypt from the blessed category (as seen during the time of Joseph) to the cursed category. This will end badly for Pharaoh and his people. Indeed, Yahweh's poetic justice is unveiled, for just as Pharaoh drowns the Hebrew baby boys (Exodus 1), so Yahweh will strike dead every Egyptian firstborn male (Exodus 12) and then drown the entire Egyptian army (Exodus 14).

WORD STUDY
WORDPLAY ON 'ABAD: SLAVE, SERVANT, OFFICIAL, SERVE, WORSHIP, CEREMONY

There is a fascinating wordplay running throughout Exodus based on the frequently occurring Hebrew word *'abad*. As a verb this word can mean "to work," "to work as a slave," or "to serve." The "serve" nuance can be used to indicate being subservient to someone in power, like Pharaoh. It can also be used for being subservient to God or for serving God, in which case it is often translated as "worship." One of the noun forms of this word refers to the person who is serving (a slave or a subordinate official). Another noun form refers to the service itself (slavery, worship, worship ceremony). This Hebrew word occurs nearly

---

[6] Hoffmeier, *Israel in Egypt*, 109. Hoffmeier also notes that a second possibility for the absence of Pharaoh's name is that in Egyptian victory inscriptions at this time it was common to omit the name of the defeated kings. Perhaps Moses was following that tradition.

100 times in Exodus, beginning in 1:13 and concluding in 39:42. We are alerted to its importance early, because it shows up five times in Exod 1:13–14, shown here with translated forms of the word *'abad* placed in bold:

> [They] **worked** them ruthlessly. They made their lives bitter with harsh **labor** in brick and mortar and with all kinds of **work** in the fields; in all their harsh **labor** the Egyptians **worked** them ruthlessly. (NIV)

As the story unfolds, noun forms of *'abad* are used to refer to the slavery of the Israelites (2:23; 6:6) but also to designate the "officials" of Pharaoh (mentioned throughout Exodus 7–14) and the "servant" of Yahweh, Moses (14:31), as well as Yahweh's servants Abraham, Isaac, and Jacob (32:13).

In 3:12, at the burning bush, Yahweh tells Moses that after he has brought the people out of Egypt, "you will all **worship** God at this mountain." Then in 6:6–7 Yahweh promises that he will rescue the Israelites "from **slavery** to them . . ." followed by "I will take you as my people." What Yahweh seems to be promising is that he will shift the Israelites from being Pharaoh's people to being his people. In this context, as Yahweh and Moses confront Pharaoh about releasing the Israelites, it is difficult to know whether to translate *'abad* as "to serve" or "to worship." For example, when Moses tells Pharaoh, "The LORD, the God of the Hebrews, has sent me to tell you: Let my people go, so that they may **worship** me" (7:16), the nuance of "serve" is certainly also present. Translating *'abad* as "worship" in this context is CSB, NIV, Tanakh, NLT, and NRSV. Translating it as "serve" is NET, NASB, KJV, NRSVue, and ESV. Yahweh and Moses seem to be telling Pharaoh, with some irony, that the Israelites will transform from **serving** Pharaoh to **serving** Yahweh (see also 7:16; 8:1, 20; 9:1, 13; 10:3). Finally, in exasperation, Pharaoh says, "Go, **worship** [serve?] the LORD" (10:24). In Exodus 12 the narrative is interrupted by the instructions from Yahweh on how to commemorate this event through the Passover. Here the noun form of *'abad* is used twice, translated as "ceremony" (12:25–26) but still probably carrying a nuance of "serving." Then once again Pharaoh tells the Israelites, "Go, **worship** [serve?] the LORD" (12:31).

After Yahweh brings the Israelites out of Egypt, he enters into a special covenant with them, identifying himself as "[Yahweh] your God, who brought you out of the land of Egypt, out of the place [Hebrew, 'house'] of **slavery**" (20:2). The Egyptian word translated as "pharaoh" literally means "great house," so the reference to Egypt as the "house of slavery" probably carries an allusion to Pharaoh's central role in that slavery. Likewise, the later references to the tabernacle as the "house of Yahweh" (23:19; 34:26) underscore the contrast as the Israelites change in which house they serve.

Then, throughout Exodus 35–39 the noun form of *'abad* is used to refer to the "work" or "service" in constructing and operating the tabernacle. In contrast to the opening repeated use of *'abad* in Exodus 1 to refer to slavery in building the store cities for Pharaoh, here at the end, in Exodus 39, *'abad* is mentioned several times (translated as "the work") in reference to constructing the tabernacle for Yahweh (39:32, 40, 42).

So, to summarize the wordplay, the Israelites will go from **serving** Pharaoh (and his **officials**) and being his **slaves** and **working** on his store cities, to **serving** Yahweh, being his holy people, following his **servant**, Moses, and **working** to make the tabernacle through which they can **serve** and **worship** Yahweh.[7] All of these terms in bold are translations of *'abad* and related forms.

Holiness, Presence, and Power: Yahweh Calls Moses from within the Burning Bush (2:1–4:17)

Exodus 2:1–10 describes the birth of Moses, and here we see Yahweh working quietly behind the scenes, again with some poetic irony. Seeking to save her baby boy from the edict about being thrown into the Nile River, the mother of Moses places him in a basket, which she puts among the reeds in the Nile River. Then the daughter of Pharaoh discovers him! Not only does she allow him to live (in defiance of her father's decree) but she takes him as her adopted son. She names him Moses, which carries meaning in both Hebrew and Egyptian. In Hebrew, as explained in Exod 2:10, the name Moses sounds like the Hebrew word for "drawing out." Not explained but no doubt obvious to early readers is the Egyptian meaning ("born of"), a meaning seen frequently in Egyptian names, especially in the names for the pharaohs, such as Thutmose (lit., "born of Thoth," an Egyptian god).

Interestingly, five women have important roles in Exod 1:1–2:10. There are the two midwives who disobey Pharaoh regarding killing Hebrew baby boys. Then there are also Moses's mother, Moses's sister, and Pharaoh's daughter, all of whom also disobey Pharaoh regarding killing baby boys. Moses's sister (later identified as

---

[7] Another important cluster of *'abad* usages occurs in Joshua 24 (fifteen times), where the focus is on "Whom will you *serve*, Yahweh or the foreign gods?"

Miriam) plays an interesting role literarily (an *inclusio*), for in this deliverance story, she shows up at the beginning (Exod 2:4–9), watching Moses being delivered from drowning in the Nile River, and then again at the end (Exod 15:20–21), leading all the Israelite women in triumphant song and praising Yahweh for drowning the Egyptians in the Sea.

When Moses grows up, he seems to realize his Hebrew identity, for he kills an Egyptian who was beating a Hebrew. Yet we see how ineffective his actions are when he does not have Yahweh's direct leading. This action only causes trouble for him, for Pharaoh now seeks to kill him. In fear, Moses flees to Midian, where he meets and then marries the daughter of a priest of Midian, settling down to live with that family (2:11–22).

Exodus 2:23–25 is an important pivot point in the story. The Israelites cry out for help because of their slavery. Yahweh hears them; recalls his covenant with Abraham, Isaac, and Jacob; and decides to act. This underscores once again the important connection between the Abrahamic covenant and the exodus. Yahweh does not deliver Israel from Egypt because they repented or became pious or made some significant sacrifices, but he delivered Israel in response to their cry for help and based on his promises to Abraham.

In Exodus 3–4 Yahweh moves from working behind the scenes to direct intervention in delivering Israel. Based on his promises to Abraham, and in response to the cry of the Israelites in 2:23–25, Yahweh now comes crashing down into human history in spectacular fashion. Moses's encounter with Yahweh in the burning bush episode is unlike any of the theophany encounters with the patriarchs in Genesis.[8] The presence of Yahweh here in Exodus 3–4 is more intense than in his encounters with the patriarchs, as Yahweh now speaks from the midst of a fire. Likewise, now holiness emanates out from his presence, requiring Moses to remove his shoes as if in a temple (3:5). In this encounter Yahweh reveals a number of very important things to Moses: (1) He calls Moses to lead the deliverance of the Israelites from Egypt, overruling all of Moses's objections; (2) he restates the promise he made to Abraham about the Promised Land; (3) he encourages Moses with the promise of his powerful presence; (4) he tells Moses that after the deliverance he and the Israelites will worship Yahweh in this same location (Mount Sinai, see Exodus 19); (5) he reveals his name and some of the character of his name; (6) he provides Moses with two miraculous signs; and

---

[8] The smoking firepot and flaming torch in Gen 15:17 is the closest parallel, but even that is quite different. See the discussion in Duvall and Hays, *God's Relational Presence*, 6–7, 24–27 (see chap. 1, n. 4).

(7) because of Moses's doubts about his public speaking ability, Yahweh appoints his brother Aaron as his spokesman.

The revelation of Yahweh's name is fascinating and filled with significant theological implications (3:5–16). In 3:12 Yahweh tells Moses, "I will certainly be with you." This phrase could also be translated as "I am with you" (*'ehyeh 'immak*). In 3:13 Moses asks him for a more specific name than just "God of your father" (3:6). Yahweh then answers, "I AM WHO I AM" (*'ehyeh 'asher 'ehyeh*; 3:14a). Next Yahweh says, "This is what you are to say to the Israelites: I AM [*'ehyeh*] has sent me" (3:14b). Then in 3:16 he identifies his divine name as "The LORD [Yahweh, *yehvah*], the God of your ancestors." The repeated terms *I AM* (or *I will be*; *'ehyeh*), along with the name Yahweh, come from the same Hebrew verb, *hayah* (to be). There is no complete consensus over what the phrase "I AM WHO I AM" means or what the exact nuance is of the name Yahweh. Yet considering the promise of Yahweh's presence in 3:12 followed by the repetition of the same word *'ehyeh* (I am) in 3:14, a number of scholars understand the meaning of Yahweh and "I Am" to be related to his divine presence, the intense kind of presence seen throughout Exodus, and associated with holiness and power.[9]

The intense divine presence of Yahweh will be a central theme in Exodus and will be closely associated with his great actions to deliver Israel from Egypt and then with the covenant he establishes with Israel at Mount Sinai. Indeed, the focus in the second half of the book (Exodus 25–40) is about building the tabernacle, where this divine presence will live.

REUEL, JETHRO, HOBAB—WHO IS THE "FATHER-IN-LAW" OF MOSES?

In Exod 2:15–22 Moses meets and marries a Midianite woman named Zipporah. In 2:18 her father is introduced as Reuel. Then in 3:1 Moses is said to be shepherding the flock of Jethro, his father-in-law (Hebrew, *hoten*), who shows up again in Exodus 18 and is called the father-in-law (*hoten*) of Moses several times (sixteen times total in Exodus). Then in Num 10:29, another man, Hobab, also seems to be referred to as "Moses' father-in-law" (NIV; Hebrew, *hoten*), although the text is not completely clear as to whom *hoten* refers. So what is going on here? The problem centers on how the Hebrew word *hoten* is translated. Most English translations translate the term as "father-in-law,"

---

[9] Thomas B. Dozeman, *Commentary on Exodus*, ECC (Grand Rapids: Eerdmans, 2009), 134–35. See the discussion in Duvall and Hays, *God's Relational Presence*, 24–27.

assuming the ancient Hebrews had similar terms for relatives as we do in the English-speaking world today (e.g., aunt, uncle, father-in-law). Yet many languages and cultures have a different range of terms for relatives, some more specific than those in English and some less so. Thus, the term *hoten* in ancient Hebrew is not as specific as "father-in-law," but rather refers to any male relative in the wife's family, her father, her uncle, or her brother.[10] Reuel is clearly identified as Zipporah's father. Hobab, however, is identified as the son of Reuel, so he would be her brother, thus still qualifying to be called *hoten*. CSB follows this understanding and translates the relationship as "relative by marriage." Jethro, referred to repeatedly as the *hoten* of Moses, is not further identified. Thus, he could be Zipporah's uncle and the brother of Reuel or perhaps another brother. The fact that Moses is said to be shepherding the flock of Jethro in 3:1 and the important mediatorial role that Jethro plays in Exodus 18 suggests that he is the major patriarch in that family and thus perhaps more likely to be Zipporah's uncle.[11]

Who Is Yahweh? The Initial Confrontation with Pharaoh (4:18–7:7)

The strange episode in Exod 4:18–26 regarding the wife of Moses and the circumcision of his sons is probably best understood in the context of the Abrahamic covenant, which drives the story. Circumcision was the sign of being part of that covenant (Gen 17:9–14) and was a strict requirement, even for the family of Moses.

In Exod 5:1–21 Moses and Aaron have their first encounter with Pharaoh. They tell him that Yahweh (the LORD), the God of Israel, says to let his people go (5:1). Pharaoh responds with arrogance, "Who is Yahweh ['the LORD'] that I should obey him . . . ? I don't know Yahweh [the LORD], and besides, I will not let Israel go" (5:2). This challenge will echo throughout the next eight chapters as Yahweh destroys Egypt. It also sets up the phrase that is repeated throughout the rest of the book: "that they might know that I am Yahweh [the LORD]" (various forms of this phrase appear in 6:7; 7:5, 17; 8:10, 22; 9:14; 10:2; 14:4, 18; 16:12; 29:46; and 31:13). Throughout the book of Exodus Yahweh is known through his actions, and he declares clearly that everyone will know that he is Yahweh—those who arrogantly defy him will know him

---

[10] Terence C. Mitchell, "The Meaning of the Noun HTN in the Old Testament," *VT* 19 (1969): 105.

[11] J. Daniel Hays, "Moses: The Private Man Behind the Public Leader," *BR* 16, no. 4 (2000): 20–21.

as punishing judge and fearsome adversary, and those who trust him will know him as the great deliverer.

As a result of this first encounter, Pharaoh responds by making the work for the enslaved Israelites even harder (5:4–18). The Israelites angrily complain to Moses (5:19–21) and he likewise complains to Yahweh (5:22–23).

Yahweh answers Moses, first by reminding Moses of Yahweh's name (6:1–3). When Yahweh states that he was not known to the patriarchs by the name Yahweh (6:3) he is not saying they were not aware of his name (they called on the name of Yahweh) but that they did not experience the essence of his name—the intense, fiery, holiness-emitting divine presence as seen in Exodus and his powerful, spectacular deliverance as demonstrated in the exodus event. Yahweh then restates his faithfulness to the Abrahamic covenant (6:4–5). Next, in a section that opens and closes with "I am Yahweh" (6:6, 8) he reminds Moses of what he is planning to do: (1) free the Israelites from slavery in Egypt, (2) redeem them, (3) take them as his own people, and (4) give them the land he promised to Abraham. In 6:7 he summarizes the result: "You will know that I am Yahweh [the LORD] your God."

The genealogy in Exod 6:14–25 opens as though it is going to cover all twelve sons of Jacob in order of birth (Reuben, Simeon, Levi), but it stops on Levi and then tracks only the descendants of Levi. The main Levite lineage being tracked is indicated by those whose wives are mentioned—Amram (6:20), Aaron (6:23), and Eleazar (6:25), with the genealogy ending with Phinehas, who is apparently the focus of the genealogy. He will play an important role later in Scripture (Numbers 25, 31; Joshua 22; Ps 106:28–31).

THE HARDENING OF PHARAOH'S HEART

In Exod 7:3–5 Yahweh says that he will harden Pharaoh's heart so that "the Egyptians will know that I am Yahweh [the LORD]." The hardening of Pharaoh's heart is a repeated theme running throughout Exodus 4–14. Yet what does it mean to harden one's heart? In Hebrew the "heart" functioned not so much as the seat of emotions, as in English, but rather as the seat of volitional will, the place where one makes decisions. At the beginning of the "Moses and Yahweh versus Pharaoh" encounters in Exodus 4–14 Yahweh states that he will (at some point, harden Pharaoh's heart (4:21; 7:3). But once the plagues start, the text states that either Pharaoh hardened his own heart (8:15, 32) or just that his heart "was hard" or "hardened" or "unyielding" (7:13, 22; 8:19; 9:7, 35). Through the first seven plagues the only time that Yahweh is explicitly said to harden

Pharaoh's heart is in 9:12, at the end of the sixth plague. At the end, however, starting in 10:1 with the eighth plague and continuing to the destruction of Pharaoh's army in the Red Sea, the text repeatedly states that Yahweh hardened Pharaoh's heart (and, sometimes, the hearts of his officials) (10:1–2, 27; 11:10; 14:4, 8). It seems as if at the beginning, Pharaoh has a real opportunity to listen to Yahweh and to obey by letting the people go. Yet he repeatedly decides otherwise, hardening his heart, changing his mind, and going back on his promises. Toward the end of the plagues, however, the time for leniency has passed. Remember that Pharaoh and the Egyptians were throwing Yahweh's baby boys into the Nile River in Exodus 1. Yahweh certainly has not forgotten, and now he seems determined to complete the total judgment on the unrepentant, arrogant Pharaoh by destroying Egypt and Pharaoh's army. Thus, at the end of the plague cycle confrontation, Yahweh hardens Pharaoh's heart once again, leading him to pursue the Israelites right into the Red Sea and final judgment.[12]

Yahweh versus Pharaoh: The First Nine Plagues (7:8–10:29)

The confrontation between Yahweh (along with his spokesmen Moses and Aaron) and Pharaoh (along with his court magicians and officials) starts in earnest in Exod 7:8–13 when Aaron's staff turns into a snake and then swallows the staffs/snakes of Pharaoh's magicians, who had replicated his initial action. In ancient Egypt, magic and snakes were closely associated. As mentioned earlier, the Egyptians also believed in a giant serpent of the underworld (Apophis), who was the god of chaos and the enemy of Ra, the sun-god and the patron deity of the pharaohs. Each day this snake would try to stop the sun from rising. The Egyptians venerated Ra and set magic spells against Apophis. The cobra, on the other hand, carried different, positive connotations in Egypt. A cobra-goddess was the patron-goddess of Lower Egypt (the northern delta region of Egypt). In fact, the typical headwear of the pharaohs at this time usually included a cobra placed right at the forehead of the pharaoh, poised to strike, symbolizing his rule over Lower Egypt. Furthermore, the staff was a symbol of power and rule; thus, when Aaron's staff-turned-snake swallowed the staffs-turned-snakes of the Egyptian magicians it probably symbolized either power greater than Apophis (to unleash chaos and destruction, as occurs in the upcoming plagues) or

---

[12] See the good discussion on the hardening of Pharaoh's heart in Terence E. Fretheim, *Exodus*, Interpretation (Louisville: John Knox, 1991), 96–103.

power over the cobra-goddess of Lower Egypt, challenging the very rule and authority of Pharaoh.[13]

Since the miracle of the snakes did not convince Pharaoh, Yahweh strikes Egypt with ten plagues. The plagues come in cycles of three, as illustrated in table 2.1:

Table 2.1: The Plague Cycles[14]

Plague	Warning to Pharaoh?	Time of Warning
#1—Blood	Yes	In the morning
#2—Frogs	Yes	No specific time
#3—Gnats or mosquitoes	No	No warning
#4—Flies	Yes	In the morning
#5—Plague on livestock	Yes	No specific time
#6—Boils on people	No	No warning
#7—Hail	Yes	In the morning
#8—Locusts	Yes	No specific time
#9—Darkness	No	No warning
#10—Death of firstborn	Yes	No specific time

In general, each plague gets worse and increases in its negative impact on Egypt. Pharaoh tries to counter. His magicians are able to replicate the miraculous action of Moses and Aaron in the beginning (changing staffs to snakes, changing water to blood, bringing frogs on the land), but note that while they might replicate the plague, they are unable to reverse it (i.e., they only bring on more frogs, adding to the judgment). By the third plague (gnats or mosquitos) the magicians are no longer able to replicate the plague and they declare, "This is the finger of God" (8:19). In 9:11, when boils come on people, the magicians are unable even to stand before Moses.

The accounts describing plagues 7 and 8 (hail and locusts) are longer than those of the earlier plagues and are described in much more detail (9:13–35; 10:1–20). Accordingly, these two plagues are perhaps the most devastating ones to date,

---

[13] Eric Alan Mitchell, "Exodus," *BIBBC*, 126–27; Shaw and Nicholson, "Apophis," "serpent, snake," *The Princeton Dictionary of Ancient Egypt*, 38–39, 295–96 (see chap. 1, n. 25).

[14] This chart is developed from the chart in Peter E. Enns, *Exodus*, NIVAC (Grand Rapids: Zondervan, 2000), 208. Enns references Nahum M. Sarna, *Exploring Exodus: The Heritage of Biblical Israel* (New York: Schocken, 1986), 76.

destroying all of the crops growing in Egypt (10:15). The ninth plague is a plague of darkness (10:21–29), and while this plague does not seem to be physically damaging like the earlier plagues, the darkness serves as a concluding climactic statement, demonstrating Yahweh's power directly over the most powerful and top Egyptian deity, Amun-Re, the sun-god. This plague has implications of both judgment and death (see the following discussion) and thus also serves to introduce the final plague, the death of the firstborn (at midnight).

The Tenth Plague, the Exodus, and Deliverance at the Red Sea (11:1–15:21)

Several important events take place in this unit. First, in the final and concluding plague, during the night Yahweh strikes dead the firstborn of the Egyptians. Remember that back in Exodus 1, Pharaoh decreed that the newborn baby boys of the Hebrews should be killed, thrown in the Nile River. Also remember the provision in Yahweh's promise to Abraham, "I will bless those who bless you, and whoever curses you I will curse" (Gen 12:3 NIV). So, this final plague seems to come as a climactic response to Pharaoh's earlier actions against the Israelite babies as well as a consequence of Pharaoh's continued obstinance, lying, and repeated refusal to let the Israelites go as Yahweh requested.

The Israelites are instructed to slaughter a lamb and spread its blood on the doorposts and lintels of their houses. The death angel would then "pass over" the houses that had blood on the doorposts and lintels (Exod 12:1–13). Right in the middle of this narrative, Yahweh interrupts the story to give instructions for how to memorialize this important event by instituting the Passover and the Festival of Unleavened Bread (12:14–28; 13:3–10).

In Exod 11:2–3 Yahweh had instructed the Israelites to ask their Egyptian neighbors for silver and gold as they were leaving. In Exod 12:35–36 the Israelites indeed do this, asking also for clothes. The Egyptians give these items to the Israelites and the text notes, "In this way they [the Israelites] plundered the Egyptians" (12:36). The exit of Israel from Egypt, therefore, is not described as a group of nomads fleeing in the night, but of a victorious army departing from a conquered country, hauling away the plunder. This picture of the departing victorious army will continue into the Red Sea episode when the Egyptian army is finally completely defeated as well.

As Israel departs, their population, according to the text, is "about six hundred *thousand* [Hebrew, *'eleph*] able-bodied men on foot, besides their families" (12:37, emphasis added). If this translation is correct, then there would be about two and a half million total people of all ages in this group. Yet how we understand this phrase depends on how we translate the Hebrew word *'eleph*, which has a wide semantic range of possible meanings. It can mean "one thousand" (Gen 20:16; Exod 18:21; Num 31:5), as translated by CSB and NIV, which is the most common meaning of the word, but it can also mean "cattle, ox, herd" (Deut 7:13; 28:4; Isa 30:24); "clans, families" (Josh 22:14, 21; Judg 6:15); or "divisions" (Num 1:16 NKJV). Douglas Stuart argues that in Exodus 12:37 the term *'eleph* refers to a small family-related military unit (like a platoon or squad). The number of people in that unit depended on the size of that family and could average as small as a dozen (or thirty or fifty, etc.). Thus, a group of 600 "*elephs*" might not contain any more than 7,200 people.[15] Or if the average size of the *'eleph* was 50, the number of fighting men would be 30,000. Scholars are divided on which meaning of *'eleph* should be understood in this passage.[16]

Exodus 12:38 states that "a mixed crowd also went up with them." The Hebrew phrase translated as "mixed crowd" is a reference to people of other nationalities or ethnicities than the Israelites. So as the Israelites are delivered out of Egypt, included among them are other ethnic groups—probably Libyans, Cushites, and Asiatics (nomads from the northeast such as Canaanites and Amorites).

As Yahweh leads the Israelites out of Egypt, several places along the route are mentioned (13:17–14:4). The text also states that Yahweh leads them "toward the Red Sea" (13:18). The Hebrew phrase translated as "the Red Sea" is *yom suph*, which literally means "Sea of Reeds." Neither the exact route nor the specific body of water that the phrase *yom suph* refers to can be determined with certainty.[17] Yet, while we tend to focus on determining the exact geographical location where these events take place, the text is perhaps more focused on theological connections. The presence of Yahweh is stressed in 13:20–24 as he travels with the Israelites in pillars of fire and cloud. When they encamp by the sea, they are in front of Baal-zephon (14:2). Baal was a Canaanite god who will figure prominently in the historical books of the Old Testament, after Israel enters Canaan, and who was also worshipped in Egypt throughout the second millennium. Baal-zephon means "lord of the north," and in Egypt,

---

[15] Douglas K. Stuart, *Exodus*, NAC (Nashville: Holman, 2006), 297–303. See also Kitchen, *On the Reliability of the Old Testament*, 264–65.

[16] Numerous commentaries reject Stuart's translation as "small military unit" and argue for 600,000, including William H. C. Propp, *Exodus 1–18*, AB (New York: Doubleday, 1998), 414; and John I. Durham, *Exodus*, WBC (Waco, TX: Word, 1987), 172.

[17] For a convincing explanation of the route and a plausible identification of the *yom suph*, see Hoffmeier, *Israel in Egypt*, 164–222; and Kitchen, *On the Reliability of the Old Testament*, 254–72.

Baal was also known as the "protector of sailors."[18] While the geographical locations are important for this historical event, the theological battle between Yahweh and the foreign gods continues as Yahweh defeats the Egyptian army of Pharaoh right in front of the worship center for Baal, who in Egyptian belief should have protected them.[19] This demonstration of Yahweh's power over Baal should have been a strong source of encouragement to the Israelites in the near future when Yahweh tells them to drive out the Canaanites, whose primary god is Baal.

In keeping with plagues 9 (darkness) and 10 (the death of firstborn), the deliverance of the Israelites through the crossing of the sea and the destruction of the Egyptian army takes place at night (14:20–21). After the destruction of the Egyptian army, the Israelites "feared the LORD and believed in him and in his servant Moses" (14:31). Moses then leads the Israelites in singing a victory celebration song and praise to Yahweh for delivering them. Particularly stressed is that Yahweh has delivered them to bring them into his presence—that is, "to your holy dwelling" (15:13), and to "the place, LORD, you made for your dwelling, the sanctuary, Lord, your hands established" (15:17 NIV). Likewise playing a prominent role in this celebration is Miriam, the sister of Moses. She is named for the first time here in 15:20, called the "the prophetess" and "Aaron's sister." Micah 6:4 is probably alluding back to this event when it states, "I brought you up out of Egypt and redeemed you from the land of slavery. I sent Moses to lead you, also Aaron and Miriam" (Mic 6:4 NIV).[20]

ANCIENT CONNECTIONS 2.1: THE PLAGUES, THE EXODUS, AND THE RELIGIOUS CONTEXT OF ANCIENT EGYPT

Set in the context of ancient Egyptian religious belief, some of the plagues appear to have been directed polemically at belittling specific Egyptian gods.[21] While this may be true, it is more likely, however, that the extended confrontation between Moses and Pharaoh and the consequential plague cycle should be viewed as a larger, cosmic kind of divine contest or battle between the gods

---

[18] Mitchell, "Exodus," 137; Hoffmeier, *Israel in Egypt*, 190.

[19] Mitchell, "Exodus," 137.

[20] Wells suggests that since women were the ones who typically composed the victory songs, Miriam was probably the author of the song that Moses sang as well. Bruce Wells, "Exodus," *ZIBBC* 1:216.

[21] John D. Currid, *Ancient Egypt and the Old Testament* (Grand Rapids: Baker, 1997), 108–13.

of Egypt (with Pharaoh as their representative) and Yahweh, the God of Israel (with Moses and Aaron as his representatives).

This battle comes to a climax in the ninth plague, the plague of darkness. The sun-god Amun-Re was the "king of the gods" and head of the Egyptian pantheon. A central belief in Egyptian religion was that in the daytime Amun-Re traveled across the sky in his boat, paralleling the movement of the sun. In the nighttime, however, Amun-Re traveled in this boat through the netherworld below, where each night he had to defeat the evil snake-god Apophis. Assisted by another god named Seth, and aided by the power from the rituals performed each day by the pharaoh, Amun-Re would defeat Apophis each night and bring about the sunrise. When Yahweh brought about darkness on the land of Egypt for three days (10:21–22) the implication was that Yahweh had defeated or overpowered Amun-Re. Verifying this was the observation that there was light where the Israelites lived (10:23). This would have been terrifying to the Egyptians.[22]

Furthermore, one of the central aspects of the ancient Egyptian religious worldview was the concept of *ma'at* (order and balance in the world). The pharaoh's primary role was to maintain *ma'at* (e.g., order brought by the regular flooding of the Nile, causing the crops to grow; the daily rising of the sun to provide sunshine) and to prevent *isft* (chaos). Interestingly, in ancient Egyptian literature, one specific cause of *isft* and lack of *ma'at* was the presence of too many foreigners in the land. In an Egyptian document named "Prophecy of Neferti" a situation of *isft* is first described, which is then corrected by the new incoming king (pharaoh) who restores *ma'at*.[23]

> The land is burdened with misfortune
> Because of those looking for food,
> Asiatics [i.e., semitic nomads from the northeast; this term would include groups such as the Israelites] roaming the land. . . .
> Asiatics have descended into Egypt. . . .
> Then a king will come from the south. . . .
> The Asiatics will fall to his slaughter. . . .
> The serpent which is on his forehead will still the traitors for him. . . .
> Then order [*ma'at*] will come into its place
> While wrongdoing [*isft*] is driven out.[24]

---

[22] Mitchell, "Exodus," 134.

[23] Hoffmeier, *Israel in Egypt*, 151–53; Mitchell, 135–36.

[24] "The Prophecies of Neferti," trans. Nili Shupak, *COS* 1.45:108–10.

Ma'at was also the name of the Egyptian goddess of order. The daughter of
Amun-Re (the sun god), she and the pharaoh (the son of Amun-Re) were
responsible for maintaining order. She is normally represented as a seated
god with an ostrich feather in her hair pointing upward. In another ancient
Egyptian document called "The Book of the Dead," recently deceased people
are depicted as standing before the judgment of the gods, a scene in which
the deceased's heart is placed in the balance pan of a weighing scale and
the feather of Ma'at is placed on the other balance pan. If the heart was
out of balance with *ma'at*, the deceased person would not enter the afterlife but rather would be devoured by the ferocious crocodile-headed god
Ammit. This judgment took place late at night after a person passed away.
In Exodus 7–10, through the nine plagues (including the plague of darkness,
which struck at the most basic element of order, the sunrise), Yahweh had
destroyed all aspects of *ma'at* in Egypt. Thus, in the tenth plague, when the
death angel descends at "about midnight" (Exod 11:4), striking dead all of
the firstborn in Egypt, it suggests an allusion to the Egyptian "judgment of
the dead" ceremony. The Egyptians would have understood this as a judgment on Egypt itself, especially on Pharaoh, on the gods of Egypt, and on
the people themselves.[25]

YAHWEH ESTABLISHES A COVENANT WITH ISRAEL AT MOUNT SINAI (15:22–24:18)

Yahweh Leads Israel from the Red Sea to Mount Sinai (15:22–18:27)

From Exod 15:22 until 17:7 the story centers on the problems of providing water and
food for the Israelites while in the desert. The main points are that (1) the Israelites
have short memories of what Yahweh has done for them and they are characterized by
frequent grumbling (15:24; 16:2, 7, 8–9, 12; 17:3), and (2) Yahweh miraculously provides food and water for them. On either end of this section are two miraculous water
episodes (15:22–27; 17:1–7) that serve as bookends for the larger miraculous food
section in the middle (16:1–36), in which Yahweh provides manna for the Israelites
each day.

---

[25] Mitchell, "Exodus," 135–36.

In Exod 17:8–16, the Israelites have their first battle with a people other than the Egyptians. In this battle episode Joshua is introduced for the first time. He will play an important role in the many battles to come, especially during the conquest of Canaan in the book of Joshua. The enemy that opposes the Israelites here is the Amalekites. Moses declares that because of this opposition, Yahweh will continually be at war against the Amalekites, a prophetic antagonism that plays a major role in 1–2 Samuel, as both King Saul (disobediently) and King David (obediently) interact with the Amalekites (1 Sam 14:48; 15:1–35; 30:1–20; 2 Sam 1:1–16).

Jethro, the "father-in-law" of Moses, comes to the Israelite camp in Exodus 18, bringing Moses's wife and two sons with him.[26] Moses apparently sent them away earlier (18:2), an event that is not mentioned elsewhere, but perhaps was the result of the peculiar episode in Exod 4:18–26. It is interesting to note that references to Moses's Midianite family (his wife, Zipporah, and his "father-in-law" Jethro) served as the prelude to his encounter with Yahweh back at the burning bush (2:15–3:1). Here in Exodus 18 they both appear again, this time before his parallel encounter with Yahweh at Mount Sinai.

Perhaps the most theologically significant part of Jethro's visit is his testimony regarding Yahweh: "Blessed be the Lord. . . . Now I know that the Lord is greater than all gods" (18:10–11). Yahweh's promise that people will "know" that he is Yahweh because of his actions in delivering Israel and judging Egypt is fulfilled through the testimony of Jethro, the Midianite. Then Jethro joins Moses and the elders of Israel in eating a meal "in God's presence" (18:12), after which he gives Moses some helpful advice on how to govern the people (18:13–26).

Holiness, Presence, and Power: Yahweh Calls Israel from Mount Sinai (19:1–25)

One of the most central, climactic events in Exodus is Israel's encounter with Yahweh on Mount Sinai in Exodus 19. The Israelites arrive at Mount Sinai in Exod 19:1, and they stay here throughout the rest of Exodus, all of Leviticus, and until Numbers 10, when they depart for the Promised Land. Recall that back in Exod 3:12, as Yahweh revealed his name to Moses, he also promised, "When you bring the people out of Egypt, you will all worship God on this mountain." Indeed, there are several parallels

---

[26] Recall the earlier discussion, in which it was argued that the term often translated as "father-in-law" is better understood as referring to a male relative of the wife. Jethro is more likely to be the uncle or brother of Moses's wife, Zipporah.

between the encounter with Yahweh in Exodus 3 and the encounter in Exodus 19, as presented in Table 2.2 below.

Table 2.2: A Comparison of the Encounters with Yahweh
at the Burning Bush and at Mount Sinai

Exodus 3 (the burning bush)	Exodus 19 (Mount Sinai)
Prelude reference to Moses's Midianite family (2:15–3:1)	Prelude reference to Moses's Midianite family (18:1–27)
At the "mountain of God" (3:1)	At the "mountain to God" (19:3, LXX, CSB)
Yahweh appears in fire in the bush (3:4)	Yahweh appears in fire on the mountain (19:18)
Hebrew word for "bush" is *seneh*	Hebrew word for "mountain" is *sinay* (Sinai)
Area around the bush is holy (3:5),	Area around the mountain is holy (19:10–23)
Due to the presence of Yahweh	Due to the presence of Yahweh
Yahweh speaks thru the angel of the Lord to Moses	Yahweh speaks through Moses to the people
Yahweh calls Moses	Yahweh calls the nation of Israel

Like the encounter in Exodus 3, the intense, powerful, and holy presence of Yahweh, often shielded from the Israelites by smoke or clouds, comes to the top of the mountain to reveal an exciting and dramatic new relationship into which Yahweh is inviting the Israelites. Moses will make several trips up and down the mountain, relaying Yahweh's words to the people while also warning them about the seriousness of Yahweh's holiness and the need to respect the physical boundaries around the base of the mountain that he has decreed.

In Yahweh's first dialogue with Moses on the mountain (19:3–6), he communicates several very important things. First, Yahweh is the one who brought the Israelites out of Egypt, but he also brought them *to himself* (19:4). This implies that the ultimate purpose of the exodus from Egypt was to bring the Israelites into relationship with Yahweh.

Second, Yahweh is going to enter into a covenant with Israel, but it is a conditional covenant that they are called to obey and keep (19:5). The Hebrew phrase that literally translates as "if you really hear my voice" implies obedience. CSB translates it as "if you will carefully listen to me," while NIV stresses the obedience nuance, "if you obey me fully." This call to "hear the voice of Yahweh" or "hear the words of Yahweh" (i.e., to obey Yahweh) will be repeated dozens of times throughout the Old Testament as a critical part of keeping the covenant (in particular, note Deut 28:1–45 and Jer 11:1–14).

Third, out of all the peoples of the world, Yahweh has chosen the "house of Jacob" (19:3), the Israelites, as his "own possession" (19:5; the NIV translates this as "treasured possession").

Fourth, Yahweh declares that the Israelites will be a "kingdom of priests" to him (19:6). This designation as priests will be important as Yahweh comes to dwell right among them (as played out in the rest of Exodus). In the ancient world, the average person was not allowed into the temples where the gods lived. Only the priests could approach the gods inside the temple. While Yahweh will still use designated special priests to enter the actual Holy Place inside the tabernacle and temple, the very fact that he will now reside in the tabernacle in the midst of the Israelites, in close proximity to them, blesses them with a certain priestly status. The priestly status also implies a mediatorial role. Because priests were the ones to mediate between the deity and the regular people, Israel as a whole seems to be given this mediatorial role, to mediate between Yahweh dwelling in their midst and the rest of the people of the world.

Finally, Yahweh pulls all the above aspects of the new relationship together in summary when he now decrees that the Israelites will be a "holy nation" (19:6). The concept of holiness with respect to people carries nuances of being separated for a special, sacred use. Yahweh has separated Israel from Egypt and has brought them to himself as a special people. Thus they are set apart to serve him. This is an important aspect of being a "holy nation." But holiness also carries ethical nuances associated with the character of God, which involves the absence of anything unclean or impure and the presence of a just and righteous behavior. Yahweh's holiness is seen emanating from his close, intense presence, both in Exodus 3 and Exodus 19. If this holy, intense presence of Yahweh is coming down to dwell right among them, then holiness will likewise emanate from his presence, requiring a certain level of holiness in the lives of his people who lived nearby. This requirement of Yahweh's for holiness will be described in more detail later, especially in Leviticus, when Yahweh stresses, "Be holy because I am holy" (Lev 11:45; 19:2; 20:26).

The verb form of the Hebrew word for "holy" is often used for the rituals that symbolize cleansing or making holy. This verb is usually translated as "consecrate," and it occurs three times in Exodus 19 (vv. 10, 14, 22) as the people prepare to meet the holy awesome Yahweh. His presence is both dangerous and terrifying (19:16–19). As Yahweh descends onto Mount Sinai, the thunder, lightning, fire, smoke, and loud trumpet blast cause the people to tremble (NIV; CSB translates "shudder"). This same Hebrew verb is used in 19:18, where not only the people but the entire mountain itself "trembled" (NIV).

Yahweh Gives the Heart of the Covenant: The Ten Commandments (20:1–21)

In the middle of the scene described in Exodus 19 (the terrifying scene of the holy, awesome Yahweh on the top of Mount Sinai in fire, smoke, lightning, thunder, and earthquakes), the story is interrupted by Yahweh presenting the Ten Commandments. This interruption probably underscores the importance of these verses, for the Ten Commandments will serve as the foundation and summary of the terms of the covenant that Yahweh is establishing with Israel, a covenant that will be formally ratified in Exodus 24. These Ten Commandments are also defining what it will mean for Israel to be a "holy nation."

The Ten Commandments contain an introductory prelude (20:2), followed by four commandments dealing with the people's relationship with Yahweh (20:4–11; that is, the vertical relationship) and then six commandments dealing with the relationship the people are to have with each other (20:12–17; that is, the horizontal relationship). In the prelude (20:2), Yahweh reminds the Israelites of who he is (Yahweh, their God) and what his prior relationship is with them (he brought them out of Egypt, the "place of slavery").

The first commandment (20:3) may be the most radical. Polytheism was common throughout the ANE, and in Egypt, where the Israelites have lived for the last 400 or so years, the people worshipped dozens of gods. Furthermore, typically people in the ANE had both national, tribal, or regional gods as well as personal household gods (e.g., Gen 31:19–35). The first commandment prohibits the Israelites from having any other gods anywhere. The phrase "before me" (NIV) is not so much a priority statement or statement of importance ranking as it is a spatial statement. Yahweh is coming to dwell in their midst, to live in the tabernacle. If the Israelites are to be a "holy nation," set aside as a special possession to serve Yahweh, they cannot have any other gods anywhere in their camp (or country).

The second commandment (do not make idols or worship and serve them, 20:4) is related to the first. In addition to forbidding the Israelites to construct idols of the pagan gods, it implies that they are not to construct any idols at all, including idols of Yahweh. This would include the construction, for example, of the golden calf (Exodus 32).

The third commandment forbids "misusing" the name of Yahweh their God. The Hebrew phrase translated as "misuse" can carry connotations of falsehood and dishonesty as well as trivializing or treating as worthless. Recall the importance assigned to the name Yahweh throughout the earlier chapters of Exodus—the revelation of the name at the burning bush (Exodus 3), the close association of the name with the deliverance of Israel from Egypt (Exodus 6), and the ongoing, plot-driving issue over "knowing Yahweh" that runs throughout Exodus 5–15. Using the name Yahweh with appropriate honor and respect will be an important part of the new covenant relationship.

Another important feature that will set Israel apart from the other nations as a "holy nation" is their keeping of the Sabbath day as "holy" (the fourth commandment, 20:8–11). The Sabbath day was introduced in the creation story (Gen 2:2–3), where God blessed the seventh day and made it holy. Besides Exod 20:8–11, further explanation regarding how to keep the Sabbath as holy will be provided in 31:12–17 and 35:1–3. Note that the fourth commandment opens and closes with a statement about the day being holy (20:8, 11).

Commandments five to ten (20:12–17) present how Yahweh wants his special, holy people to relate to one another—they must honor their parents, not murder, not commit adultery, not steal, not give false testimony, and not covet anything that belongs to their neighbor. These commandments establish a strong social order, specifically relating to the family and the community, and illustrate that Yahweh is very concerned not only that his people worship him correctly but that they interact with one another in a correct and holy manner. This strong interconnection between how one understands God and worships him (theology proper) and how one interacts with his or her family and community (social and personal ethics) will continue to be stressed throughout the rest of the Old Testament and into the New Testament.

Note that after the Ten Commandments are stated, the story returns to the scene of the narrative that was interrupted after 19:25, which includes thunder, lightning, and smoke, along with trembling and fear (20:18–21). Moses tells the Israelites not to be afraid, and then he informs them of Yahweh's purpose behind this fearful encounter—"the fear of God will be with you to keep you from sinning" (20:20 NIV).

The Book of the Covenant: Revealed, Written, and Ratified (20:22–24:18)

Following closely after the Ten Commandments, the next three chapters (20:22–23:19) include further explanation, elaboration, and implications of those commandments. The general topics include idol-making (20:22–26); treatment of servants (21:2–11); homicides and personal injury (21:12–36); stealing, borrowing, and property rights (22:1–15); miscellaneous social interactions (22:16–31); justice and legal proceedings (23:1–9); Sabbath observance (23:10–13); and the three major worship festivals (23:14–19). Looking back, in light of the large amount of text in the book of Genesis devoted to the story of how the sons of Jacob "kidnapped" Joseph and sold him into slavery (Gen 37:12–50:21), Yahweh's serious prohibition against kidnapping struck very close to home: "Anyone who kidnaps someone is to be put to death, whether the victim has been sold or is still in the kidnapper's possession" (Exod 21:16 NIV). Likewise, looking forward, this elaboration and expansion of the Ten Commandments introduce the obligation to care for the rights and well-being of residing foreigners (22:21; 23:9), widows (22:22), orphans (22:22), and the poor (23:6–8).[27] The responsibility of Yahweh's people to care for this triad (residing foreigners, widows, and orphans), with the poor occasionally added as well, will be repeated frequently throughout the rest of the Old Testament, especially in Deuteronomy and the Prophets. They seem to represent the socioeconomic underclass, those who do not have adequate power to defend themselves and care for themselves and who are thus very vulnerable if the society becomes self-centered and loses its concern for Yahweh's justice.

In Exod 23:20–33 Yahweh explains that he will empower the Israelites to successfully conquer the land he is giving them. He also describes the large boundaries of the land he is giving them (23:31–33). The Hebrew word *'abad* occurs three times in this section, as Yahweh warns them not to worship or serve the gods that the inhabitants of the land worship or serve (23:24, 25, 33).

Back in Exod 19:5 Yahweh alluded to a covenant relationship with Israel and the importance of obeying and keeping the covenant. After presenting the terms of the covenant (20:1–23:19), Yahweh now moves to formally ratify the covenant. First, after Moses presents "all the commands of the LORD and all the ordinances," the people respond unanimously that they will obey it (24:3). Moses then "[writes] down all the words of the LORD" (24:4), which probably includes everything in Exod 20:1–23:19.

---

[27] CSB translates the Hebrew term *ger* as "resident alien" and *yatom* as "the fatherless." Throughout this book we will use the terms *residing foreigner* for *ger* and *orphan* for *yatom*.

Next, Moses builds an altar at the bottom of Mount Sinai and places twelve stone pillars there as a memorial for the twelve tribes. The Israelites then sacrifice bulls (24:5). Moses takes blood from this sacrifice, splashes half on the altar, and reads "the Book of the Covenant" (24:7 NIV; i.e., the text he just wrote down in 24:4). The people formally agree again to obey everything in that covenant document, and then Moses sprinkles the rest of the blood from the sacrifice on them (24:8), formally ratifying the covenant between Yahweh and the people of Israel.

Yahweh then invites Moses to come to the top of the mountain, where Yahweh is, to receive the tablets of stone that Yahweh has written (i.e., the Ten Commandments; 24:12). There is a special stress on the "glory" of Yahweh, appearing as a consuming fire within a thick cloud that covered the top of the mountain. Moses goes into the cloud and stays there in the presence of Yahweh for forty days (24:16–18). This paragraph concludes the first half of the book of Exodus and will parallel the ending of the book in Exod 40:34–38. In Exod 24:9–18 the glory of Yahweh is on top of Mount Sinai and the entire mountain is covered with a cloud. In Exod 40:34–38 the same glory of Yahweh fills the tabernacle and the cloud covers the tabernacle.

Yahweh Guides the Israelites in Constructing the Tabernacle, the Dwelling Place for His Presence (25:1–40:38)

At the heart of the covenant relationship that Yahweh has just inaugurated with Israel is the reality that he will now dwell in their midst. Thus he will need a place to reside. The entire second half of Exodus (excluding the golden calf interruption in Exodus 32–34) deals with constructing the tabernacle, the place where Yahweh will reside. At the end of Exodus, Yahweh does indeed come and enter the tabernacle to dwell right in the midst of Israel, his kingdom of priests, his holy nation.

In Exodus 25–31 Yahweh tells Moses and the Israelites how to make the tabernacle. Then in Exodus 35–40 they construct the tabernacle, carefully following Yahweh's instructions. Exodus 25–40 is not so much an account describing what the tabernacle looked like as it is an account of the construction of the tabernacle. Related to this, note that this section likewise has numerous parallels and allusions to the creation account in Genesis 1–2. For example, the creation account is structured around the statement "God said," which occurs seven times (Gen 1:3, 6, 9, 14, 20, 24, 26). In the instructions for building the tabernacle we see a similar sevenfold repetition of "Yahweh said" (Exod 25:1; 30:11, 17, 22, 34; 31:1, 12). In addition, both accounts mention gold (Gen 2:11–12; Exod 25:18), precious jewels (Gen 2:12; Exod 25:7); and cherubim (Gen 3:24; Exod 25:18). Also, just as the creation account

concluded with God resting on the seventh day (Gen 2:2), so the instructions for
the tabernacle conclude with a reminder of observing the Sabbath (Exod 31:12–18).
Likewise, both accounts have a "rebellion and fall" (Genesis 3; Exodus 32). Just as
God's relational presence was in the garden with Adam and Eve (Gen 3:8), at the end
of Exodus Yahweh's relational presence comes to dwell in the midst of Israel (Exod
40:34–38). The implication is that the construction of the tabernacle is described in
a way that suggests it represents in some sense a reconstruction (or memory) of the
garden; that is, the place where Yahweh first dwelt among his people and interacted
with them.[28]

YAHWEH GIVES INSTRUCTIONS FOR BUILDING THE TABERNACLE (25:1–31:18)

Yahweh Gives Instructions for Constructing the Tabernacle and the Items Inside and Outside the Tabernacle (25:1–27:19)

Exodus 25:1–9 introduces the large following unit that describes the construction
of the tabernacle (25:10–31:18; 35:1–40:38). In 25:8–9 Yahweh tells Moses, "They
are to make a sanctuary [Hebrew, *miqdash*, 'holy place'] for me so that I may dwell
[Hebrew, *shakan*] among them. You must make it according to all that I show you—
the pattern of the tabernacle [Hebrew, *mishkan*, 'dwelling place'] as well as the pattern
of all its furnishings."

Yahweh starts the actual instructions by describing the sacred items (that is, "holy"
or "set apart for special use" items) that will be inside the tabernacle. The tabernacle
was basically a rectangular tent-like structure that was divided into two rooms—the
Most Holy Place and the Holy Place. The tabernacle had three corresponding levels
of emanating holiness—the Most Holy Place (where Yahweh resided and where holiness was most intense), the Holy Place (adjacent but screened off from the Most Holy
Place), and the tabernacle courtyard outside. As Yahweh describes the items associated with the tabernacle, he follows this same order of descending levels of holiness:
He first describes how to build the ark of the covenant, which will be in the Most
Holy Place (25:10–22). Then he moves to the items in the Holy Place, the table of
the Bread of the Presence and the lampstand (25:23–40). Then he describes the tabernacle structure itself (26:1–37), followed by the altar outside in the front (27:1–8)
and the courtyard (27:9–19).

---

[28] John H. Sailhamer, *The Pentateuch as Narrative* (Grand Rapids: Zondervan, 1992),
298–99; Hays, *The Temple and the Tabernacle*, 36 (see chap. 1, n. 16).

Next, Yahweh describes the priests—their duties, dress and consecration (28:1–30:28). In this section Yahweh will also describe how to construct the altar of incense (30:1–6), an item also located in the Holy Place. Twice Yahweh will remind Moses to make the items exactly like the pattern he was shown on the mountain (25:40; 27:8), so apparently Yahweh gave very explicit instructions and perhaps even let Moses see a visual model of the tabernacle and its furnishings while he was with Yahweh on Mount Sinai, perhaps during his forty-day stay there (24:18).

Each item, of course, carries theological significance. The ark represents the intense focal point of Yahweh's presence and resides in the Most Holy Place. Thus, it is to be treated as extremely holy, and there are strict rules about how to handle it and move it. It is a small wood box (approximately 3 feet, 9 inches long by 2 feet, 4 inches wide by 2 feet, 4 inches high) covered inside and outside with gold. Inside the ark are the Ten Commandments (25:16, 21–22), symbolizing the terms of the covenant, and a jarful of manna, a reminder of how Yahweh sustained the Israelites after he delivered them from Egypt (16:31–34).[29] The lid to the box is a sculpted gold cover (25:17–22), the "atonement cover" (NIV; often translated as "mercy seat," as in CSB), where the blood from the Day of Atonement ceremony will be smeared (see the discussion for Leviticus 16). Two winged cherubim are to be sculpted into the cover and thus stand above the ark. Cherubim (the word is plural) were angelic-like winged composite beings (the ones in Ezek 1:5–10 and 10:12–14 combine physical elements of humans, birds, oxen or calves, lions, and eagles) who were associated, somewhat like guards, with access to the presence of Yahweh. When Adam and Eve were driven out of the garden, Yahweh posted cherubim at the entrance to the garden as armed guards (Gen 3:24). Visually, Yahweh is often described in the Old Testament as seated above the cherubim, as on a throne. After describing the ark, in Exod 25:22 Yahweh tells Moses, "I will meet with you there above the mercy seat, between the two cherubim that are over the ark of the testimony; I will speak with you from there about all that I command you regarding the Israelites."[30]

Described next is a wooden table covered with gold, which will hold the Bread of the Presence, to be located in the Holy Place (25:23–30). Leviticus 24:5–9 adds additional details about the bread. This bread symbolizes the close, relational table fellowship with Yahweh that the Israelites enjoy as partners in the covenant.

---

[29] In Num 17:10–11 Yahweh tells Moses to put Aaron's staff in the ark as well. See also Heb 9:3–4.

[30] For a detailed discussion on the purpose and function of the ark, see Hays, *The Temple and the Tabernacle*, 36–43.

Yahweh is coming to dwell in their midst, not just to rule over them, but to fellowship with them.

Also to be located in the Holy Place was the golden lampstand (25:31–40) (Hebrew, *menōrāh*). Although this lampstand was to have seven branches, this ancient menorah in the tabernacle is described as having the appearance of a tree in blossom, thus looking quite a bit different from the traditional menorah we think of today, the seven-branched candelabrum that serves as one of the national symbols of Israel. This lampstand did not hold candles but rather burned a special olive oil to produce light. The treelike appearance of this lampstand placed right before the presence of Yahweh suggests a sacred or holy tree, so it is probably symbolic of the tree of life in the garden, stressing the close connection between the presence of Yahweh and life itself. The lamps burning in this tree also recall the burning bush of Exodus 3. So, while the tree symbolizes life, the fire-burning lamps are reminders of Yahweh's holiness and the dangers associated with being in the presence of his holiness. Light is also very symbolic throughout the Bible. Light was the first thing created in Genesis 1; it is often associated with Yahweh's glory, presence, holiness, and creative power.[31]

In Exod 26:1–37 Yahweh gives instructions on how to build the tabernacle structure itself. Overall, it was to be about forty-five feet long and about fifteen feet wide, broken down into two rooms. The Most Holy Place was to be fifteen feet by fifteen feet, and the Holy Place was to be thirty feet long and fifteen feet wide. The structure would have a pole frame of wooden poles wrapped with gold, covered with four layers of fabric. Considerable detail is added for how to construct the curtain that separated the Most Holy Place from the Holy Place. The fabric used for the interior was to be the finest quality and very expensive linen, producing a bright white appearance. Cherubim were to be embroidered on the white linen with colorful wool yarn.

In the courtyard immediately in front of the entrance to the tabernacle would be the altar of burnt offering (27:1–8), a square structure (7 feet, 6 inches by 7 feet, 6 inches, and 4 feet, 6 inches high) constructed of acacia wood and covered in bronze. This altar was to be used for almost all the sacrifices described in Leviticus 1–7 and summarized in Lev 7:37.

The courtyard itself is described in Exod 26:9–19. The courtyard was to be 75 feet wide and 150 feet long. It would have a 7-foot, 6-inch-high linen fence enclosure, strung on wooden posts that would have silver bands and bronze bases, along with bronze tent pegs. In general, the metals used increase in value as one moved closer to

---

[31] See the discussion in Hays, 44–48.

the presence of Yahweh: first bronze and silver (in the courtyard), then gold (Holy Place and Most Holy Place).

Yahweh Gives Instructions for the Priests and for Operating the Tabernacle (27:20–30:38)

Having described most of the items associated with the tabernacle, Yahweh next moves to describe the special garments and special consecration required for those who would minister in the tabernacle and in the courtyard. There is a specific focus on the high priests, especially on Aaron and his sons. All the people can come into the courtyard (like a kingdom of priests), but only a special group of further consecrated (i.e., "set apart for special service") people (the Levitical priests, and especially the high priests) can come into the Holy Place and the Most Holy Place of the tabernacle.

The unit starts with a description of one of the priests' most important ongoing daily functions: keeping the lamp in the Holy Place filled with high quality oil (27:20–21). Next, Yahweh describes the intricate garments the high priests are to wear, which includes the special ephod containing the breastpiece with the Urim and Thummim for making decisions, as well as the special robe and turban that go with the ephod (28:1–43). There are to be specific, detailed ceremonies involved in consecrating the high priests, which Yahweh describes in 29:1–46, underscoring the ongoing pervasive concern with Yahweh's holiness. Yahweh concludes this section on the high priests by restating the basic terms of the covenant: "I will dwell among the Israelites and be their God. And they will know that I am the LORD their God, who brought them out of the land of Egypt, so that I might dwell among them. I am the LORD their God" (29:45–46).

In Exodus 30 Yahweh describes how to construct the incense altar that will be placed inside the tabernacle in the Holy Place, right in front of the curtain of the Most Holy Place. The incense will create a fragrant cloud of smoke and probably also serve as a protective veil between the ministering high priest and the holiness of Yahweh. Remember that it was dangerous for sinful people to come into close, direct contact with the holiness of Yahweh. Aaron (the high priest) was to burn incense daily on this altar as he serviced the lampstand in the Holy Place, and he was also to use this altar for special incense when entering the Most Holy Place on the Day of Atonement (see Leviticus 16). In addition, Yahweh explains how to construct the bronze washbasin out in the courtyard (30:17–21). He also describes the required atonement money (30:11–16), special atonement oil used for consecrating, and the sacred incense to be used on the incense altar (30:22–38). Running throughout all these instructions is the high concern for Yahweh's holiness and the need for consecrating (i.e., making holy or setting apart for special use) those who would come into his presence.

Yahweh Selects the Lead Workers and Restates the Importance of Sabbath Observance (31:1–18)

This large section in which Yahweh gives instructions on how to build the tabernacle (25:1–31:18) is brought to a conclusion with three short, important events. First, Yahweh informs Moses that he has selected two men, Bezalel and Oholiab, to be the lead craftsmen for the construction of the tabernacle (31:1–11). Yahweh then restates the importance of observing the Sabbath (31:12–17; "Whoever profanes it must be put to death. If anyone does work on it, that person must be cut off from his people," v. 14), and then he gives Moses "the two tablets of the testimony, stone tablets inscribed by the finger of God" (31:18).

AN UNEXPECTED INTERRUPTION: SINFUL REBELLION AND COVENANT RESTORATION (32:1–34:35)

The Golden Calf Episode Jeopardizes Israel's Covenant Relationship with Yahweh and His Presence with Them (32:1–10)

While Moses is up on Mount Sinai, receiving special instructions from Yahweh on how to construct the tabernacle so that Yahweh can come and dwell among them, the people of Israel do the unthinkable—they reject the foundational elements of the covenant relationship, violating the first two of the Ten Commandments (32:1–6). Even Aaron, who plays such an important role in Yahweh's instructions for the priesthood in Exodus 28–29, gets swept away with this terrible act of disobedience. Yahweh refers to the people as "your [Moses's] people" (32:7) and then tells Moses, "Now leave me alone, so that my anger can burn against them and I can destroy them. Then I will make you into a great nation" (32:10). Yahweh appears to be threatening to end the covenant he has with Israel.

Moses Intercedes, and Yahweh Reestablishes His Covenant Relationship and Presence with Israel (32:11–34:35)

With Israel's covenant relationship with Yahweh hanging in the balance, Moses intercedes, reminding Yahweh of his promise to Abraham, Isaac, and Israel (Jacob), beseeching him to relent from his decision to destroy Israel (32:11–13). In response, Yahweh does indeed relent (32:14). Yet when Moses returns to the Israelite camp and sees the idolatry firsthand, he also becomes angry, throwing the stone tablets with the Ten Commandments to the ground, breaking them. After Moses and the Levites kill 3,000 of the offenders (32:25–29), however, and after Yahweh strikes the camp with a plague (32:35), Yahweh tells Moses to continue with their trip to the Promised Land. Unfortunately, Yahweh states, underscoring the change in covenant relational status, he will no longer go with them (33:1–3). Moses intervenes once again, and Yahweh once again relents, agreeing, "My presence will go with you" (33:14).

In Exodus 34 the stone tablets with the Ten Commandments are replaced and the covenant relationship is restored between Yahweh and Israel. Stressing the special role that Moses has as intercessor and mediator, he now appears with a face so radiant from being in the presence of Yahweh that he has to cover his face with a veil (34:29–35).

Exodus 32–34 illustrates the tight interconnectedness of Yahweh's name, his glory, his holiness, his presence, and the blessings that come with his presence. Likewise, this unit underscores how sin and rebellion as an offense against Yahweh's holiness can threaten his ongoing presence and blessings. Only due to the grace of Yahweh and through the intercession of his servant Moses was disaster for Israel averted.[32]

Moses and Israel Complete the Tabernacle according to Yahweh's Instructions, and Yahweh Comes to Reside There (35:1–40:38)

The Tabernacle Is Built Exactly as Yahweh Instructed (35:1–40:33)

With the covenant relationship now restored, the story picks back up from chapters 25–31 and continues the account of the tabernacle construction. In Exodus 25–31 Yahweh had given instructions about how to build the tabernacle. Now in Exodus 35–40 the Israelites actually build it in accordance with those instructions. Thus, most of the items included in the instructions described in Exodus 25–31 are referenced again in Exodus 35–40. As mentioned earlier, the account in Exodus 25–31 and 35–40 is not so much a description of the tabernacle itself as it is of how the tabernacle was built. After a brief reminder about the Sabbath observance (35:1–3), the text describes

---

[32] Duvall and Hays, *God's Relational Presence*, 35–38.

how the people willingly donated the needed materials for the tabernacle (35:4–29) and how Yahweh's chosen chief craftsmen, Bezalel and Oholiab, led the project (35:30–36:7). Then the story recounts that the following were each constructed: the tabernacle (36:8–38); the ark (37:1–9); the table for the Bread of the Presence (37:10–16); the lampstand (37:17–24); the altar of incense (37:25–29); the altar of burnt offering (38:1–7); the bronze washbasin (38:8); and the courtyard (38:9–20).

Also included are a summary of the expensive materials donated and used in the construction of the tabernacle (38:21–31) and a description of how Yahweh's instructions about the high priest were carried out. This covers the making of the priestly garments (39:1); the ephod (39:2–7); the breastpiece (39:8–21); and the robe, garments, and holy diadem on the turban (39:22–31). Running throughout this section describing the priestly accoutrements is the repeated statement that the people completed this "as the LORD had commanded Moses" (39:1, 5, 7, 21, 26, 29, 31). In the next section (39:32–43), Moses inspects the work and sees that it has been done just as the LORD commanded. The text also states twice, redundantly, that the Israelites did everything just as the LORD had commanded Moses, stressing their obedience.

Recall our earlier word study on the Hebrew word 'abad. The noun form of this word 'abad occurs several times in this summary passage, in reference to the "work" or "service" in building the tabernacle. This includes 39:32, "So all the *work* for the tabernacle, the tent of meeting, was finished"; 39:40, "and all the furnishings for the *service* of the tabernacle"; and 39:42, "The Israelites had done all the *work* according to everything the LORD had commanded Moses" (emphasis added in each). As noted above, this repetition of 'abad at the end of Exodus is probably an intentional contrast with the repeated use of 'abad in the opening scene (1:13–14). Now, however, the Israelites are not *serving* Pharaoh and building his store cities but rather *serving* Yahweh and building his residence, a residence filled with items designed to assist the Israelites in their *worship* (*service*) of Yahweh, their God.

With all the items and materials completed, Moses now oversees putting it all together (40:1–33). Once again, running repeatedly throughout this section is the refrain that Moses did everything just as Yahweh had commanded him (40:16, 19, 21, 23, 25, 27, 29, 32).

The Glory of Yahweh Fills the Tabernacle (40:34–38)

This brief paragraph at the end of the book is, in fact, the climax of the exodus story. In the first half of the book Yahweh delivered the Israelites from Egypt, brought them to himself at Mount Sinai, and entered a special covenant relationship with them that centered on his promise to personally dwell among them. In the second half of the book, Yahweh guided the Israelites in constructing his dwelling place. Now, at the end of Exodus, and in spectacular fashion, Yahweh, in his glory, takes up residence in the tabernacle. A cloud covers the tabernacle (probably to veil the people from the intensity of Yahweh's glory) and Yahweh's glory fills the tabernacle. The final three verses note that Yahweh's glory in the tabernacle went with the Israelites on their travels.

Biblical Connections

The importance of the exodus event throughout the Bible cannot be overstated. It is the central paradigmatic picture of deliverance in the Old Testament. Throughout the Old Testament the many multifaceted components of Yahweh's great deliverance are referenced repeatedly, both implicitly and explicitly. These components include the following: Yahweh reveals the character of his name, delivers Israel from slavery and oppression, judges the hostile oppressors, brings the Israelites into covenant relationship with him as his people, gives them the written terms of the covenant, establishes the important centrality of blood sacrifice in the relationship, forbids idolatry, and comes to dwell in their midst as he takes them to the Promised Land. Indeed, the Old Testament contains more than 100 clear references to these events, found especially in the Prophets and in Psalms.

Yet in identifying biblical connections we must start with Genesis, for the exodus event continues the story from the end of Genesis. Indeed, many of the main events in Exodus are presented as a fulfillment of the Abrahamic covenant (e.g., Gen 12:1–3; 15:1–21; Exod 2:24–25; 3:6–8, 16–17; 6:8; 33:1). Likewise, the following books in the Pentateuch (Leviticus, Numbers, and Deuteronomy) all assume the events in the book of Exodus and continue the story. Forty years after the exodus, as the Israelites approach the Promised Land once again, and as Moses restates the covenant terms by which Yahweh will dwell in their midst and bless them (Deuteronomy), Moses recalls the events of the exodus as he summarizes Yahweh's history with Israel (Deut 4:32–38; 5:2–6, 15, 22–33). Similarly, Moses identifies the major motive for obedience to Yahweh as: "We were slaves of Pharaoh in Egypt, but the LORD brought us out of Egypt with a strong hand" (Deut 6:21). This reminder that Yahweh is the one who brought Israel out of Egypt will echo throughout the Old Testament, indicting wayward Israel, warning her to be faithful, and calling on Yahweh for forgiveness (e.g.,

Judg 2:1, 12; 1 Sam 10:18–19; 12:8; 1 Kgs 9:8–9; Neh 9:9–19; Ps 78:12–53; 81:10–12; Ezek 20:5–12; Dan 9:11–16; Hos 13:4–5; Amos 2:10; Mic 6:3–4).

Not only are the blessings of Yahweh's deliverance in the book of Exodus cited frequently, but the judgment on Egypt is referenced frequently as well, especially the plagues. These usually are cited as warnings for Israel. For example, in the warning section of Deuteronomy 28, Moses chides, "The LORD will afflict you with the boils of Egypt" (28:27). See also Deut 28:60 and Amos 4:10.

In the book of Joshua, Yahweh tells Joshua that he would be with him as he was with Moses. Likewise he instructs Joshua and the people to obey all the laws that Moses gave them (Josh 1:1–18). Joshua leading the Israelites across the Jordan River alludes to the earlier parallel event of crossing the Red Sea. Central to their success in crossing the Jordan and in defeating Jericho is the ark of the covenant, representing the powerful presence of Yahweh, as described in Exodus.

In the opening chapters of 1–2 Samuel, Yahweh is residing in the tabernacle, as described in Exodus. The ark of the covenant reappears to play a central role in three different episodes in 1–2 Samuel, driving the main storyline (1 Sam 4:1–7; 2 Sam 6:1–23; 15:24–29).

First Kings 1–11, which describes the reign of King Solomon, is filled with numerous direct and indirect allusions to the exodus event. For example, mentioned in this account of Solomon are the daughter of Pharaoh (1 Kgs 3:1), the Red Sea (9:26), store cities (9:19), forced labor (5:13–16), construction of Yahweh's dwelling place (5:1–6:38), and the cloud and the glory of Yahweh filling his dwelling place (8:10–11). First Kings 5–8 deals with Solomon's construction of the temple, which will replace the tabernacle as the place where Yahweh will dwell. Indeed, 1 Kgs 6:1 even dates the construction of the new temple in relation to the exodus. The narrative account of Solomon in 1 Kings 1–11 seems to invite the reader to make a direct comparison and contrast between Moses's construction of the tabernacle and Solomon's construction of the temple. When viewed together, however, the Exodus account of building the tabernacle (Exod 25–40) stands in stark contrast to the account of Solomon's construction of the temple, suggesting with some subtlety that things may not be quite right with the reign of Solomon. That is, the account of constructing the temple in 1 Kings 5–8 contains quite a number of glaring negative contrasts with the account of building the tabernacle in Exodus 25–40. First Kings 5–8, for example, includes no direct word from Yahweh on how to build the temple and no repeated references to completing it exactly as Yahweh has decreed; the people do not work voluntarily but as forced labor; and Canaanite craftsmen are used instead of Israelites chosen by Yahweh.[33] The account of the tabernacle construction in Exodus 25–40, built exactly as Yahweh instructed and according to what Yahweh showed Moses on Mount Sinai, appears to be the true model of what Yahweh desires—and not necessarily the larger, flashier temple that Solomon built even as his heart slipped away from Yahweh to worship other gods.[34]

In Psalms, Yahweh is praised repeatedly for his great saving acts of deliverance seen in Exodus (see especially Ps 66:6–12; 68; 105; 106:7–12; 114; 135:8–9). The miraculous crossing of the Red Sea is specifically mentioned numerous times (66:6; 74:13–14; 77:16–20; 78:13, 53; 106:9–11, 22; 114:3–5; 136:13–15). While the psalmists typically cite the great deliverance events in praise of Yahweh, they also frequently call for repentance and faithful obedience. Psalm 95:8, for example, exhorts the Israelites, "Do not harden your hearts as at Meribah, as on that day at Massah," referencing the grumbling and rebelling of Israel in Exod 17:1–7. In essence the psalmists are saying, "Remember the great way that Yahweh saved your ancestors and thus be faithful to him."[35]

In the Prophets the events in Exodus, along with the closely related decrees of Deuteronomy, are referenced repeatedly. As in Psalms, the Prophets refer time after time to the great saving acts of Yahweh as seen in Exodus. Yet the Prophets usually make the point that because Yahweh has delivered Israel and been faithful to them, Israel should faithfully obey Yahweh and desist from their idolatry and injustices. Jeremiah 7 is typical:

> "For when I brought your ancestors out of the land of Egypt . . . I did give them this command: 'Obey me, and then I will be your God, and you will be my people. . . . Yet they didn't listen or pay attention but followed their . . .

---

[33] While the account in 1 Kings 5–8 leaves Yahweh completely silent on how to build the temple, 1 Chr 28:11–19 recounts that when David gave Solomon plans for the temple, he perhaps claimed that the plans came from Yahweh. But there is some ambiguity in these texts, and neither 28:11 nor 28:19 clearly states that the plans came from Yahweh. At any rate, there is no repeated "and Yahweh said" (as in Exodus 25–40) in the accounts of building the temple in 1 Kings 5–8, 1 Chr 28:1–21, or 2 Chr 2:1–5:1.

[34] See J. Daniel Hays, "Has the Narrator Come to Praise Solomon or to Bury Him? Narrative Subtlety in 1 Kings 1–11," *JSOT* 23 (2003): 149–74. This negative picture of Solomon will emerge again in our discussion of Deut 17:14–20, for Solomon violated all the guidelines for the monarchy decreed in Deut 17:14–20.

[35] Rikki E. Watts, "Exodus," in *New Dictionary of Biblical Theology*, ed. T. Desmond Alexander and Brian S. Rosner (Downers Grove, IL: IVP, 2000), 484.

own stubborn, evil heart. . . . Since the day your ancestors came out of the land of Egypt until today, I have sent all my servants the prophets to you time and time again. However, my people . . . did more evil than their ancestors." (vv. 22–26)

Likewise, earlier in Jeremiah 7 Yahweh indicts Israel for violating the Ten Commandments (7:9) as well as the prohibition in Exod 22:21–22 against oppressing residing foreigners, widows, and orphans (Jer 7:5–6).

Connected to this is the imagery of Yahweh as the husband, Israel the unfaithful wife, and the establishment of the covenant at Mount Sinai as the marriage ceremony. For example, consider Jeremiah 2:

"I remember the loyalty of your youth,
your love as a bride—
how you followed me in the wilderness. . . .
What fault did your ancestors find in me
that they . . .
followed worthless idols . . . ?
They stopped asking, 'Where is the LORD
who brought us from the land of Egypt . . . ?'
Can a young woman forget her jewelry
or a bride her wedding sash?
Yet my people have forgotten me." (vv. 2–6, 32)

Furthermore, the paradigmatic nature of the exodus, as the pattern of Yahweh's great deliverance, lies behind much of the deliverance imagery of Isaiah. This is especially true in Isaiah 40–66, in which Yahweh uses the imagery of a New Exodus to describe the future deliverance. In addition to references to the big picture—that is, the paradigmatic deliverance—are numerous allusions to some of the details in Exodus. When Isa 40:5, for example, states that "the glory of the LORD will appear, and all humanity together will see it," it is no doubt alluding back to the revelation of Yahweh's glory in Exodus, particularly in the tabernacle (Exod 40:34). In the New Exodus, however, as Isaiah points out, "all humanity" will see it, and not just Moses.

Several times in Isaiah the past events of the exodus will be referred to as "the former things" (NIV; "past events," CSB). As spectacular as these wonderful acts of Yahweh were, the coming deliverance (i.e., the New Exodus) will be bigger and more spectacular. This is demonstrated, for example, in Isa 43:16–21:

This is what the L\ord says—
who makes a way in the sea,
and a path through raging water,
who brings out the chariot and horse,
the army and the mighty one together
(they lie down, they do not rise again . . .)
"Do not remember the past events,
pay no attention to things of old.
Look, I am about to do something new;
even now it is coming."

Adding to the close relationship in Isaiah of the New Exodus to the Old Exodus ("the past events") is the highly significant term "servant." In the four Servant Songs of Isaiah (42:1–7; 49:1–6; 50:4–10; 52:13–53:12) a suffering servant is presented as the one who will bring about the glorious New Exodus. While David is often called Yahweh's servant (a few others are referred to as Yahweh's servants in brief references), Moses is referred to as the servant of Yahweh more than forty times throughout the Old Testament (in Exodus, Deuteronomy, Joshua, 2 Samuel, 1–2 Kings, 1–2 Chronicles, Nehemiah, Psalms, and Malachi). Thus the suffering servant of Yahweh ("his servant") in Isaiah is presented as the "new Moses," the leader and mediator for the New Exodus.[36] Yet Isaiah's addition of "suffering" to the servant concept adds a whole new level of meaning that goes beyond Moses (i.e., the substitutionary, sacrificial connotations). Also, as discussed below, Heb 3:5–6 argues that while Moses was a faithful servant in God's household, Christ was a faithful Son in God's household and thus far superior to Moses.

Focusing on the character of Yahweh as revealed in Exodus are the many allusions to Exodus in the book of Ezekiel. Throughout Exodus Yahweh frequently declared, "I am Yahweh"; "I am Yahweh, your God"; or "You will know that I am Yahweh." Indeed, one of the central themes in Exodus is that everyone will know who Yahweh is, either as his blessed and delivered covenant people or as his judged and destroyed enemy. The book of Ezekiel uses the same phrases ("I am Yahweh"; or "You will know that I am Yahweh") repeatedly (more than seventy times). Ezekiel is clearly connecting back to Exodus, exhorting his readers "to know Yahweh as the God of the exodus, who still acts, in covenant, to judge and to deliver."[37]

---

[36] L. Michael Morales, *Exodus Old and New: A Biblical Theology of Redemption*, ESBT (Downers Grove, IL: IVP, 2020), 77–90, 148–51.

[37] John F. Evans, *You Shall Know That I Am Yahweh: An Inner-Biblical Interpretation of Ezekiel's Recognition Formula*, BBRSup 25 (University Park, PA: Eisenbrauns, 2019), 8.

In the New Testament, allusions to and direct quotations of Exodus are just as ubiquitous as in the Old Testament. For example, throughout the Synoptic Gospels, numerous allusions and quotes parallel Jesus with Moses, presenting him as the "new Moses," only even bigger and better than Moses. Thus just as Pharaoh was killing babies at the time of Moses's birth, threatening his survival (Exodus 1–2), so King Herod is killing babies at the time of Jesus's birth, likewise posing a threat to his survival (Matt 2:13–18). Ironically, Jesus's parents flee with him to Egypt. In Matt 5:1 Jesus went up on the mountain (like Moses). He did not bring the law back down on tablets like Moses, but Jesus taught authoritatively about the law, particularly critical aspects of the Ten Commandments (i.e., murder, adultery, lying). Indeed, Jesus sounds very much like Yahweh in Exodus when he says, "teaching them to observe everything I have commanded you" (Matt 28:20). Most dramatically, he states that he has come to fulfill the Law (5:17). In addition, just as Moses fed the Israelites manna in the wilderness, so Jesus feeds the crowds (Mark 6:30–44; 8:1–10). Likewise, the account of the transfiguration in Luke 9:28–36 is filled with allusions to Moses and his actions in Exodus. For example, Jesus goes up on a mountain, and the appearance of his face changes. In Luke's account, Moses shows up too, talking with Jesus about his "departure" (CSB, NIV). The Greek word translated as "departure" is *exodos*. Other similar, highly significant terminology reminiscent of Exodus is used throughout the transfiguration account—glory, cloud, and voice from the cloud.

As the "new Moses," Jesus is presented as the one who will lead the New Exodus that Isaiah prophesied. This is strongly implied by the opening of Mark, which quotes Isa 40:3, a verse in Isaiah that introduces one of the central New Exodus passages.[38] The New Exodus theme is continued throughout the book of Acts as well.[39]

Early in the Gospel of John a clear connection is made to God's glory and the indwelling presence of God, a central theme in Exodus. Connecting to Exod 40:34–35 and referring to Jesus, John 1:14–17 states, "The Word became flesh and dwelt among us. We observed his glory, the glory as the one and only Son from the Father, full of grace and truth . . . for the law was given through Moses; grace and truth came through Jesus Christ." The Greek word CSB translates as "dwelt" in 1:14 is the same Greek word use to translate "tabernacle" in the LXX translation of Exodus. In this context, this verse could be rendered, "The Word became flesh and *tabernacled* among us."

---

[38] For a good discussion on the Isaianic New Exodus in the Gospels, see Rikki E. Watts, *Isaiah's New Exodus in Mark* (Grand Rapids: Baker, 2000); and "Exodus," 484–85.

[39] David W. Pao, *Acts and the Isaianic New Exodus* (Grand Rapids: Baker, 2002).

The Passover (Exod 12:1–23) is also alluded to, directly and indirectly, several times in the Gospel of John. A few verses after the tabernacle reference in John 1:14–17, John the Baptist will identify Jesus as "the Lamb of God, who takes away the sin of the world," a reference to Jesus as the Passover Lamb (1:29). In both John and the Synoptic Gospels the Last Supper takes place on the Passover, likewise indicating that Jesus was the Passover Lamb. Furthermore, at the crucifixion of Christ, John 19:36 cites the Passover criteria for the sacrificed lamb, "Not one of his bones will be broken" (Exod 12:46; see also Num 9:12; Ps 34:20).[40]

Another connection to Exodus in the book of John is the "I am" statements (John 6:35; 8:12; 10:7, 11; 11:25; 14:6; 15:1; and especially 8:58). When Moses encountered Yahweh at the burning bush, Yahweh identified himself as "I AM WHO I AM" (Exod 3:14). Thus, when Jesus declares, "before Abraham was, I am" (John 8:58), he is claiming a status of deity, like Yahweh. The other "I am" statements of Jesus likewise probably allude back to Exod 3:14, implying Jesus's claim of deity. This is particularly clear in the first "I am" statement in John 6:35 ("I am the bread of life"), where the book of Exodus is already in the immediate context. Leading up to this declaration is a discussion regarding the manna that God provided during the time of Moses (citing Exod 16:4). Jesus's phrase "bread of life" connects not only to the manna provided in the wilderness, but probably also to the "Bread of the Presence" placed on the table in the Holy Place of the tabernacle. Likewise, his next claim ("I am the light of the world; 8:12) probably alludes to the symbolism of the lampstand, also in the Holy Place of the tabernacle (see Rev 1:12–16).

The book of Hebrews makes several theological connections to Exodus. For example, in the warning against unbelief, Heb 3:7–19 cites Ps 95:7–11, a reference to Israel's grumbling and disbelief in Exodus 17 (and beyond). Also repeatedly in Hebrews, specific details are alluded to, to demonstrate the superiority of Jesus Christ and the covenant he brings over Moses and the covenant inaugurated at Mount Sinai in Exodus. Thus Heb 3:1–6 argues that Christ, "a Son over his [God's] household," is superior to Moses, who was merely "a servant in all God's household." Likewise, Christ is a greater high priest than those high priests in the order of Aaron (Heb 7:11–28; Exodus 28–29). Furthermore, the tabernacle in which Christ serves is the true heavenly tabernacle and is thus greater than the one Moses built in Exodus, a mere copy of the true one. Related to this, Hebrews declares that Christ mediates a better covenant than Moses did and offers a greater blood sacrifice than the human priests in the old tabernacle could (Heb 8:1–9:28).

---

[40] Paul also identifies Christ as the Passover Lamb in 1 Cor 5:7.

The imagery in the book of Revelation also draws frequently from the book of Exodus, especially from the account of the plagues (Exodus 7–11; Revelation 8–9; 16). Allusions to the parting of the Red Sea and the song of Moses (Exodus 14–15) can likewise be seen in Rev 15:1–4 and perhaps in 16:12. The phenomenon that accompanied Israel's encounter with Yahweh at Mount Sinai in Exodus 19–24 (lightning, thunder, earthquakes, trumpets) is suggested several times in Revelation (4:5; 8:5; 11:19; and 16:18–21). In addition, one of the most central images of Christ occurring throughout Revelation is that of "the Lamb who was slain" (5:6–12 NIV), imagery that draws from the Passover lamb of Exodus 12. As the slain Lamb is introduced in Revelation 5, the text (5:9–10) declares that "you purchased people for God by your blood" (see the redemption of the firstborn with a lamb in Exod 13:1–16) and that "you made them a kingdom and priests to our God" (see Exod 19:6, "you will be my kingdom of priests"). Finally, the presence of God in the temple described in Rev 15:8 is described in similar terms as Yahweh in the tabernacle in Exod 40:34–35.[41] In addition, central to Exodus was Yahweh's interrelated three-part covenant promise of "I will be your God," "You will be my people," and "I will dwell among them" (see Exod 6:7; 25:8). At the culmination of the biblical story, in the new heaven and the new earth, a loud voice declares, "Look! God's dwelling place is now among the people, and he will dwell with them. They will be his people, and God himself will be with them and be their God" (Rev 21:3 NIV).

Gospel Connections

Many of the critical theological concepts underlying the gospel are introduced in the book of Exodus, either through the big-picture, paradigmatic overview of deliverance or through specific symbolic details, such as the Passover or the items associated with the tabernacle. As mentioned earlier, the exodus event is the Old Testament picture of what salvation and deliverance is all about. In Exodus, God saves his people from their enslavement, not based on their worthiness, but based on his grace and his promises. This salvation or deliverance is not just to save them from their oppressive situation (although it certainly does that), but to bring them to the presence of God, where he will enter into a close and personal relationship with them. Thus, tightly connected to the purpose of deliverance is to have a close relationship with

---

[41] G. K. Beale and Sean M. McDonough, "Revelation," in *Commentary of the New Testament Use of the Old Testament*, ed. G. K. Beale and D. A. Carson (Grand Rapids: Baker, 2007), 1082, 1110–17, 1133–37.

God. Indeed, in Exodus he will dwell in their midst, and his presence will bless them and protect them. His glory and his holiness, however, must be respected, and the presence of his glory and holiness amid a sinful people presents challenges that have to be met through distancing, veiling, and sacrificing. This challenge will continue throughout the Old Testament until Christ comes. Indeed, the salvation and deliverance that Jesus Christ brings will be greater than that of this first exodus. Christ delivers his people from enslavement to sin and death, likewise bringing them into a close personal relationship with the triune God. The challenge of close presence in light of God's glory and holiness, however, is now overcome by the cleansing from sin and the imputation of righteousness that Christ provides through his superior and perfect sacrifice. The presence of God is no longer in a tabernacle in the midst of the nation. Because of what Christ has accomplished, God now dwells directly within his people through the indwelling Holy Spirit, both individually (1 Cor 6:19) and collectively (3:16–17).

Exodus also introduces and teaches the necessity of the blood from the Passover lamb sacrifice, as well as the necessity for redeeming life with a sacrifice. Not only is blood necessary for forgiveness and for cleansing from sin, but blood is necessary for ratifying covenant relationships. Thus, at the Last Supper when Jesus declares, "This is my blood of the covenant, which is poured out for many for the forgiveness of sins" (Matt 26:28 NIV), he is alluding back to the blood ratification of the covenant in Exod 24:8. Furthermore, as mentioned earlier, in the Passover context of the Last Supper, blood is also a reference to the blood from the Passover lamb (Exodus 12).

Finally, Moses's role in Exodus as the powerful and privileged mediator between the people and the presence of God is now superseded in the New Testament by the superior Mediator, Jesus Christ, the Son of God, who sits at the right hand of God.

Life Connections

Exodus is filled with important and relevant theology from which many personal life connections can be made. Space only allows a few. First, note that God saves and delivers people so that they can serve him and have a close relationship with him as he indwells among them. For us today, as Christians, he now indwells in each of us. Thus, when we profess faith in Christ, we are saved from the judgment on our sin, but we are also called to a close, ongoing, all-consuming servant-oriented relationship with God as the people of God. At the heart of this relationship is the call to serve God. He is a jealous God (Exod 34:14) and demands our total worship and our complete loyalty. Furthermore, as his people, we are called to serve others and care for them.

Another important lesson to learn from Exodus relates to God's timing. The book of Exodus recounts the biggest and most spectacular story of deliverance in the entire Old Testament, culminating with God himself in his glory coming to dwell with his people. Yet note that this did not happen all at once, and it did not happen in chapter 1. Likewise, eighty-plus years went by in Exod 2:1–22, and deliverance from God did not come. Exodus 2:24, however, states that "God heard their groaning," and in response, according to his timing, the great story of the exodus deliverance began to unfold. No doubt the Israelites wanted to be delivered immediately and simply. God, however, had big plans that went beyond the simple deliverance of Israel. Likewise, we are often like the Israelites, unable to see beyond our most pressing immediate need and unable to grasp the larger work that God is undertaking and of which we are part.

Leaders can draw strength and courage from the character of Moses, especially from his reliance on God. The people in Exodus grumble, lose heart, and cry out in despair ready to accept defeat, while Moses exhorts them, "Don't be afraid. Stand firm and see the LORD's salvation that he will accomplish for you today" (Exod 14:13).

Finally, the hero of the story in Exodus is Yahweh. As we engage with the book of Exodus, we are confronted with a tremendous amount of text in which Yahweh appears and reveals himself—he speaks, he acts, he listens, he gets angry, he loves, and so on. He also has a bit of poetic flair in the way he judges his enemies. He describes himself as "The LORD . . . a compassionate and gracious God, slow to anger and abounding in faithful love and truth, maintaining faithful love to a thousand generations, forgiving iniquity, rebellion, and sin. But," he warns, "he will not leave the guilty unpunished" (34:6–7). We can learn much about the character of God, thus deepening our relationship with him, by paying attention to what he says and does.

Likewise stressed throughout Exodus is the holiness of God and the splendor of his glory. Even though we as believers in Christ have been made holy and imputed with righteousness, allowing us to have a close access to the presence of God in a way that no one in Exodus could, we should never lose our wonder and respect—even fear, perhaps—of the holy, awesome God surrounded by his spectacular glory.

Interactive Questions

2-1. Compare the women who are mentioned in Exodus 1–2 and the role that they play in the story.

2-2. Using a concordance, locate the places in Exodus where Abraham is referenced. Based on these texts, discuss the role that Abraham plays in Exodus.

2-3. From Exod 3:1–22 and 6:1–8, discuss the name *Yahweh* and explain what it means and how it relates to the story.

2-4. Locate two or three articles from reputable Bible dictionaries or encyclopedias on the gods of Egypt and give an overview of religious views in ancient Egypt.[42] How does understanding this religious context help us in understanding Exodus?

2-5. Discuss the interaction and actions taken by Moses, Pharaoh, and Pharaoh's ministers, officials, and magicians in the plague narratives (Exodus 7–11).

2-6. Describe and evaluate the virtues for leadership we can see in Moses in Exod 14:1–17:7.

2-7. Practically speaking, how should Christians today observe the Sabbath? Is Sunday parallel to the Sabbath? What can Christians do on the Sabbath, and what activities, if any, should they avoid?

2-8. Describe the tabernacle, and explain the impact of Yahweh's holiness both on the structure and on the priestly activities within the tabernacle.

2-9. Describe the Passover and the Feast of Unleavened Bread in Exodus 12 and explain the meaning of the two.

2-10. Discuss the presence of Yahweh dwelling among his people in Exodus. How does it come about? What does Yahweh say about it? How is it described?

Recommended Resources

Dozeman, Thomas B. *Exodus*. ECC. Grand Rapids: Eerdmans, 2009.

Durham, John I. *Exodus*. WBC. Waco, TX: Word, 1987.

Duvall, J. Scott, and J. Daniel Hays. *God's Relational Presence: The Cohesive Center of Biblical Theology*. Grand Rapids: Baker, 2019.

Enns, Peter E. *Exodus*. NIVAC. Grand Rapids: Zondervan, 2000.

Hays, J. Daniel. *The Temple and the Tabernacle*. Grand Rapids: Baker, 2016.

Hoffmeier, James K. *Ancient Israel in Sinai: The Evidence for the Authenticity of the Wilderness Tradition*. Oxford: Oxford University Press, 2005.

---

[42] For a list of good Bible dictionaries and encyclopedias, see Duvall and Hays, *Grasping God's Word*, 512–13 (see chap. 1, n. 5).

————. *Israel in Egypt: The Evidence for the Authenticity of the Exodus Tradition.* Oxford: Oxford University Press, 1996.

Janzen, Mark D., ed. *Five Views on the Exodus: Historicity, Chronology, and Theological Implications.* Grand Rapids: Zondervan, 2021.

Mitchell, Eric Alan. "Exodus." In *The Baker Illustrated Bible Background Commentary.* Edited by J. Scott Duvall and J. Daniel Hays, 120–47. Grand Rapids: Baker, 2020.

Morales, Michael L. *Exodus Old and New: A Biblical Theology of Redemption.* ESBT. Downers Grove, IL: IVP, 2020.

Stuart, Douglas K. *Exodus.* NAC. Nashville: Holman, 2006.

Wells, Bruce. "Exodus." In *ZIBBC.* Edited by John H. Walton, 160–283. Grand Rapids: Zondervan, 2009.

Wright, Christopher J. H. *Exodus.* SGBC. Grand Rapids: Zondervan, 2021.

3

Leviticus

"Be holy because I, the LORD your God, am holy."

—LEVITICUS 19:2

Outline

I.   The sacrifices for individual worship (1:1–7:38)
II. The inauguration and shortcomings of the priesthood (8:1–10:20)
    A. The inauguration of the priesthood and the altar (8:1–9:24)
    B. The priesthood's violation of Yahweh's sacrificial commands (10:1–20)
III. Ritual uncleanness and its treatment (11:1–15:33)
IV. The Day of Atonement—the national sacrifice (16:1–34)
V.   Laws for holy living (17:1–22:33)
VI. Sacred times—national worship (23:1–25:55)
    A. Sacred times—the appointed festivals and sacred assemblies (23:1–24)
    B. The lamps, the Bread of the Presence, and blasphemers (24:1–23)
    C. Sacred times—the Sabbath Year and Year of Jubilee (25:1–55)

VII.   Covenant blessings and covenant curses (26:1–46)

VIII.   Dedication offerings (27:1–34)[1]

Author, Date, and Message

Author and Date

As discussed in the introduction, the view reflected in this book is that Moses is the human author of the Pentateuch, with the understanding that perhaps some later grammatical and place-name updates were made, along with the account of Moses's death. Sequentially, the events in Leviticus take place right after the events in Exodus. Thus, the date for Leviticus is tied to the date for Exodus (either 1446 BC or 1270–1260 BC; see the discussion in the chapter on Exodus).

In the Hebrew Bible the name of this book translates as "And he called." As with the other four books of the Pentateuch (Torah) in the Hebrew Bible, the title comes from the first phrase of the book (Lev 1:1). The Septuagint, the Greek translation of the Hebrew Bible, titled this book *Leuitikon* ("that which concerns the Levites, i.e., the priests"). The Septuagint title carries a meaning akin to "The Priestly Things." Leviticus, the title in our English translations, is a transliteration of the Latin Vulgate's translation of the Greek into Latin.

Numerous scholars have noted that within the structural arrangement of the five-book Pentateuch, Leviticus stands at the center, with Leviticus 16 (the Day of Atonement) at the center of Leviticus. Indeed, a chiastic pattern of sorts can be seen:

(A) Genesis, the prologue (blessings, land, descendants)

(B) Exodus, leaving Egypt and preparing to build the tabernacle

(C) Leviticus, focused on how to operate the tabernacle and live with Yahweh in their midst

(B') Numbers, dedicating the tabernacle and preparing to enter Canaan

(A') Deuteronomy, the epilogue (blessings, land, descendants) [2]

---

[1] This outline has been developed and expanded from Hays and Duvall, *BIBH*, 81.

[2] This suggested chiasm is developed from the discussion by L. Michael Morales, *Who Shall Ascend the Mountain of the Lord? A Biblical Theology of the Book of Leviticus*, NSBT (Downers Grove, IL: IVP, 2015), 24–27. Morales draws on A. C. Leder, *Waiting for the Land: The Story Line of the Pentateuch* (Phillipsburg, NJ: P&R, 2010), 34–35; and Moshe Kline, "The Literary Structure of Leviticus," *Biblical Historian* 2, no. 1 (2006): 11–28.

The Message of Leviticus

In Exodus, Yahweh delivered the Israelites from Egypt and then brought them to Mount Sinai, where he entered a personal covenant relationship with them. At the heart of the covenant was Yahweh's three-part promise: "I will be your God . . . I will take you as my people . . . I will dwell [in your midst]" (6:7; 29:45). If Yahweh is coming to actually dwell in the midst of the Israelites, then he will need a place to reside. Thus, the second half of Exodus deals with the construction of the tabernacle, the place where Yahweh will dwell. At the end of Exodus (40:34–38), Yahweh did indeed come down and fill the Most Holy Place of the tabernacle with his glorious presence. In fulfillment of his covenant promise to dwell among the Israelites, Yahweh will now reside there in the tabernacle, in the midst of his people.

As the story moves from Exodus to Leviticus, Yahweh is residing in the tabernacle, and he will now speak from there, not from the top of Mount Sinai as in Exodus. Moses still mediates and takes the message of Yahweh to the people. Indeed, most of Leviticus consists of direct quotations of material spoken by Yahweh to Moses that he then delivers to the Israelites. The exceptions are the two chapters of narrative texts about priests, especially the death of two of them (Lev 9:1–10:20) and the narrative story of the death of a person who blasphemed Yahweh (24:10–23). Yet even the direct quotation material is introduced with narrative style introduction ("Then the LORD summoned Moses and spoke to him from the tent of meeting"; 1:1), thus embedding all of the instructions and procedures into the narrative story. That is, the instructions and procedures of Leviticus are tied to the narrative historical and theological context that continues from Genesis and Exodus. They are given at a particular time and in a particular situation—right on the heels of Yahweh's great exodus deliverance of Israel, in the context of the covenant he has just enacted with Israel, and in response to his indwelling in the tabernacle to be their God living in their midst.

With the holy, powerful presence of Yahweh dwelling right in the midst of the Israelites, how can they appropriately worship him? How can they deal with their sin so that his holiness does not destroy them? How can they live as holy people serving a holy God? The book of Leviticus answers these questions. With the real, actual presence of the holy and glorious Yahweh living in close physical proximity to them, Yahweh wants them to be completely oriented to that reality. In fact, in light of that reality, Yahweh tells them that everything in their life will change. Yahweh wants them to be constantly focused on him, always aware of his holy presence throughout all aspects of their lives. Their lives are to be lived within the context of what is clean and what is unclean, what is holy and what is profane, an orientation that inter-connects to all aspects of life (e.g., worship, work, family, relationships).

Out of this context, four primary themes emerge from Leviticus: (1) the presence of Yahweh, (2) holiness, (3) the role of sacrifice, and (4) how to worship Yahweh and be obedient to the covenant (and thus enjoy living in his presence).

Interpretive Overview

The Sacrifices for Individual Worship (1:1–7:38)

The opening verse in Leviticus ("the LORD summoned Moses and spoke to him from the tent of meeting") and the repeated quotations from Yahweh throughout the book are strong reminders that the instructions given in Leviticus are from Yahweh. That is, he institutes the sacrificial system that Israel is called to follow if they are indeed to be his special people, a kingdom of priests (Exod 19:4–6).

The first seven chapters of Leviticus cover sacrifices that individual people make (as opposed to national sacrifices, such as in Leviticus 16). Instructions for how to carry out these sacrifices are given first regarding the role of individual Israelites in making the sacrifice (1:1–6:7), followed by the role of the priests in facilitating the sacrifice of these individuals (6:8–7:38). At the end of this section (7:38) is a narrative summary noting that these are the regulations for the many different types of sacrifices that Yahweh gave to Moses at Mount Sinai, underscoring the tight narrative connection between Leviticus and Exodus.

In Leviticus 1–7 two main categories composed of five different types of sacrifices are described. The first category consists of voluntary fellowship and thanksgiving sacrifices. When these are burned, the ascending smoke is described as "a pleasing aroma to the LORD" (1:9, 13, 17; 2:2, 9; 3:5; 6:15, 21; see also 3:16). Three sacrifices fall into the voluntary fellowship and thanksgiving sacrifice category: (1) the burnt offering sacrifice (1:1–17; 6:8–13), offered ritually to indicate one's dedication or devotion to Yahweh; (2) the grain offering (2:1–16; 6:14–23), given in thanksgiving for Yahweh's blessings in meeting daily needs, recognizing him as the source of all agricultural produce and food; and (3) the fellowship offering (3:1–17; 7:11–36), given as part of a vow or in thanksgiving for a specific or general act of Yahweh.

The second category is different because the two sacrifices in this category were not voluntary but mandatory. They were required whenever one sinned (or when someone became ritually unclean). In this category there is no mention of the "pleasing aroma." One of the sacrifices in this category is the fourth type: (4) the sin offering

(4:1–5:13; 6:24–30), required by people who had sinned unintentionally or who had become ceremonially unclean. The sin offering (4:1–5:13) is described in reference to four different groups or situations: "If the anointed priest sins" (4:1–12); "Now if the whole community of Israel errs" (4:13–21); "When a leader sins" (4:22–26); and "Now if any of the common people sins" (4:27–35). The other sacrifice in the "mandatory" category is (5) the guilt offering (5:14–6:7; 7:1–6), necessary for unintentional sin and inadvertent sin, not only sin against Yahweh, but also against other people.

The typical procedure for the animal sacrifices was for the worshiper first to lay his hand on the head of the animal (3:2, 8, 13; 4:4, 15, 24, 29, 33). This served to identify the worshiper with the animal, symbolizing the transfer of sins, culpability, or uncleanness from the worshiper to the animal, who will die as a substitute for the worshiper. The individual worshiper would then kill the animal himself, after which the priests would take the blood of the animal and sprinkle it on or around the altar, which was in front of the tabernacle entrance ("before the Lord").[3] The worshiper would then skin the animal and cut it up into parts, washing some of the parts. The priests would maintain the fire on the altar, take the parts, arrange them on the altar, and burn them completely. The Hebrew word translated as "burnt offering" (e.g., 1:3) is derived from a verb that means "to go up." The image conveyed is that of the sacrifice going up as smoke before the Lord.

WORD STUDY
THE "DRAWING NEAR TO/IN THE PRESENCE OF YAHWEH" TERMINOLOGY FOR SACRIFICING IN LEVITICUS

Leviticus is replete with terminology stressing the close presence of Yahweh in the tabernacle. For example, after the introductory verse (1:1), the opening verses (1:2–3) use these terms or phrases several times, stressing the close presence of Yahweh and setting the tone for the rest of the book. The Hebrew verb *qarab* means "to draw near, or to bring near." Sometimes it is translated into English simply as "bring," but it normally carries connotations of "bringing near." The noun derived from this verb, *qarban*, carries a nuanced meaning of "that which is brought near." The nuance is often lost in its frequent English translation simply as "offering." The phrase *lipne Yahweh* is usually translated as "before the Lord," but it stresses the spatial presence of Yahweh. It would perhaps be better translated as "in the presence of the Lord." It is the major

[3] Mark F. Rooker, *Leviticus*, NAC (Nashville: B&H, 2000), 87–88.

phrase used to refer to the presence of Yahweh in the Old Testament. The opening verses in Leviticus use the verb *qarab* four times and the noun *qarban* three times, followed by *lipne Yahweh*. The English translated words for these terms are in bold below:

> "Speak to the Israelites and tell them: When any of you **brings** [*qarab*] an **offering** [*qarban*] to the LORD from the livestock, you may **bring** [*qarab*] your **offering** [*qarban*] from the herd or flock. If his **offering** [*qarab*] is a burnt offering from the herd, he is to **bring** [*qarab*] an unblemished male. He will **bring** [*qarab*] it to the entrance to the tent of meeting so that he may be accepted **by the** LORD [*lipne Yahweh*; that is, in the presence of Yahweh]." (Lev 1:2–3)

This terminology is repeated throughout Leviticus. The verb *qarab* occurs 102 times, and the noun *qarban* occurs 80 times. The phrase *lipne Yahweh* occurs more than 60 times (e.g., 1:5, 11; 3:1, 7, 12). Nearly all the sacrifices and other rituals that Yahweh prescribes for Israel are to take place "before Yahweh"—that is, in front of his indwelling presence in the tabernacle. Indeed, the indwelling presence of Yahweh in the tabernacle was central to the entire sacrificial system. Neither Leviticus nor Numbers makes any reference to Yahweh sitting on a throne in heaven with his footstool in the tabernacle.[4]

ANCIENT CONNECTIONS SIDEBAR 3.1: THE RITUALS OF WORSHIP IN THE ANCIENT NEAR EAST

Many of the rituals that Yahweh asked the Israelites to perform in worshipping him and in living in his presence were not unlike the religious rituals practiced by people and priests throughout the ANE. We find evidence of this in non-Israelite ancient literary documents as well as in the ancient religious artifacts discovered by archaeologists—temples, animal sacrificial altars, incense altars, libation altars (for liquids such as oil, water, and wine), special lamps, and incense shovels. The ancient people around Israel commonly interacted with their gods through animal sacrifice, bread offerings, libations, and incense burning, usually via priests as mediators at temples. In addition, often back

---

[4] Duvall and Hays, *God's Relational Presence*, 39–42 (see chap. 1, n. 4).

at home people had smaller, household gods that they also worshipped and tried to appease. "Burnt offerings," numerous in Leviticus, were also commonly practiced in Syria-Palestine and Anatolia but were not common in Egypt and Mesopotamia. Literary similarities from the ANE abound. A few examples are listed here, by category.

Regarding sacrifices:

> On the day of fullness, they will slaughter bulls to Moon. On the tenth (day of the month), a sacrifice for Baal of Zaphon; two ewes and a city dove; and two kidneys and a ram for . . . ; and a liver and a ram for Shalim; and a bull-liver and a ram for Baal of Zaphon; a ewe for Zaphon as a burnt offering. And as peace offerings, the same.[5]

Concerning a bread offering and the purification of priests:

> Let those who make the daily bread be clean. Let them be washed and trimmed. . . . Let them be clothed in clean garments.[6]

Regarding festivals:

> Further: The festival of the month, the festival of the year, the festival of the stag, the festival of autumn, the festival of spring, the festival of thunder. . . . If you do not perform them with all the cattle, sheep, bread, beer and wine set up . . . you will cause them [the offerings] to fall short of the will of the gods.[7]

Regarding the high priest's portion of the sacrifices:

> From the sheep of the king's sacrifices of the entire year: [the high priest will receive] the loins, the skin, the hind-quarters, the muscles, half the stomach, half the intestines, two knuckle-bones, and a vessel of meat-broth; From the sacrifices of cattle and sheep of the worshipper: [the high priest's portion is to be] as above.[8]

---

[5] "God and Sacrifice Lists from Ugarit," trans. Michael D. Coogan, in *A Reader of Ancient Near Eastern Texts*, ed. Michael D. Coogan (Oxford: Oxford University Press, 2013), 6.117.b.

[6] "Instructions to Priests and Temple Officials," trans. Gregory McMahon, *COS* 1.83:2.

[7] "Instructions to Priests and Temple Officials," 1.83:4.

[8] "The 'Sun Disk' Tablet of NABÛ-APLA-IDDINA," trans. Victor Hurowitz, *COS* 2.135:iv.35–vi.16.

Most of the people in the ANE embraced a religious worldview that was filled with a multitude of both benevolent gods and dangerous, hostile gods and demons who had power over life, death, sickness, crop growth, animal health, and rainfall. Much of the religious ritual performed by the royal courts, the priests, and the people at large involved seeking to keep the benevolent gods happy through care and feeding, and seeking to keep the evil, hostile gods and demons at bay by enlisting supernatural help.

While the rituals Yahweh prescribed for Israel were like those practiced throughout the region, the purpose for the ritual as well as the relationship the ritual maintained were quite different. With the all-powerful Yahweh dwelling in their midst, the Israelites were freed from the superstitious fear of evil gods and demons lurking everywhere as their neighbors feared. Furthermore, in contrast to the practices of most other peoples in the ANE, the offerings and sacrifices prescribed by Yahweh were not for the purpose of feeding him, but for maintaining their relationship through atonement, reconciliation, dedication, and worship. In addition, the worship rituals Yahweh gave Israel were part of the covenant relationship with him, the One who made moral and ethical obedience part of the requirement, something unique in the religious milieu of the ANE.[9]

The Inauguration and Shortcomings of the Priesthood (8:1–10:20)

THE INAUGURATION OF THE PRIESTHOOD AND THE ALTAR (8:1–9:24)

Leviticus 8 is closely connected to Exodus 29. In Exodus 29, as part of his instructions for constructing the tabernacle, Yahweh also gave directions to Moses regarding how to consecrate (to make "holy") the priests, who would serve in and around the tabernacle. In Leviticus 8–10, and especially in Leviticus 8, Moses carries out these instructions. His strict obedience is stressed by the repetition of the phrase "Moses did as the LORD commanded him" (Lev 8:4; 9:10; see also 8:5, 9, 13, 17, 21, 29, 34, 36; 9:6, 7, 21; 10:7, 13, 15). Note the similarly repeated phrase in Exodus 38–40, where Moses constructs the tabernacle exactly as Yahweh commanded him in Exodus 25–31. In the consecration ceremony for Aaron and his sons, Moses plays the role of priest and mediator, because he is the one to take the blood from the slain animals and sprinkle it on the altar as well as on Aaron and his sons. Moses is

[9] Roy E. Gane, "Leviticus," *ZIBBC* 1:287–88.

also the one who anoints the tabernacle and its appurtenances with oil before also anointing Aaron with oil.

In Leviticus 9 a formal, official transition takes place when Aaron begins his ministry as high priest. He makes a sacrifice for himself and then for the people. Aaron and Moses then both go into the tabernacle ("tent of meeting"), and when they emerge, all the people see the glory of Yahweh. Fire comes out from Yahweh in the tabernacle and burns up the sacrifice on the altar. The sacrificial system and the worship of Yahweh who is dwelling with them in the tabernacle is now officially underway.

THE PRIESTHOOD'S VIOLATION OF YAHWEH'S SACRIFICIAL COMMANDS (10:1–20)

Just as the sacrificial system is officially inaugurated, disaster strikes. Aaron's sons Nadab and Abihu, who have just been consecrated by Moses (Leviticus 8), bring "unauthorized fire" into the presence of Yahweh ("before the LORD"), violating the strict instructions Yahweh has given them (10:1). The exact nature of the offense is not entirely clear. Leviticus 10:8 suggests that perhaps they are drunk; Lev 16:1 suggests that they might have gone into the Most Holy Place with their incense, which was only allowed on the Day of Atonement. Yet 10:1–2 indicates that it is the fire (i.e., coals) that they use to burn the incense that is wrong. Perhaps, for convenience, they have brought hot coals from somewhere other than the specified altar.[10] Fire then comes out from Yahweh and consumes them completely, just as the fire consumes the sacrifice on the altar in Lev 9:24.

As in Lev 1:1–3, in 10:1–3 terms for being in proximity to Yahweh are used repeatedly:

> Aaron's sons Nadab and Abihu each took his own firepan, put fire in it, placed incense on it, and **presented** [*qarab*] unauthorized fire **before the LORD** [*lipne Yahweh*], which he had not commanded them to do. Then fire came **from the LORD** [*lipne Yahweh*] and consumed them, and they died **before the LORD** [*lipne Yahweh*]. Moses said to Aaron, "This is what the LORD has spoken:
>
> > "I will demonstrate my holiness
> > to those who **are near** me [*qarab*]."

---

[10] See the discussion by Jacob Milgrom, *Leviticus 1–16*, AB (New York: Doubleday, 1991), 598–99.

Yahweh makes it crystal clear that he and he alone determines the manner in which his dangerous and holy presence can be properly approached. Even top priests like the sons of Aaron are not excused from following Yahweh's strict guidelines; they are not free to modify Yahweh's strict commands regarding how to approach and serve him.

ANCIENT CONNECTIONS SIDEBAR 3.2: PRIESTLY INSTRUCTIONS IN THE ANCIENT NEAR EAST

Throughout the ANE, whether in Egypt, Syria-Palestine, Mesopotamia, or Anatolia, there were numerous temples for the many gods worshipped. These temples were commonly staffed by a special group of people called *priests*. Instructions, guidelines, and warnings for these priests appear in several ancient literary works. For example, in a Hittite document titled "Instructions to Priests and Temple Officials," the priests are warned against taking food for themselves that was intended for the gods, or substituting a thin, scrawny animal for a healthy one and then keeping the healthy one for themselves. The text reads:

> Or if you take them [the offerings] when set up, and do not bring them forth for the pleasure of the gods, [but rather] carry them away to your own houses, and your wives, children, and servants eat them up . . . You are taking them from the pleasure of the god. . . . He who does . . . shall die. . . . If some ox or sheep [is] driven in for the gods to eat, but you take away either the fattened ox or fattened sheep; and you substitute a thin one which you have slaughtered; [and] either you eat up that ox, or you put it into a pen, or you put it under a yoke . . . You are withholding [a morsel] from the mouth of the god.[11]

Ritual Uncleanness and Its Treatment (11:1–15:33)

This section deals with things that are clean and unclean and how to make something that has become unclean to be clean again. These chapters connect back to 10:10 ("You must distinguish between the holy and the common, and the clean and the unclean"), and they connect forward to the Day of Atonement in Leviticus 16, which

---

[11] "Instructions to Priests and Temple Officials," trans. Gregory McMahon, *COS* 1.83:217–18).

in 16:16 references the uncleanness problem: "He will make atonement for the most holy place in this way for all their sins because of the Israelites' *impurities* [the Hebrew word used here is the word translated as "unclean" throughout Leviticus 11–15] and rebellious acts."[12] These concepts of clean and unclean are related to the holiness of Yahweh, who now dwells in the midst of the Israelites. Unclean things or unclean people cannot come into the presence of Yahweh (this probably implies a prohibition from even entering the courtyard of the tabernacle) until they are made clean again. Once something or someone is clean, that person or object can then be "consecrated" (made holy) for special use in and around the tabernacle. Thus, there are three stages: unclean, clean, consecrated. Recall that in Exod 19:6 Yahweh called Israel to be a "holy nation," implying that they were to be set apart (consecrated, made holy) for service and worship. Many areas of clean and unclean that are addressed in Leviticus 11–15 would serve to separate Israel from the religious practices of her neighbors and to make her different (i.e., set apart). For example, these guidelines certainly eliminated aberrant, immoral sexual activities and veneration of the dead as acceptable worship practices, things that the Canaanites were known to have practiced.[13]

The division of things into the categories of clean and unclean have puzzled interpreters over the years, especially regarding the food laws in Leviticus 11 (why some animals are clean and others unclean). Wenham and others discuss several approaches (e.g., the food distinctions are for the purpose of separating from Canaanite ritualistic practice, or the distinctions are for health and hygienic reasons), noting that most of the proposed approaches seem inconsistent and inadequate.[14] Keep in mind that the concepts of clean and unclean are largely metaphorical or symbolic, even though strict adherence was required. Modern readers, for example, are probably missing the point if they focus on trying to discover logical scientific explanations relating to health and hygiene in determining which animals are clean and unclean. It is highly unlikely that the New Testament would have declared all foods as clean if the Levitical clean and unclean distinctions were based on health.[15] For example, Jesus stated, "It's not what

---

[12] Gordon J. Wenham, *The Book of Leviticus*, NICOT (Grand Rapids: Eerdmans, 1979), 161.

[13] John E. Hartley, *Leviticus*, WBC (Dallas: Word Books, 1992), 139–47.

[14] Wenham, *Leviticus*, 166–69. Wenham suggests that the divisions are related to the notion that "holiness and cleanness" are connected to "wholeness and normality." Thus cows, sheep, and goats set the norm for land animals (all clean), while camels, rabbits, and pigs are outside of this "normal" category and thus are unclean.

[15] Joe M. Sprinkle, *Biblical Law and Its Relevance* (Lanham, MD: University Press of America, 2006), 111–12.

goes into the mouth that defiles a person, but what comes out of the mouth" (Matt 15:11; see also Mark 7:15; Acts 10:9–15; Rom 14:14).

Note also that Lev 20:25–26 connects the clean and unclean distinction to the set-apart status that separated Israel from the Gentiles (nations):

> "Therefore you are to distinguish the clean animal from the unclean one, and the unclean bird from the clean one. Do not become contaminated by any land animal, bird, or whatever crawls on the ground; I have set these apart as unclean for you. You are to be holy to me because I, the LORD, am holy, and I have set you apart from the nations to be mine."

Working off of that observation, Joe Sprinkle notes that in Leviticus 1–7, some animals are also designated as not just clean, but holy (i.e., permissible for sacrificing). He thus suggests that the gradation of animals parallels the gradation of space and of people, all driven by holiness and set apartness. This can be illustrated in table 3.1:

Table 3.1: The Gradation of Unclean, Clean, and Holy regarding Space, People, and Animals

Category	Space	People	Animals
Holy and clean	The tabernacle	The priests	Sacrificeable animals
Clean and common	Land of Israel	Ordinary Israelites	Edible animals
Unclean	Lands of the Gentiles	Gentiles	Unclean, unedible animals

Thus, the food laws also symbolize and define the separation between Israel and the Gentiles, a concept that seems to be present in Peter's vision and explanation in Acts 10:9–11:18.[16]

Furthermore, the emphasis on clean and unclean categories delineated throughout Leviticus 11–15 served to shape a general worldview or outlook for Yahweh's people. That is, in the context of his holy presence living in their midst, he wants the Israelites to be constantly conscious of this holy presence and thus to view everything in life in that context: Is this clean or unclean? That is, how does this item or action relate to the holiness of Yahweh? In Lev 11:44–45 Yahweh connects the call for Israel

---

[16] Joe M. Sprinkle, *Leviticus and Numbers*, TTCS (Grand Rapids: Baker, 2015), 73.

to be holy to the fact that he is holy and that he is the one who brought them up out of Egypt: "For I am the LORD your God, so you must consecrate yourselves and be holy because I am holy. . . . For I am the LORD, who brought you up from the land of Egypt to be your God, so you must be holy because I am holy."

Covering a wide variety of activities in life, this unit addresses dietary laws (Leviticus 11); childbirth (Leviticus 12); growths on skin, garments, and walls (Leviticus 13–14); and bodily discharges (Leviticus 15). The arrangement and structure of Leviticus 11–14 follows the pattern of increasing length of time that someone or something is unclean and how long it takes to make it clean. Then Leviticus 15 includes all of the different ranges of time. This is illustrated in table 3.2:

Table 3.2: Uncleanness in Leviticus 11–15 and the
Time Required to Be Made Clean

Activities	Time Required
Dietary laws (Leviticus 11)	Hours
Childbirth (Leviticus 12)	Months
Growth on skin, garments, and walls (Leviticus 13–14)	Years
Bodily discharges (Leviticus 15)	Hours, weeks, or years[17]

Wenham observes a movement from external causes of uncleanness (dead animals, Leviticus 11) to internal, personal causes (childbirth, skin growths, bodily discharges, Leviticus 12–15). He also suggests that this movement is instructive and symbolic, paralleling the nature of uncleanness and Israel's challenge to be holy. That is, the problem of uncleanness (and thus the inability to approach Yahweh in his holiness) is not just something external that can be avoided (e.g., a dead animal). It is inextricably interconnected to their personal lives and their personal failures. This set the stage for the sacrifice in Leviticus 16, the national Day of Atonement.[18]

The Day of Atonement—the National Sacrifice (16:1–34)

In Leviticus 16 Yahweh gives Moses the requirements, procedure, and purpose for the Day of Atonement. Recall that the book of Leviticus stands at the center of the

---

[17] Hartley, *Leviticus*, 139.
[18] Wenham, *Leviticus*, 186.

Pentateuch (Torah) and that Leviticus 16 stands at the center of Leviticus. This literary positioning underscores the high importance and significance of this special day.[19] Also, *lipne Yahweh* ("before the LORD"; i.e., in "the presence of" Yahweh) occurs repeatedly (16:1, 7, 12, 13, 18, 30) in this chapter, a reminder of the important role that the presence of Yahweh plays in the purpose and function of the Day of Atonement.

Leviticus 16 opens by making a narrative connection to the death of Aaron's sons in Leviticus 10 and continues the story from there. This *inclusio*-type connection provides another indicator that Leviticus 11–15, the ritual purity regulations, function as introductory material for Leviticus 16, the Day of Atonement. The reminder pointing back to Leviticus 10 and the priests' violation of Yahweh's prescribed manner of worship provides additional context for Yahweh's instructions for the Day of Atonement, underscoring that it must be observed accurately.

The Language of Atonement

The Hebrew verb translated by CSB as "make atonement" or "atonement will be made" is *kipper*. Of the 101 occurrences of this verb in the Old Testament, 81 are in the books of Leviticus, Numbers, and Ezekiel. This verb is used fourteen times in Leviticus 16, stressing the importance of the concept of atonement in this chapter. Although scholars disagree over the exact meaning of this word, it clearly is related to the removal of sin, the removal of the guilt of sin, and cleansing from the contamination of sin.[20] There is a strong argument that it also carries the nuance of substitution. That is, *kipper* means to "deliver or ransom someone by substitution."[21] Many scholars see the stress as being on the concept of expiation (the removal of sin),[22] while some point out that atonement also carries a propitiation function (the appeasement of God's wrath on sin).[23] These two concepts are not exclusive, and *kipper* is used in such a wide range of contexts that it does seem to carry nuances of both

---

[19] Hartley, *Leviticus*, 217.

[20] See the discussion in Hartley, *Leviticus*, 64–65; and B. Lang, "כִּפֶּר *kipper*," *TDOT* VII:288–303.

[21] Walter C. Kaiser Jr., *The Promise-Plan of God: A Biblical Theology of the Old and New Testaments* (Grand Rapids: Zondervan, 2008), 84.

[22] See Hartley, *Leviticus*, 65, for example.

[23] See Nobuyoshi Kiuchi, *Leviticus*, AOTC (Nottingham, UK: Apollos, 2007), 47, 56–57, 295.

expiation and propitiation, with context determining which is in focus for each particular instance.[24]

The noun form of *kipper* is *kapporet*, the term used frequently in Exodus 25–40 to refer to the top cover for the ark of the covenant, made of gold, with the two cherubim on either side. It is the focal spot for Yahweh's holy indwelling presence in the tabernacle, and it is the place where the high priest would sprinkle blood to make atonement on the special Day of Atonement. Some English Bibles translate this term as "mercy seat" (CSB, ESV, KJV), even though the word *kapporet* by itself does not carry nuances of either "mercy" or of a "seat," unless "seat" is understood as the "*place* of mercy." Since this piece of the ark served as the cover, and since it was a primary place associated with atonement, several translations render it as "atonement cover" (NIV, NLT, NRSV). The updated edition of NRSV (NRSVue) just renders it as "cover." The Day of Atonement is still a special day in the Jewish calendar, known as *Yom Kippur*, *yom* being the Hebrew word for "day."

The high priest cannot enter the Most Holy Place whenever he chooses (16:2) but is allowed to go in only once per year, on the Day of Atonement. On that special day, first the high priest is to sacrifice a bull as a sin offering and a ram as a burnt offering (16:3). He then fills the Most Holy Place with smoke by burning incense (which provides a safety "screen" of sorts between him and Yahweh), takes blood from the bull, enters the Most Holy Place, and sprinkles the blood on the atonement cover, making atonement for himself and his family (16:11–14).

Next, he selects two goats. One goat, selected by lot, is to be sacrificed, and the high priest is to sprinkle the blood from this goat on the atonement cover, making atonement "for all their sins because of the Israelites' impurities and rebellious acts" (16:16; see vv. 8–10, 15–19).

The high priest is to place his hands on the head of the other goat, "and confess over it all the Israelites' iniquities and rebellious acts—all their sins" (16:21). Following the confession of sin (and the symbolic transfer of sin), the goat is sent away into the wilderness.

In Lev 16:8 the text states that one of these goats, the one chosen by lot to be sacrificed, is "for the LORD," while the other goat is for "an uninhabitable place" (CSB). The Hebrew term translated as "an uninhabitable place" is *azazel*. There is no consensus regarding the meaning of *azazel*, but scholars have identified three plausible

---

[24] Kiuchi, *Leviticus*, 57.

possibilities: (1) *Azazel* was the proper name of a goat-demon who lived in the desert
(ESV, ASV, NRSVue, NET); (2) *azazel* refers to a desolate or steep rocky place (CSB,
"uninhabitable"); or (3) *azazel* means "the sent-away goat," often translated as "scape-
goat" (KJV, NASB, NIV, NLB; see also LXX). The point of this ritual was that the sin
of the Israelites was removed from them and taken far away.[25]

Not only will the high priest make atonement for himself, his family, and all of
Israel, but he will also "make atonement" (and here the stress seems to be on cleansing) for the different components of the tabernacle—the Most Holy Place, the tent
of meeting (the tabernacle), and the altar just outside of the tabernacle (16:16–19).

Yahweh summarizes the overall purpose of the Day of Atonement in 16:30:
"Atonement will be made for you on this day to cleanse you, and you will be clean
from all your sins before the LORD." In Hebrew all of the second-person pronouns
(i.e., *you, your*) in this verse are plural. So while individual Israelites were expected to
keep up with their individual sins throughout the year with the sacrifices prescribed
in Leviticus 1–7, once a year, on the Day of Atonement, a national, corporate sacrifice
would be made and forgiveness and cleansing would be provided for all the Israelites
as a people.

At this same time, the high priest and the tabernacle would be cleansed as well.
This maintained the covenant relationship between Yahweh and Israel, allowing
Yahweh to continue to reside in the Israelites' midst, even though he was holy and
they were sinful, while also allowing Israel to continue to worship him through the
high priest and the tabernacle. Thus Yahweh does not continue to be present in their
midst in just a powerful way but also in a relational way.

Laws for Holy Living (17:1–22:33)

In this unit Yahweh speaks through Moses to address Aaron, his sons, and the entire
Israelite population on the topic of holy living. The focus in Leviticus 1–16 is on
how Israel was to relate in a holy manner to Yahweh living in their midst. This unit,
Leviticus 17–22, focuses on how they were to relate in a holy manner to each other,
underscoring the reality that how people relate to each other is also an issue of holiness. This unit is sometimes referred to as "The Holiness Collection" because of its
stress on holiness and the repetition of variations of the command "Be holy because
I, the LORD your God, am holy" (19:2; see also 20:7, 26; 21:6–8; cf. 11:45). A related

---

[25] Note the similarity to Zech 5:5–11, where the iniquity of the people is put into a basket
and removed to Babylon.

phrase that is repeated in this unit is "I am the LORD who sets him [or them] apart" (CSB; "makes [them] holy," NIV; 21:15, 23; 22:9, 16, 32).

Leviticus 17 opens the unit with Yahweh's regulations regarding blood sacrifices and blood in general. In Israel and across the ANE, blood was a symbol of both life and death, carrying connotations of both clean and unclean. Yet while some cultures of the ANE practiced blood purification rites, the numerous, detailed regulations given by Yahweh to Israel concerning how to handle blood and how to use it in sacrifice and worship are unparalleled. Furthermore, in contrast to some of the surrounding pagan cultures, the consumption of blood by the Israelites was strictly forbidden.[26]

In Leviticus 18, Yahweh stresses that Israel is not to embrace the sexual ethics of their neighbors, especially the Egyptians and the Canaanites. Part of being "holy"— that is, being "set apart to serve Yahweh"—is living by higher standards regarding marriage and sexual ethics than that practiced by the other surrounding cultures. Indeed, proper sexual behavior—defined as sex between a husband and wife—is a very important criterium for how Yahweh wants his people to live and be set apart. Sexual aberrations, as practiced by the Canaanites and Egyptians, are strictly forbidden. These include incest (18:6–18), adultery (18:20), homosexuality (18:22), and bestiality (18:23). The punishment for these sins is quite serious (death), described in Lev 20:10–21.

Leviticus 19 focuses on interpersonal relationships between the Israelites. In 19:18 we find the famous verse quoted by Jesus, "Love your neighbor as yourself." Building off the Ten Commandments, in this chapter Yahweh teaches that holy living involves concern and care for the poor (19:9–10) and disadvantaged (19:14). It also underscores the importance of justice in holy living (19:15), including the fair treatment of workers (19:13), care and concern for residing foreigners (19:33–34), and honesty in business transactions (19:35–36).

Capital offenses, those that are punishable by death, are the focus of Leviticus 20. At the top of the list is the prohibition against the horrific pagan practice of sacrificing children to Molek (often spelled Molech), a pagan god associated with child sacrifice. There is a strong relationship between Leviticus 20 and Leviticus 18. The prohibitions are spelled out in Leviticus 18, while the punishment for these offenses are stipulated in Leviticus 20.

Leviticus 21–22 is directed at Aaron and his sons and prescribes additional regulations regarding the priests and how they were to live and to make sacrifices. At the

---

[26] R. Dennis Cole, "Leviticus," *BIBBC*, 160.

end of this section Yahweh gives a summary for the unit, declaring, "Keep my commands and follow them. I am the LORD. Do not profane my *holy* name, for I must be acknowledged as *holy* by the Israelites. I am the LORD, who made you *holy* and who brought you up out of Egypt to be your God. I am the LORD" (22:31–33 NIV, italics added).

Sacred Times: National Worship (23:1–25:55)

SACRED TIMES: THE APPOINTED FESTIVALS AND SACRED ASSEMBLIES (23:1–24)

Leviticus 23 describes the sacred calendar for the Israelites—those special days in the year when they would all gather to worship, sacrifice, and remember what Yahweh has done for them, celebrating the relationship they have with him under the covenant. These special days are also described in other places as well, especially Exodus 12, Leviticus 16, Numbers 28–29, and Deuteronomy 16. In the introduction to this section (Lev 23:1–2), Yahweh refers to these special days with two phrases: (1) "my appointed festivals" (NIV; CSB renders the term as "my appointed times") and (2) "sacred assemblies." Instructions regarding the Sabbath day, first on the list here (23:3), are also presented numerous times elsewhere throughout the Pentateuch.

After a brief word exhorting the Israelites to keep the Sabbath (23:3), followed by another brief introduction (23:4), Yahweh then gives the times and the procedures for celebrating seven appointed festivals and sacred assemblies: the Passover (23:5), the Festival of Unleavened Bread (23:6–8), the Offering of the Firstfruits (23:9–14), the Festival of Weeks (23:15–22), the Festival of Trumpets (23:23–25), the Day of Atonement (23:26–32), and the Festival of Tabernacles (23:33–43).

THE LAMPS, THE BREAD OF THE PRESENCE, AND BLASPHEMERS (24:1–23)

In the context of special sacred days such as the weekly Sabbath and the annual festivals, Yahweh adds some additional guidelines for the acts of fellowship and worship that would regularly occur in the Holy Place of the tabernacle. Here Yahweh provides guidance to the high priest for maintaining daily the fires of the golden lampstand (24:1–4) and for setting out the Bread of the Presence weekly, along with guidelines regarding how to eat it (24:5–9).

Then the ongoing dialogue of Yahweh's instructions is interrupted by the narrative account of a serious case of blasphemy (24:10–23), just as his earlier instructions had been interrupted by the narrative of the sin of Nadab and Abihu (10:1–20)—and as the golden calf of Exodus 32 interrupted Yahweh's instructions to Moses on Mount Sinai. Within this narrative event (the blasphemer is to be stoned to death), Yahweh restates the legal principle of *lex talionis*, that punishment should be equivalent to the crime (e.g., "eye for eye"). The principle of *lex talionis*, reflected frequently in Exodus, Numbers, Leviticus, and Deuteronomy, functions as a limitation on the severity of punishment.

SACRED TIMES: THE SABBATH YEAR AND YEAR OF JUBILEE (25:1–55)

After presenting the guidelines for the special days and special weeks, Yahweh now gives instructions for special years—the Sabbath Year (25:1–7) and the Year of Jubilee (25:8–54). Underlying these instructions is the reality that both the land and the people in the land belong to Yahweh (25:23, 55). The Sabbath Year guidelines underscore that the land, like the people, need a time of rest. Thus, fields are to lie fallow every seven years. The Year of Jubilee decrees that every fifty years all Israelite indentured servants are to be set free. Likewise, all land that has been sold is to return to the original person or clan who owned it. Yahweh gives his reasoning for returning land in the Year of Jubilee, stating, "The land must not be sold permanently, because the land is mine and you reside in my land as foreigners and strangers" (25:23 NIV). Similarly, he states his reason for freeing servants and slaves in the Year of Jubilee: "They and their children are to be released in the Year of Jubilee, for the Israelites belong to me as servants . . . whom I brought out of Egypt. I am the LORD your God" (25:54–55 NIV).

Covenant Blessings and Covenant Curses (26:1–46)

In Exodus, Yahweh delivered the Israelites from Egypt (Exodus 1–18), brought them to Mount Sinai (Exodus 19), and entered into a covenant agreement with them. Just about everything from Exodus 20 to Leviticus 25 deals with the terms of this covenant—the stipulations, requirements, and guidelines whereby the Israelites can worship the holy and powerful Yahweh as he dwells among them and thus find tremendous blessings under his protection and rule in the Promised Land. Leviticus 26 (like Deuteronomy 28) presents the choice that lies ahead for Israel. If they obey Yahweh and keep his decrees and commands (as presented in Exodus 20–Leviticus 25), they will experience tremendous blessings in the land—plentiful rain, bountiful crops, and an abundance of food; safety and peace; an increase in population; and Yahweh dwelling with them (Lev 26:1–13).

On the other hand, Yahweh warns ominously, if they will not listen to him and follow his commands, then they will experience terrible curses—enemies who steal the produce of the land and rule over them; wild animals; diseases, plagues, and famine; and even exile out of the land (26:14–39). Not only will Yahweh no longer protect them and defend them from their enemies, but he himself will fight against them (26:17, 24–25, 33).

Yet even despite this anticipated disobedience, covenant violation, and judgment, Yahweh promises to remember the covenant he made with Abraham, Isaac, and Jacob. While terrible judgment will come on Israel, Yahweh states that he will not destroy them completely. Even though Israel has broken (i.e., shattered, annulled) the covenant made in Exodus and Leviticus, if in the future they will confess their sins, Yahweh will restore his relationship with them, based on his fidelity to the covenant (26:40–46).

Dedication Offerings (27:1–34)

In the concluding chapter (Leviticus 27), Yahweh explains how people can voluntarily dedicate things to him. This is an appropriate way to conclude a book dealing with holiness (being set apart), for complete dedication and devotion to Yahweh is the essence of holy living. Recall that Leviticus opens with a description of voluntary sacrifices as acts of worship (Leviticus 1–3). Thus Leviticus opens and closes with voluntary acts of worship. In Leviticus 27 Yahweh explains that declarations of dedication must be sincere and not hypocritical. Yahweh also points out that some things, like the firstborn of animals and the tithe, cannot be dedicated to him because he owns them already (27:26–33).

The final verse summarizes all of Leviticus: "These are the commands the LORD gave Moses at Mount Sinai for the Israelites" (27:34 NIV).

Biblical Connections

The covenant relationship between Yahweh and Israel described in Exodus 20–Leviticus 27, along with his indwelling presence in the tabernacle (and later in the temple) and the worship system required to allow the Israelites to stay in proximity to his holy presence, provides the cultural, ritualistic, and theological background for the entire remaining Old Testament biblical story. That is, most of the references throughout the rest of the Old Testament to sacrifices, Levites, priests, the tabernacle and its furnishings, and festivals can only be properly understood from the context of Exodus 20–Leviticus 27 (along with Numbers).

For example, consider the dramatic story of how Yahweh calls the young boy Samuel in 1 Samuel 2–3. It is helpful to remember that the opening scene for "the calling of Samuel" occurs in the Holy Place of the tabernacle. The boy Samuel is spending the night here in the Holy Place, apparently caring for the special lamp (the menorah) there, a task that was supposed to be fulfilled by the high priest Eli (1 Sam 2:18; 3:1–18; Lev 24:1–4). Likewise, the account of the terrible sins of Eli's wicked sons, who were serving as priests at the tabernacle (1 Sam 2:12–17), should be understood in light of the serious warnings in Leviticus. That is, while the people were sacrificing, these two sons took the fat portions of the sacrificed animal for themselves (1 Sam 2:15–16, 29), that part of the sacrifice that belonged to Yahweh and was to be burned before Yahweh ("all fat belongs to the Lord," Lev 3:16). Likewise, carrying into 1 Samuel 2–4 is the account of the death of Aaron's two sons, who, like Eli's two sons, ignored the warnings and thus perished (Leviticus 9–10; 1 Sam 2:12–36; 4:1–22).

The Old Testament prophets, following Leviticus 26 (and Deuteronomy 28) proclaim to Israel and Judah that they have violated the covenant by worshipping idols (even in close proximity to Yahweh in the temple). Because of this and their complete abandonment of Yahweh's laws relating to "love your neighbor as yourself," the prophets inform Israel and Judah that Yahweh views their sacrifices as hypocritical and meaningless.

As Lev 26:33 warns, the continued sin and disobedience of the Israelites eventually drives Yahweh to banish them from the land (and from his presence). Both this cause (covenant disobedience) and this effect (judgment and exile) are recounted repeatedly in the Prophets as well as in 2 Kings, 2 Chronicles, Psalms, and Lamentations.

Likewise, the promise of future restoration and the need for confession in Lev 26:40–45 provides the background for the prayer of confession by Nehemiah (Neh 1:5–11) and the story of the return of the exiles in Ezra-Nehemiah.

In the New Testament, especially in the Gospels, the sacrificial system described in Leviticus provides extensive cultural, ritual, and theological background for understanding the life of Jesus and his teachings. Right after the birth of Jesus, for example, Joseph and Mary present Jesus at the temple and they "offer a sacrifice (according to what is stated in the law of the Lord, **a pair of turtledoves or two young pigeons**)" (Luke 2:24, quoting Lev 12:8). For another example, when John the Baptist points to Jesus and cries out, "Look, the Lamb of God!" (John 1:36), it is Leviticus (and Exodus) that provides the background for understanding that statement. Likewise, throughout the Gospels and even in Acts, the Levitical calendar, stressing the Sabbath and the festivals (Leviticus 23), is ever present throughout the story. Not only is the Sabbath referenced frequently, but also the Feast of Tabernacles, the Feast of Unleavened Bread, the Feast of the Passover, and the Feast of Weeks (Pentecost) are mentioned in the background of the New Testament story.

The Year of Jubilee (Leviticus 25) carries eschatological connotations and thus echoes through the Prophets into the Gospels. Isaiah 61:1–2 uses terminology and concepts that allude to Leviticus 25 ("good news to the poor," "freedom," "release," "the year of the LORD's favor").[27] Thus, when Jesus cites this text at the inauguration of his public ministry in Luke 4:18–19 he is implying some type of eschatological fulfillment (through his ministry) for the Year of Jubilee ("the year of the Lord's favor").[28]

When Jesus is asked, "Teacher, which command in the law is the greatest?" he answers first by quoting Deut 6:5, **"Love the Lord your God with all your heart, with all your soul, and with all your mind.** This is the greatest and most important command." Then Jesus continues, quoting Lev 19:18b, "The second is like it: **Love your neighbor as yourself.** *All the Law and the Prophets depend on these two commands*" (Matt 22:36–40, italics added). Notice the huge importance Jesus assigns to Lev 19:18b and Deut 6:5. In fact, in the New Testament, Lev 19:18b is one of the most quoted Old Testament verses (Matt 19:19; 22:39; Mark 12:31–33; Luke 10:27; Rom 13:9; Gal 5:14; Jas 2:8). Notice what Jesus is saying in citing these two commandments as summary statements. First and foremost, he stresses our vertical relationship with God, thus "Love the Lord your God." Second, but relatedly, he underscores the importance of our horizontal relationship with other people, thus "Love your neighbor as yourself." Often, we summarize Leviticus as being about sacrifices and priestly duties regarding worshipping Yahweh. Jesus, however, quotes from the Holiness Collection (Leviticus 17–22), the section teaching that holy living requires Yahweh's people to be holy in how they relate to each other.

Another important biblical connection to Leviticus is that the imagery of Jesus's death as a blood sacrifice is rooted in the blood sacrifices described in Leviticus, especially the Day of Atonement sacrifice (Leviticus 16) and the guilt offering sacrifice (Leviticus 5–6), along with the Passover sacrifice in Exodus. This connection is at the

---

[27] Brevard S. Childs, *Isaiah*, OTL (Louisville: Westminster John Knox, 2001), 505.

[28] Christopher J. H. Wright, "Jubilee, Year of," *ABD* 3:1028–29; Joel B. Green, *The Gospel of Luke*, NICNT (Grand Rapids: Eerdmans, 1997), 212.

heart of New Testament theology and runs throughout the New Testament, as illustrated in the following representative passages:

> In him we have redemption through his blood. (Eph 1:7)

> You who were far away have been brought near by the blood of Christ. (Eph 2:13)

> To those chosen . . . to be sprinkled with the blood of Jesus Christ. (1 Pet 1:1–2)

> The blood of Jesus his Son cleanses us from all sin. (1 John 1:7)

> To him who loves us and has set us free from our sins by his blood . . . (Rev 1:5)

It is the book of Hebrews, however, that draws on Leviticus most extensively, referring especially to the Day of Atonement. One of the major themes and purposes of Hebrews is to demonstrate that the priesthood and sacrifice of Jesus Christ is completely superior to the priesthood and sacrificial system described in Leviticus (see especially Heb 4:14–10:25); indeed, Jesus is the culmination and the ultimate reality to which Leviticus points.

Gospel Connections

Quite a bit of essential Christian theology, especially relating to Christology and soteriology, is taught in the book of Hebrews by comparing the ministry and new covenant of Jesus Christ to the sacrificial system connected to the tabernacle and the old covenant, as presented in Exodus 20–Leviticus 27. For example, Hebrews points out that Jesus is greater than Moses, for Moses served as a servant in God's house while Jesus is the Son over God's house (Heb 3:1–6). Furthermore, Jesus as the great High Priest is superior to the high priests who served in the tabernacle. Jesus was selected from a greater, eternal priesthood (the priesthood of Melchizedek; 5:5–10; 7:1–28). In addition, he did not have to offer the prerequisite and preliminary sin sacrifices for himself, because he was without sin (4:14–16). Also, while the other high priests all died, Jesus lives forever as the permanent high priest, always interceding for his people (7:23–25). While the human high priests in the tabernacle had to offer sacrifices over and over, day after day and year after year, Jesus offered one ultimate sacrifice (himself) that serves for all time (9:11–14; 10:11–14), making his people perfectly holy (10:14). Finally, Jesus is the mediator and guarantor of a new and better covenant that was ratified by a better blood sacrifice (himself) and has better promises (7:22; 8:6–13; 9:15; 10:16–18).

Leviticus also provides a wealth of information about the holiness of God, a foundational aspect of his eternal character that has not changed. Leviticus (and Exodus) also reveals to us that God wants a close, personal relationship with his people. That is, he wants to dwell closely with his people. Because his holiness restricted the access to him by sinful people, the tabernacle was provided and the Levitical system of sacrifices was implemented, allowing God to live in the midst of his people—even though they sinned—without compromising his holiness. Similarly, while the gospel message certainly includes the forgiveness of sins, it is not only about the forgiveness of sins. As in Leviticus, the holy God desires to provide access to his people so that he can have a personal and close relationship with them. Yet in contrast to the limitations of the system in Leviticus, Jesus Christ, through his once-for-all-time death and resurrection, forgives and cleanses his people from sin, making them holy, and thus allowing special access to and relationship with God (especially through the indwelling Holy Spirit).

Likewise, the book of Leviticus teaches emphatically that God is the one who dictates and determines how people can approach him and have a relationship with him. Even esteemed priests like Nadab and Abihu, sons of Aaron, cannot abuse or ignore God's regulations about how to deal with his holiness (Leviticus 10). The Nadab and Abihu episode combines with the disastrous golden calf episode of Exodus 32 to stress that God does not give people the option of determining on their own, or in accordance with widespread human cultural norms, how to approach him and worship him or how to deal with their own sin. They *must* follow the approach he requires (and graciously provides). The New Testament affirms this and puts it at the heart of the gospel, as Jesus declares, "I am the way, the truth, and the life. No one comes to the Father except through me" (John 14:6).

HOW WERE PEOPLE IN THE OLD TESTAMENT SAVED AND FORGIVEN OF THEIR SINS?

For Christians, the study of the sacrificial system in Leviticus naturally raises several questions. How does the Levitical sacrificial system relate to actual forgiveness of sins? That is, how were the people in the Old Testament saved since they lived before the death and resurrection of Jesus Christ? How were they forgiven of their sins? How were they made righteous? In attempting to answer this, we will consider two interrelated aspects: (1) How was corporate Israel, God's people, saved? (2) How were individual people within this group saved?

As mentioned in the discussion on Exodus, the exodus event was the Old Testament paradigm of what salvation and deliverance looked like. From the exodus story we can make several observations about deliverance and salvation. First, the entire exodus saving event was rooted in the loving grace of God and in his faithfulness to his covenant with Abraham. The Israelites (and the other people with them) were not delivered based on any works they did or on any high moral standing they had (Exod 2:24–25). Also, notice the components of this great deliverance: God rescues them from their oppressors in Egypt, passes over judging them due to the blood of the Passover lamb on their doorways (and instead destroys their enemies), brings them out of Egypt to himself at Mount Sinai, makes a covenant with them, and then moves into the tabernacle to dwell among them in close relationship with them. This is a picture of "corporate deliverance" in that God delivers Israel as a nation (along with other peoples who are with them—Exod 12:38) and then brings them to himself as "his people" in a covenant relationship that is sealed with "the blood of the covenant" (Exod 24:4–8).

Related to the individual aspect of deliverance and salvation in the Old Testament exodus model, note that Exod 12:3–4 stresses that each individual family or household was required to smear the blood of the Passover lamb on their own doorframe. Thus, the blood sacrifice and blood covering were required at the individual family level.

In the book of Romans, Paul adds more detail to our understanding of this topic by focusing more on individuals. First, Paul underscores the importance of Abraham's personal faith ("Abraham believed God, and it was credited to him as righteousness," 4:3 NIV; see Gen 15:6), stressing that righteousness can only come as a result of faith and never as a result of works, whether it be circumcision or keeping the law (Rom 4:1–5). Paul continues by pointing out that what Abraham put his faith in was the promise of God—that is, those things that God had revealed to him, that he would have many descendants and that he would be the father of many nations (Rom 4:16–25). So, faith was a critical component in Abraham's righteousness, and the object of that faith was God's revelation and promise.

But what about the sacrifices that are described as so important in Leviticus? Hebrews 10 helps us to understand how this relates to New Testament theology, stating, "Since the law has only a shadow of the good things to come, and not the reality of those things, it can never perfect the worshipers by the same sacrifices they continually offer year after year. . . . But in the sacrifices there is a reminder of sins year after year. For it is impossible for the blood of bulls and goats to take away sins" (10:1–4). Therefore, the Levitical sacrificial system in and of itself did not remove the sin of the Israelites in the Old Testament era. But as a shadow that pointed to the later reality of Jesus Christ, who would come as the perfect sacrifice and who would remove sin, the Levitical sacrificial system provided an expression of faith in the revelation that God had given them at Mount Sinai as part of their covenant relationship with him. As such, this faith appears to be a valid faith, much as Abraham's was.

Paul gives us further insight into how God made them righteous, especially from a forensic point of view, writing, "For all have sinned and fall short of the glory of God. They are justified freely by his grace through the redemption that is in Christ Jesus. God presented him as . . . [an atoning sacrifice in] his blood, [received] through faith, to demonstrate his righteousness, *because in his restraint God passed over the sins previously committed*" (Rom 3:23–25, italics added). The phrase "in his restraint God passed over the sins previous committed" apparently applies to those in the Old Testament living under the old covenant. Douglas Moo writes, "This does not mean that God failed to punish or 'overlooked' sins committed before Christ; nor does it mean that God did not really 'forgive' sins under the Old Covenant. Paul's meaning is rather that God 'postponed' the full penalty due sins under the Old Covenant."[29] In the Old Testament God accepted their sacrifices through their faith and, based on that, held off on the punishment for their sin until the death of Christ, who died as an atonement for sin both for those in the past who came to God through faith in his revealed truth (the sacrificial system) and for those in the future who will come to God through faith in his revealed truth (the death and resurrection of Christ).[30]

Life Connections

If one of our goals as Christians is "to know God," Leviticus connects to our journey in numerous ways, for it teaches us much about the character of God. Indeed, Leviticus enables us to grow in our knowledge of and relationship with him. For example, from Leviticus we see that God is holy and that he never compromises his holiness. Yet he loves us and wants to relate to us, so he sacrifices his son as an atonement to enable us

---

[29] Douglas Moo, *The Epistle to the Romans*, NICNT (Grand Rapids: Eerdmans, 1996), 238–40.

[30] Kaiser, *The Promise-Plan of God*, 85.

to overcome the holiness barrier; through his death Jesus declares us to be righteous and holy.

Yet in Leviticus the call to be holy is not only about how to relate vertically to God, but about how to relate horizontally to other people. Jesus underscores this when he cites Lev 19:18b ("love your neighbor as yourself") as one of the two verses that synthesizes the entire Old Testament. God calls on us to "be holy because I, the LORD your God, am holy" (Lev 19:2), and he then defines holy living throughout the rest of Leviticus 19 and the following chapters. God not only restates most of the Ten Commandments, but he elaborates and adds more detail, especially to the horizontal human relationships. He addresses economic relationships (19:13–15), particularly concerning how his people treat hired workers (19:13), and the others who are the most vulnerable in the society—the poor and the residing foreigner (19:9–10, 15, 33–34). God exhorts his people to treat residing foreigners as if they were native born, instructing the Israelites to "love him as yourself" (19:33–34), using the same terminology as in 19:18b (love your neighbor as yourself).[31] All of this has application for us today as we strive to be faithful followers of Christ in how we treat people in our modern workplace and especially how we treat those who are poor and residing foreigners.

Thus a basic starting point for us as New Testament Christians in determining how to be obedient in regard to holy living is to grasp both our vertical relationship with the always-holy God, made possible for us through the death of Christ, and our horizontal relationship with other people (our call to follow Christ in obedience), especially in regard to those who are vulnerable in the society. We are to love others—our neighbor, hired workers, the poor, and foreigners—as we love ourselves.

Interactive Questions

3-1. Discuss the flow of the story from Abraham to the end of Leviticus.

3-2. Why do you think it was important that the Israelites offered their sacrifices "before the LORD"—that is, close to the presence of Yahweh himself?

3-3. Based on Leviticus 1–9, explain the role that the priests played in the sacrificial system.

---

[31] For a good discussion on how Lev 19:18b connects to other texts, especially in Exodus, Leviticus, and Deuteronomy, see Gary E. Schnittjer, "Going Vertical with Love Thy Neighbor: Exegetical Use of Scripture in Leviticus 19:18b," *JSOT* 47, no. 1 (2022): 114–42.

3-4. In Leviticus 10, why does Yahweh kill Nadab and Abihu? What does God want us to learn from that episode?

3-5. What are the implications in our life from God's repeated statement to "be holy, because I . . . am holy"?

3-6. Do some background research on Hansen's disease (leprosy). What are the symptoms? How does it spread? Is there an effective treatment for it? In this context, discuss the various diseases (especially the symptoms) described in Leviticus 13. Note that the Hebrew word *tsara'at* occurs repeatedly throughout this chapter (vv. 2, 3, 8, 9, 11, 12, 13, 15, 20, 25, 27, 30, 42, 43, 47, 49, 51, 52, 59), yet no consensus has been reached on how to translate this word. The KJV and ESV translate it as "leprosy" or "a leprous disease," while others, such as NIV, NRSVue, and CSB, avoid the term *leprosy* and translate it as "a skin disease," "defiling skin disease," "defiling disease," or "a serious disease." Study the chapter and decide which translation is best. Is Leviticus 13 talking about leprosy or not? Give reasons for your answer.

3-7. Explain what it means for us today to "love your neighbor as yourself" (Lev 19:18). In Luke 10, after the reference to this verse, an expert in the law asks Jesus, "And who is my neighbor?" (v. 29). What does Jesus tell him? How does this factor into how we obey Lev 19:18?

3-8. Explain how we as Christians today should apply Lev 19:33–34 in our own lives. How does Luke 10:25–37 factor in to how we obey Lev 19:33–34?

3-9. Briefly summarize the festivals discussed in Leviticus 23. Which of these festivals did the early church continue to observe? Does the church today observe any comparable festivals? Is it beneficial to gather God's people together in large groups? In what contexts does the church practice gathering in large groups?

3-10. Contrast the good things Yahweh promises in Lev 26:3–13 for obedience and faithfulness with the bad things he promises in Lev 26:14–39 for disobedience and unfaithfulness.

Recommended Resources

Hartley, John E. *Leviticus*. WBC. Dallas: Word Books, 1992.
Kiuchi, Nobuyoshi. *Leviticus*. AOTC. Nottingham, UK: Apollos, 2007.
Milgram, Jacob. *Leviticus 1–16*. AB. New York: Doubleday, 1991.
———. *Leviticus 17–22*. AB. New York: Doubleday, 2000.

———. *Leviticus 23–27*. AB. New York: Doubleday, 2000.

Morales, L. Michael. *Who Shall Ascend the Mountain of the Lord?: A Biblical Theology of the Book of Leviticus*. NSBT. Downers Grove, IL: IVP, 2015.

Rooker, Mark R. *Leviticus*. NAC. Nashville: B & H, 2000.

Shepherd, Jerry E. *Leviticus*. SGBC. Grand Rapids: Zondervan, 2021.

Sprinkle, Joe M. *Leviticus and Numbers*. TTCS. Grand Rapids: Baker, 2015.

Wenham, Gordon J. *The Book of Leviticus*. NICOT. Grand Rapids: Eerdmans, 1979.

4

Numbers

"'May the LORD bless you and protect you;
may the LORD make his face shine on you
and be gracious to you;
may the LORD look with favor on you
and give you peace.'
In this way they will pronounce my name over
the Israelites, and I will bless them."

—NUMBERS 6:24–27

Outline

I. The disobedient generation (1:1–25:18)

    A. Yahweh organizes and prepares Israel for the trip to the Promised Land (1:1–10:10)

        1. The first census, organization of the camp, and leaders (1:1–2:34)

2. How the Israelites should worship and experience blessing
   while traveling with Yahweh in their midst (3:1–9:14)

3. Yahweh's cloud and the two trumpets: divine guidance for
   traveling to the Promised Land (9:15–10:10)

B. Rebellion and rejection of the Promised Land (10:11–14:45)

1. The trip begins but is characterized by refusal, grumbling, and
   rebellion (10:11–12:16)

2. Arriving at the Promised Land, the people anger Yahweh
   by refusing to enter and conquer the good land, but Moses
   intercedes for them (13:1–14:45)

C. The consequences—the Israelites wander in the wilderness, yet
   Yahweh blesses them in spite of rebellions (15:1–25:18)

1. Future offerings in the land and the special status of the priests
   serving in the holy tabernacle are contrasted with a priestly
   rebellion against Moses (15:1–19:22)

2. More rebellions; the death of Miriam and Aaron; and
   opposition from Balaam, Moab, and Midian; but Yahweh still
   protects his people (20:1–25:18)

II. The obedient generation (26:1–36:13)

A. The generational transition—a new generation and new leaders
   (26:1–27:23)

B. Reminder of offerings, festival days, and special vows (28:1–30:16)

C. The defeat and plunder of Midian and the death of Balaam
   (31:1–54)

D. Preparations for entering the Promised Land (32:1–36:13)[1]

Author, Date, and Message

Author and Date

As explained in the introduction, this book follows the traditional understanding that
Moses was the human author of the book of Numbers. Chronologically, Num 1:1
connects the book of Numbers very tightly to the exodus event: "The LORD spoke to

---

[1] This outline has been developed from that in Hays and Duvall, *BIBH*, 94. Also proposing
that the two census accounts and the two related generations are key to the structure and
meaning of the book are Dennis T. Olson, *Numbers*, Interpretation (Louisville: John Knox,
1996), 4–7; and R. Dennis Cole, *Numbers*, NAC (Nashville: B&H, 2000), 40–41.

Moses in the tent of meeting in the Wilderness of Sinai, on the first day of the second month of the second year after Israel's departure from the land of Egypt." That is, Numbers picks up the story a little more than one year after the exodus, with Israel still at Mount Sinai, where they have been since Exod 19:1. As with Leviticus, the date for the events in Numbers is tied to the date for the exodus (either 1446 BC or 1270–1260 BC). The book of Numbers covers roughly forty years, as noted in Num 32:13: "The LORD's anger burned against Israel and he made them wander in the wilderness forty years, until the whole generation of those who had done evil in his sight was gone" (NIV).

In the Hebrew Bible this book is titled *Bemidbar* ("in the wilderness"), an apt description of the contents. When it was translated into Greek (the Septuagint) it was titled *Arithmoi*, and then when it was later translated into Latin, it was titled *Numeri*. Both these words mean "numbers," and thus our English translations follow the Latin and Greek titles.

The Message of Numbers

The book of Numbers continues the narrative story that began in Genesis 12 with Abraham—a story that is driven by Yahweh's faithfulness to the promise he made to the patriarchs, a promise of land, descendants, and blessings. The descendant fulfillment was seen in the proliferation described in Exodus 1 and is further stressed by the census in Numbers 1 and 26. The blessing fulfillment is seen especially through the deliverance of the exodus event and the ensuing indwelling presence of Yahweh in the tabernacle, highlighted in Exodus and Leviticus, and continued throughout Numbers. It receives specific renewed emphasis in Num 6:22–27 through the priestly blessing. One of the remaining final components of Yahweh's patriarchal promise is for the Israelites to move into the Promised Land and live there with Yahweh dwelling in their midst, blessing them with his powerful and personal presence. Numbers begins with this final component (the land) as the immediate goal.

As noted in the outline, the story in Numbers breaks down into two primary parts, each one introduced with a census. In the first part (Numbers 1–25) the story opens with Yahweh making the final preparations for Israel to travel with him to the Promised Land. Yet, when they get there, the unthinkable happens—they refuse to go in and conquer the land! Gripped with fear of the fortified Canaanite cities, the Israelites whine that it would have been better if they had died in the wilderness. "Fine," Yahweh seems to respond with irony, "go die in the wilderness." The Israelites will then wander in the wilderness for the next forty years until that entire disobedient generation dies off. In the second part of Numbers (26–36), with a new generation, a new census, and new leaders, Yahweh takes Israel back to the Promised Land and makes preparation for the conquest.

One of the most important theological teachings emerging from Numbers is the dramatic depiction of the character of Yahweh, who speaks repeatedly throughout the book. As Israel continually disobeys and becomes unfaithful, we see Yahweh's righteous anger expressed, but also his graciousness and his faithfulness to his promises as he refuses to abandon disobedient Israel.

Interpretive Overview

The Disobedient Generation (1:1–25:18)

YAHWEH ORGANIZES AND PREPARES ISRAEL FOR THE TRIP TO THE PROMISED LAND (1:1–10:10)

The First Census, Organization of the Camp, and Leaders (1:1–2:34)

The book of Numbers opens with the phrase "The LORD spoke to Moses," and this phrase, along with some variations of it, will be used frequently throughout the book. Indeed, most of the literary units in Numbers open with this phrase, underscoring that much of the book is presented as the spoken word of Yahweh. This is in keeping with the central theme of the book that Yahweh now dwells in the midst of Israel and has an ongoing, intimate relationship with them. It also highlights the central importance of Moses as the mediator between Yahweh and Yahweh's covenant people.

In Numbers 1 Yahweh instructs Moses to take a census and count all men over the age of twenty, those who are able to fight in the army. Yahweh also identifies leaders from each tribe to assist him. The Levites, however, are not counted as soldiers for the army; they are assigned to caring for and transporting the tabernacle. Yahweh also assigns the camp locations for each tribe, placing three tribes on each of the four sides of the tabernacle, with the Levites in the middle. Remember that there are actually thirteen tribes. In Genesis, the patriarch Jacob had twelve sons whose descendants become tribes, except that Joseph's descendants become two tribes (Manasseh and Ephraim), thus the thirteen. In general, Numbers treats Israel as twelve tribes plus the Levites, because their situation is regularly different (e.g., they have no land inheritance).

The census in Numbers 1 will also play a role in determining the culpability of those who later rebel against Yahweh and refuse to enter the Promised Land

(Numbers 14). It is precisely those who are over twenty, counted and recorded in this first census, whom Yahweh holds responsible and who will die off in the wilderness after their rebellion (Num 14:29; 32:11–13).

ANCIENT CONNECTIONS SIDEBAR 4.1: THE KETEF HINNOM AMULETS

During excavations of a burial cave on the hillside overlooking the valley of Hinnom in Jerusalem, archaeologists discovered two small rolled-up silver scrolls. Dating to the early sixth century BC, these scrolls appear to be jewelry, probably amulets. They both contain written blessings in Hebrew that remarkably resemble the blessing in Num 6:24–26. Amulet 2, the one that is most complete, reads:

> May Yahweh bless you and keep you.
> May Yahweh cause his face to shine on you and give you peace.[2]

How the Israelites Should Worship and Experience Blessing while Traveling with Yahweh in Their Midst (3:1–9:14)

As Yahweh prepares Israel for traveling, one of the more complicated required tasks will be dismantling, packing, moving, and then reassembling the tabernacle, the holy dwelling place of Yahweh, while retaining its sanctity. Numbers 3:1–4:49 focuses on this and especially on the important role of the Levites in this regard. Also, the special set-apart status of the Levites in relation to the other tribes is stressed as Yahweh declares, "See, I have taken the Levites from the Israelites in place of every firstborn Israelite from the womb" (3:12). This refers to Exod 13:1–16, where at the beginning of the exodus Yahweh stated that every firstborn Israelite should be consecrated to him because every firstborn was his. Thus, a census is also taken of the Levites (Num 3:39), not as candidates for the army, but to verify that there are enough of them to serve as substitutes for the firstborn of the rest of Israel (3:39–51). Levi had three sons, so the Levites are divided into three clans: Gershon, Kohath, and Merari. Each clan is given specific assignments regarding moving the tabernacle. In the census for the other twelve tribes, all men over twenty were counted, identifying those who

---

[2] "The Ketef Hinnom Amulets," trans. P. Kyle McCarter, *COS* 2.83.5–12.

could serve in the army. When counting the Levites, the age qualification used is "men from thirty years old to fifty years old—everyone who is qualified to work at the tent of meeting [the tabernacle]" (4:3; see also 4:23, 30).

In Numbers 5 Yahweh reminds Israel of the importance of purity, since he himself dwells in their camp. As part of this, there is an unusually long section (5:11–31) on how to convict or vindicate as innocent a wife suspected of being unfaithful. This passage may carry some ironic and prophetic foreshadowing, for the Old Testament prophets in the future will depict Israel metaphorically as an unfaithful wife to Yahweh (e.g., Jer 3:1–20; Ezek 16:1–63; Hos 2:2–23), and the story in Numbers, while positive in the opening chapters, is but a few chapters away from Israel's grumbling, unfaithfulness, and disobedience in following Yahweh.

While the Levites are set aside for special service to Yahweh, Num 6:1–21 describes how other people can take a special vow (the Nazarite vow) to be set apart for special service. Significant leaders in Israel's history who will be under this vow include Samson and probably Samuel.

One of the important roles Yahweh assigns to Aaron and his priestly sons is the pronouncement of his divine blessing on Israel. Yahweh gives specific instructions as to the major content of this blessing in Num 6:24–27.[3] The two central aspects of this blessing are the presence of Yahweh and the name of Yahweh. As discussed earlier, when used of Yahweh, many of the frequent occurrences of the Hebrew word for "face" and the idioms derived from this word are references to the real, "near," presence of Yahweh amid the Israelites. Phrases in our English Bibles such as "before the LORD" and "in the presence of the LORD" are translations of the idioms conveyed by the word for "face"—that is, "before the face of Yahweh"—and they stress the nearness of Yahweh. In the priestly blessing of Num 6:24–27, verses 25a and 26a are parallel, both employing the Hebrew word for "face." A literal translation would read:

May Yahweh shine his face on you . . .
May Yahweh lift up his face toward you.

---

[3] Timothy R. Ashley views Leviticus 1–Num 6:21 as a prescriptive unit. Thus, he understands the blessing of Num 6:22–27 to be the concluding benediction of that large section. Then Num 7:1 picks back up on the tabernacle construction story from the end of Exodus. See Ashley, *The Book of Numbers*, NICOT (Grand Rapids: Eerdmans, 1993), 149. Ashley, along with several other scholars, also notes that Num 6:22–27 may reflect the content of the blessing given by Aaron in Lev 9:22. See, for example, Puttagunta Satyavani, *Seeing the Face of God: Exploring an Old Testament Theme* (Carlisle, UK: Langham, 2014), 208.

The image conveyed is that of Yahweh looking out favorably from his dwelling place in the tabernacle. Another critical aspect of this blessing is the stress on the name of Yahweh (the Lord). The name *Yahweh* is stated in each of the three verses of the blessing (6:24–26). Then, in the summary (6:27), Yahweh declares, "In this way they will pronounce my *name* over the Israelites, and I will bless them" (italics added). Specific benefits flowing out of the blessing provided by Yahweh looking out favorably from his dwelling place in the tabernacle on the people who carry his name include: protection (6:24), grace (6:25), and peace (6:26).[4]

WORD STUDY
BARAK ("TO BLESS")

The Hebrew verb *barak* ("to bless") and the related noun *berakah* ("blessing") are critically important theological terms used repeatedly throughout the Pentateuch, the verb *barak* occurring over 130 times and the noun *berakah* occurring over thirty times. Yet the usage is not evenly spaced. *Barak*, for example, occurs seventy-two times in Genesis, seven times in Numbers, and thirty-nine times in Deuteronomy, but only six times in Exodus and twice in Leviticus. Furthermore, as discussed below, the occurrences often come in clusters, such that the word is used several times within a short passage. Throughout the Pentateuch *barak* most frequently means to invoke, to ask for, or bring upon an individual or group (often Israel) Yahweh's favor, with the intention that this person will experience favorable circumstances in the near future.[5] This blessing is almost always founded on the relationship one has with Yahweh, and the blessing resulting from this relationship is usually a very tangible and concrete benefit such as fertility, prosperity, authority, or safety.[6]

An early important cluster text is Gen 12:2–3, where the terms (*barak, barakah*) occur five times. Yahweh tells Abraham, "I will bless you . . . you will be

---

[4] For a further discussion on the tight connection between the priestly benediction and the indwelling presence of Yahweh in the tabernacle or temple, see Duvall and Hays, *God's Relational Presence*, 44–45 (see chap. 1, n. 4); and Jeremy D. Smoak, *The Priestly Blessing in Inscription and Scripture: The Early History of Numbers 6:24–26* (Oxford: Oxford University Press, 2016), 89–110.

[5] James Swanson, *"barak," Dictionary of Biblical Languages with Semantic Domains: Hebrew (Old Testament)* (Oak Harbor, WA: Logos Research Systems, 1997).

[6] James McKeown, "Blessings and Curses," in *Dictionary of the Old Testament: Pentateuch*, 84–86 (see intro., n. 12).

a blessing. I will bless those who bless you . . . all the peoples on earth will be blessed through you." Connecting tightly to this promise of blessing to Abraham, in Lev 9:22–23, as Aaron the high priest actually begins his official ministry, he and then also Moses bless the people, followed by the appearance of the fiery glory of Yahweh, stressing the close personal relationship. As suggested above, Num 6:22–27 probably reflects the content of Aaron's blessing in Lev 9:22–23. In Num 6:22–27 the word "bless" is used three times (6:23, 24, 27), and its effect is for Yahweh to continue his close intimate relationship with the Israelites and to provide protection, safety, and peace.

In Numbers 22–24, however, Yahweh's ongoing blessing of Israel—indeed, his relationship with Israel and his ability to protect them—is challenged, as Balaam is called on to curse the Israelites. Yet, as discussed below, try as he may, Balaam is unable to curse Israel but must instead bless them. He declares, "I have indeed received a command to bless; since he has blessed, I cannot change it" (23:20). Then, in a direct connection to Gen 12:2–3, Balaam states, "Those who bless you will be blessed, and those who curse you will be cursed" (Num 24:9).

The first main cluster in Deuteronomy comes in Deuteronomy 15, where blessing from Yahweh is stated both as the reason for Israel's care and compassion for the poor and needy as well as the consequence of that compassion (15:4, 6, 10, 14, 18). The second cluster is in Deuteronomy 28, which describes the wonderful blessings resulting from Yahweh's relational presence dwelling with Israel in the Promised Land (28:3, 4, 5, 6, 8, 12). The final cluster comes at the end, in Deuteronomy 33, when Moses gives his final blessings on the Israelites like a patriarchal father, ending with, "Blessed are you, Israel! Who is like you, a people saved by the Lord?" (33:29 NIV).

Numbers 7:1 picks up the story from the end of Exodus. After Moses sets up the tabernacle and consecrates it, each tribe, led by their tribal leaders, brings a special dedication offering to Yahweh in the tabernacle (7:1–89). Numbers 7:89 clarifies that when Yahweh would speak to Moses, he would speak to him from the Most Holy Place, from above the ark of the covenant. Numbers 8:1–4 then differentiates the ministry of Aaron in comparison to that of Moses, for Aaron's ministry is in the Holy Place, especially involving the care and operation of the golden lampstand. The Levites as a group then go through a special consecration process, getting them ready to serve in the holy tabernacle and to be able to handle the materials in the tabernacle as Israel moved.

In Num 9:1–14, since it is the first month of the second year (the month of the Passover, given in Exod 12:1–28), Israel celebrates the Passover and receives some additional details as to what is ceremonially clean or unclean and how that status affects one's participation in the Passover. This is a fitting final act of worship and remembrance by Israel at Mount Sinai before setting out on the trip to the Promised Land.

Yahweh's Cloud and the Two Trumpets: Divine Guidance for Traveling to the Promised Land (9:15–10:10)

At the end of Exodus, after the tabernacle was completed, the glory of Yahweh filled the tabernacle and a special cloud covered it. The location of the cloud would tell Israel when to break camp and start traveling and when to stay in camp (Exod 40:34–38). Numbers 9:15–23 picks up from this story in Exod 40:34–38 and adds more detail about the cloud. If the cloud is over the tabernacle, the Israelites are to stay encamped. If it moves off the tabernacle, they are to break camp and "set out." The Hebrew word *nasa*ʿ ("to set out") is used repeatedly throughout the beginning of the travel narrative, occurring nine times in Num 9:15–23 and sixteen times in Num 10:1–36. In 10:1–10 Yahweh instructs Moses to make two silver trumpets to assist in the travel organization. These trumpets are to be used to give the specific signal for when each tribe is to set out. These trumpets could also be used to signal special meetings for the leaders.

REBELLION AND REJECTION OF THE PROMISED LAND (10:11–14:45)

The Trip Begins but Is Characterized by Refusal, Grumbling, and Rebellion (10:11–12:16)

In Num 10:11 the cloud of Yahweh lifts from the tabernacle, and the Israelites finally set out on their trip to the Promised Land, following the order and the procedure Yahweh has given them. The spectacular nature of the beginning of the trip, however, is quickly marred by several negative events. First, in 10:29–32 Moses invites his Midianite in-law relative Hobab (probably the brother of Jethro, the relative who visited Moses in Exod 18:1–27; see the discussion on Exodus 18) to go with the Israelites to the Promised Land and to serve along the way as a scout, since he would know where to camp in the wilderness. This request is quite peculiar and unexpected since the previous section had stressed Yahweh's guidance through the wilderness. At

any rate, Hobab refuses Moses's offer and instead insists on returning to his own people.[7] This is an ominous decision, for later in the story the Midianites will be one of
Israel's most hostile enemies and will align themselves with the Moabites in opposing
Israel's travel to the Promised Land and in seeking to lead Israel away from Yahweh
to worship other gods. Following Yahweh's command, Moses will destroy them completely (22:4, 7; 25:6–18; 31:1–54).

The second negative event is the Israelites' complaint about their food (the manna
provided by Yahweh), a complaint that annoys both Yahweh and Moses. Yahweh,
however, in his grace provides quail for the grumbling Israelites.

The third negative event is the opposition by Miriam, the sister of Moses, and
by Aaron, his brother, to Moses's recent marriage to a Cushite woman. The text is
somewhat ambiguous about what happened to Zipporah, the Midianite wife Moses
married in Exodus 2. Jethro, apparently the functioning patriarch of this Midianite
priestly family, brought her back to Moses in Exodus 18. While there is no specific mention of her in Numbers, Hobab, as noted earlier, probably another patriarch
from this family (Jethro's brother, perhaps), refuses to join Israel and become part of
Yahweh's people. Instead, he returns to his own people. This probably signals a rift
between Moses and the Midianite family he had earlier married into, and it is quite
probable that Hobab takes Moses's Midianite wife back to Midian with him.

The woman Moses marries in Numbers 12, identified clearly as a Cushite, is different from the Midianite woman he married in Exodus 2.[8] This Cushite woman was
probably part of the "mixed crowd" that went out of Egypt with the Israelites (Exod
12:38), and she would certainly qualify as a "residing foreigner." The main point of the
passage is that Miriam and Aaron oppose Moses over this marriage. Since the Cushites
were black Africans, some have assumed that this opposition was racially motivated,
but it is more likely that it is related to issues of leadership and power. (However, based
on the amount of text in Exodus-Deuteronomy that addresses the issue, there does
seem to have been some ongoing resentment and prejudice against the "residing foreigners.") Moses, who has just defeated Egypt, a leading world power, could now claim
the status and prestige like that of the Egyptian pharaohs. Marriages in the royal families of the ANE were often viewed as political alliances, and the wives of ruling monarchs such as the pharaoh often had considerable power. Aaron, and especially Miriam,

---

[7] The text in 10:32 is somewhat ambiguous about Hobab's final decision, after Moses
pleads with him in 10:31–32, but the silence in the text seems to indicate that Hobab does not
change his mind and returns to Midian.

[8] See the discussion in Hays, *From Every People and Nation*, 70–81 (see chap. 1, n. 31); and
Edwin M. Yamauchi, *Africa and the Bible* (Grand Rapids: Baker, 2004), 35–75.

are probably feeling that this new Cushite wife will challenge their power and their role in leading Israel with Moses. They are rebuked rather strongly by Yahweh, however, who reaffirms his close relationship with Moses as well as Moses's high status as "my servant" and as the one "faithful in all my household." Yahweh even adds, "I speak with him directly, openly, and not in riddles; he sees the form of the LORD" (Num 12:7–8).

ANCIENT CONNECTIONS SIDEBAR 4.2: WHO ARE THE CUSHITES?

In Num 12:1, Moses marries a Cushite woman. Who are the Cushites? The Hebrew root word *Cush* (the place) or *Cushi* (the people)—sometimes transliterated into English with a "k" (*Kush/Kushi*)—occurs fifty-four times in the Old Testament, so this was a very important ethnic group in the Old Testament. Some English translations, however, are occasionally inconsistent in how they translate this Hebrew term. The ancient Greeks referred to the entire region south of Egypt (i.e., all of black Africa) as "Ethiopia." Thus, some English translations (e.g., KJV) translate the Hebrew word *Cush* as "Ethiopia." Note, however, that ancient Cush is unrelated geographically to the region currently designated in the modern world as Ethiopia. Further confusing the issue is the fact that often historians will refer to ancient Cush as "Nubia," a later Latin term, and occasionally some English Bible translations (and commentators) will translate "Cush" as "Nubia." Most English translations, however, have come to the correct understanding of this region and now usually translate the Hebrew word as "Cush" (NIV, CSB, NRSVue, NASB).[9]

Cush was a powerful and important kingdom in Africa along the Nile River, south of Egypt, in the country now known as Sudan. It is an identifiable entity from around 2000 BC until AD 350. The kingdom of Cush was particularly famous for its productive gold mines and mercenary soldiers, who served in armies throughout the ANE. Because of its gold mines, Cush's powerful neighbor to the north, Egypt, was constantly striving to control Cush and to extract the gold from Cush for its own use and power. Indeed, at the time of Moses,

---

[9] The NIV (2011) and NASB (2020) translate as "Cush/Cushite" throughout the Old Testament except for Jer 13:23, which peculiarly both render as "Ethiopian." The ESV is particularly inconsistent on this term, translating "Cush/Cushite" in Numbers, 1–2 Samuel, Ezra-Nehemiah, Isaiah, Ezekiel, Daniel, Amos, and Zephaniah, but translating "Ethiopia/Ethiopian" in 1–2 Chronicles, Jeremiah, and Esther.

Cush was under Egyptian control. At the end of the eighth century BC, however, during the time of Isaiah, the Cushites had defeated Egypt, and they ruled over Egypt for a short time, coming into conflict with the powerful Assyrians (cf. 2 Kgs 19:8–9; Isa 37:8–9).

Because of the ongoing close relationship between Egypt and Cush throughout the Old Testament period, the Cushites appear frequently, not only in the Old Testament, but also in Egyptian literature and especially in Egyptian art (on stone monuments and in tomb paintings). Kamose, for example, pharaoh over Egypt in the sixteenth century BC, proclaims on his stone victory steles how he overcame the conspiracy between the Asiatics to the north and the Cushites (Kushites) to the south. Here is a short excerpt:

> To what effect do I perceive it, my might, while a ruler is in Avaris and another in Kush, I sitting joined with an Asiatic and a Nubian, each man having his (own) portion of this Egypt, sharing the land with me. . . . For it was on the upland way of the oasis that I captured his messenger going south to Kush with a written letter. I found on it saying in writing: From the ruler of Avaris . . . greetings to the son of the ruler of Kush: Why have you arisen as ruler without letting me know? Do you see what Egypt has done against me?[10]

Egyptian art consistently depicts the Cushites as black Africans. There is little doubt that the Cushite woman Moses marries in Numbers 12 is a black African from the nation of Cush, along the Nile River, to the south of Egypt.[11]

Arriving at the Promised Land, the People Anger Yahweh by Refusing to Enter and Conquer the Good Land, but Moses Intercedes for Them (13:1–14:45)

In Numbers 13, following Yahweh's instructions, Moses selects one leader from each of the twelve tribes (excluding the Levites) and sends them into the land of Canaan

---

[10] "The Kamose Texts," trans. William Kelly Simpson, in *The Literature of Ancient Egypt*, 346, 349 (see intro., n. 17).

[11] Hays, *From Every People and Nation*, 70–81; Yamauchi, *Africa and the Bible*, 35–75. See also J. Daniel Hays, "The Cushites: A Black Nation in Ancient History," *BSac* 153, no. 611 (July 1996): 270–80; "The Cushites: A Black Nation in the Bible," *BSac* 153, no. 612 (October 1996): 396–409; and "Moses: The Private Man Behind the Public Leader," *BR* 16 (August 2000): 16–26, 60–63.

to explore it, especially regarding the fertility of the land and the military strength of its inhabitants. For forty days they explore the land, and then they return to give their report. The land, they report, is exceedingly bountiful, but the inhabitants are very powerful and their fortified cities are large. Two of the leaders, Caleb and Joshua, urge the people to proceed immediately and attack the land, but the other ten spies give in to fear and convince the people that the inhabitants are just too strong for them.

Thus, in Numbers 14 the unthinkable happens. Yahweh delivered Israel from Egypt, crushing the Egyptians, and brought Israel to Mount Sinai, where he established his covenant with Israel and came down in spectacular fashion to dwell among them in the tabernacle. The next crucial part of Yahweh's plan, and in fulfillment of his covenant promise to Abraham, is for Israel to move into Canaan, take possession of it, and live in this good land with Yahweh blessing them as he dwells with them. Yet, incredibly, the Israelites now refuse to enter the land. They turn against the leadership of Moses, Aaron, Caleb, and Joshua, even threatening to stone them, and declare it would have been better if they had died in the wilderness.

The glory of Yahweh then appears at the tabernacle in the view of the Israelites. Yahweh tells Moses that he will destroy all the Israelites and make Moses into a new nation. Once again, Moses intercedes on Israel's behalf (even though only a few verses earlier they were talking of stoning him), and, as a result, Yahweh does forgive them and not destroy them. However, there are consequences. Yahweh, who heard them say it would have been better to die in the wilderness, now sends them into the wilderness to die. His ironic poetic justice is further illustrated as he says that no one over twenty (the age used for the census in Num 1:3) will ever see the Promised Land, because they will all die in the wilderness as they wander there for forty years (paralleling the forty days spent exploring the land). The exceptions, of course, would be Caleb and Joshua. For the ten unfaithful spies who persuaded the people not to enter the land, however, judgment comes immediately, and they all die of a plague "before the Lord" (14:37 NIV).

The Consequences: The Israelites Wander in the Wilderness, yet Yahweh Blesses Them in Spite of Rebellions (15:1–25:18)

Future Offerings in the Land and the Special Status of the Priests Serving in the Holy Tabernacle Are Contrasted with a Priestly Rebellion against Moses (15:1–19:22)

Yahweh's communication with Moses in Numbers 15 comes somewhat as a surprise, underscoring once again the tremendous grace of Yahweh. In 15:1–21 Yahweh discusses special thanksgiving offerings that the Israelites are to offer in the future after they do enter the land. Thus right after the declaration of severe punishment for refusing to enter the land, Yahweh is already looking to the future, when the Israelites would obediently conquer and occupy the land. Numbers 15:22–31 then discusses an offering for when the community sins "unintentionally," an ironic discussion since in the previous chapter Israel commits one of the most blatant intentional acts of disobedience in their history. Numbers 15 concludes with a short narrative about the importance of keeping the Sabbath even while in the wilderness (15:32–36), followed by Yahweh's instructions to put tassels on the corner of their garments to help the people remember and keep Yahweh's commands, to be holy to him, and to always remember that he is Yahweh their God who brought them out of Egypt (15:37–41).

In contrast, Numbers 16 describes a rebellion against Moses led by the priest Korah and supported by the Reubenites Dathan and Abiram. Once again, Yahweh responds with quick, severe judgment, and once again his response is moderated by the intercession of Moses. In contrast to Numbers 16, the next few chapters will reaffirm the important role Yahweh has for the Levitical priests. Numbers 17 reaffirms the special status of Aaron, as Yahweh miraculously causes Aaron's staff to bud and produce almonds. Numbers 18:1–7 underscores the important and special responsibility that the Levites bear in caring for the tabernacle and protecting the holiness of the tabernacle. Then 18:8–32 describes the procedure for providing for the priests. Finally, Numbers 19 discusses a special sacrifice of a red cow, followed by more guidelines on how one is made clean after becoming unclean.

Throughout this unit, Eleazar, the son of Aaron, starts to appear in the story, taking on more and more responsibility (16:37, 39; 19:3–4). This anticipates the death of Aaron in Numbers 20, after which his son Eleazar and Eleazar's son Phinehas will serve as the high priestly Levitical leaders throughout the rest of the book.

More Rebellions; the Death of Miriam and Aaron; and Opposition from Balaam, Moab, and Midian; but Yahweh Still Protects His People (20:1–25:18)

In Numbers 20 the people once again quarrel with Moses and Aaron, this time about the lack of water. Yahweh instructs Moses and Aaron to "speak to the rock," for then water will miraculously flow out. Moses, however, strikes the rock instead of speaking to it (20:9–11). Water did indeed flow out of the rock, but Yahweh is displeased with Moses and Aaron because they did not trust him enough to obey him specifically. Thus, here we see that even Moses must obey Yahweh's specific instructions. The consequence, Yahweh declares, is that Moses will lose the privilege of personally leading Israel into the Promised Land (20:12).

The short episode in Num 20:14–21 describes the nation of Edom's refusal to allow Israel to pass through their territory peacefully. Moses makes the request as "your brother" (20:14), recalling that the Edomites are descendants of Esau, the son of Isaac and the brother of Jacob, who had become Israel (Gen 25:21–34; 27:1–45; 32:1–33:16). Edom, however, refuses safe passage, foreshadowing the future deep, ongoing hostility between Israel/Judah and Edom that is prevalent in the time of the Prophets (e.g., Jer 49:7–22).

Keep in mind that time is passing, even though the long forty years of wandering is barely recounted in any detail. In Numbers 20 a generational shift in leadership unfolds, because both Miriam (20:1) and Aaron (20:23–29) die. As mentioned earlier, Eleazar, the son of Aaron, takes over his father's role as high priest (20:27–28). Numbers 33, which presents an overview of the travels of Israel from the time of the exodus until they arrive on the plains of Moab, helps us with the chronology of these chapters, for Num 33:38 notes that Aaron died in the fifth month of the fortieth year. Thus, the forty-year wandering is drawing to an end, and in the chapters that follow, Yahweh is leading Israel back to the Promised Land.

In Num 21:1–3 the Israelites, under immediate pressure from an attack by the Canaanite king of Arad, a city on the southern edge of the Promised Land, make a vow before Yahweh, requesting that he deliver the people of Arad into their hands. While this vow is perhaps unnecessary, and probably Yahweh would have given the Israelites the victory over Arad if they had simply trusted him, Yahweh nonetheless listens to them and provides them with a significant victory over Arad.

The Israelites, however, return to their grumbling and rebellion against Moses in Num 21:4–5, declaring, "Why have you led us up from Egypt to die in the wilderness? There is no bread or water, and we detest this wretched food" (21:5). Note that the "wretched food" they so detest is the manna and quail divinely provided for them by Yahweh. In response, Yahweh sends deadly venomous snakes (lit., "fiery snakes"; the adjective *fiery* probably refers to the pain of the bite or the red inflammation that results; 21:6 NASB). The Israelites quickly turn to Moses, repenting of their sin and begging him to intercede with Yahweh (21:7). Moses prays on their behalf, and Yahweh instructs him to make a bronze snake and elevate it on a pole, so all can see it. Everyone who has been snake-bitten and who looks at the bronze snake will recover from the snakebite. The bronze snake does not prevent the people from being bit, but once they have repented of their sin, they will recover from the consequences of their sin by obeying Yahweh and looking at the snake on the pole.[12]

Perhaps the snake on the pole was impaled, symbolizing death and serving in a similar way as a sacrifice. Or perhaps these snakes in general were to be associated with Egypt (see the discussion on snakes as a symbol of Egypt in the section on Exod 7:8–10:29), and this event was to remind them of how deadly it was for them back in Egypt and of how Yahweh had defeated Egypt.[13]

ANCIENT CONNECTIONS SIDEBAR 4.3: COPPER SNAKES AND WORSHIP IN THE ANCIENT NEAR EAST

About fifteen miles north of the current southernmost Israelite city of Elath, in a temple to Hathor in the ancient city of Timna, a city known for its copper mines, archaeologists discovered a five-inch-long copper snake in the ruins of a Midianite era temple. The snake probably represented a deity that was worshipped. Another similar copper snake was found in the excavations of Tel Mevorakh in the coastal plain of Israel. In ancient Egypt small models of snakes were worn as amulets to prevent snakebites.[14] The snake that Moses made, however, served neither as the representation of a pagan god nor as a prevention for snakebites but rather as a divine means that involved obedience that could heal the snakebites. Later in history, however, the Israelites apparently fell back into the pagan practice of venerating snake idols, because they were said to have been offering incense to this very snake that Moses made (2 Kgs 18:4).

Yahweh continues to lead Israel closer back to the Promised Land, but in so doing he leads them around the southern side of the Dead Sea and then up through the area east of the Dead Sea and the Jordan River valley, an area known as the Transjordan.

---

[12] Gordon Wenham suggests that the symbolism involved in the snake was akin to that seen in the principles behind the sacrifices and purification rites in the Old Testament. That is, in these rituals there was an "inversion" of sorts in which "animals are killed, so that sinful men who deserve to die may live." Wenham also argues that the snake was made of a reddish-colored copper, not to match the inflammation of the bites, but "because red is the colour that symbolizes atonement and purification." Gordon J. Wenham, *Numbers*, TOTC (Downers Grove, IL: IVP, 1981), 157–58.

[13] Naselli, *The Serpent and the Serpent Slayer*, 76–77 (see chap. 1, n. 44).

[14] R. Dennis Cole, "Numbers," *ZIBBC* 1:375; R. K. Joines, "The Bronze Serpent in the Israelite Cult," *JBL* 87 (1968): 245–56.

Under Yahweh's leading, the Israelites defeat two powerful kings: Sihon, king of the Amorites (in the southern part of the Transjordan), and Og, king of Bashan (in the northern part of the Transjordan; Num 21:21–35). With these victories fresh under their belts, the Israelites arrive on the plains of Moab and camp there, on the east side of the Jordan River across from Jericho (22:1).

With the Israelites already camping in Moabite territory, the Moabites, alarmed and frightened, form an alliance with the Midianites (the former in-laws of Moses) to counter the Israelites. Rather than confront the Israelites militarily, Balak, the king of Moab, decides to hire a famous sorcerer, magician, and prophet from Mesopotamia, named Balaam, to come and put a curse on Israel. The Midianites are likewise involved in this scheme (22:4, 7). The account of this theological/magical battle between Balaam and Yahweh runs from Num 22:1 until 25:18.

At the heart of this confrontation is the question of who has the power to curse and to bless. Balak sends messengers to Mesopotamia to convince Balaam to come, offering him money and stating his belief that whomever Balaam blesses is blessed and whomever Balaam curses is cursed (22:6). Recalling his promise to Abraham in Gen 12:3, Yahweh tells Balaam not to curse Israel, because they are blessed (Num 22:12). After first telling Balaam not to go, Yahweh allows Balaam to go with the messengers but with strict instructions to "only do what I tell you" (22:20). The fact that Yahweh speaks to and through Balaam does not necessarily imply that he is a true believer. Ultimately, his attitude toward Yahweh and Israel is hostile (see Num 31:8, 16), and throughout the rest of Scripture, references to him are quite negative.

Although the story is somewhat ambiguous, it appears that Balaam thinks he can cleverly accomplish both goals—obey Yahweh but still help Balak defeat Israel and thus collect the fortune Balak offered. An angel of Yahweh confronts Balaam along the way to warn him how dangerous this plan is, cautioning him again to be sure to "say only what I tell you" (22:35). The amusing episode of Balaam's talking donkey underscores the foolishness of Balaam's plan. Ironically, his donkey can see the angel of Yahweh blocking the way (and thus the danger of Balaam's plan) while Balaam, perhaps the most powerful sorcerer and seer in the world, cannot see the angel at all, thus continuing his headlong path to destruction.

After Balaam arrives, Balak tries several times to get him to curse Israel, but each time Balaam ends up blessing Israel instead, saying things such as "How can I curse someone God has not cursed?" (23:8), and "God brought them out of Egypt; he is like the horns of a wild ox for them. There is no magic curse against Jacob and no divination against Israel" (23:22–23).

In 24:25 it appears as if Balaam and Balak both give up on this endeavor. Yet in Num 25:1–18 we see a new tactic, employed by the Moabites and Midianites. Here they use their women to sexually seduce the Israelite men, convincing them to worship Baal (the "worship" activities for this fertility god probably involved sexual acts). Numbers 31:16 explains that this attempt to lead Israel away from Yahweh through sexual enticements was actually Balaam's idea! It appears that Balaam has concluded that since Yahweh will not allow him to curse Israel directly, perhaps he can lead them away from Yahweh and then let Yahweh punish them—or at least remove Yahweh's protection of them so the Moabites and Midianites can defeat them.

A number of Israelites are indeed seduced and start to worship Baal (25:3). Yahweh responds quickly and angrily to this appalling apostasy. The Israelites are ordered to put to death all who have "aligned themselves with Baal" (25:5), and Yahweh also sends a plague on them (25:9), perhaps suggesting that they were not expeditious in executing the ones who had joined in the Baal worship. A dramatic and specific event is recounted, in which an Israelite man blatantly and defiantly brings a Midianite woman into his tent even as Moses and many of the Israelites were weeping over this apostasy in front of the tabernacle (25:6). Phinehas, the son of Eleazar and grandson of Aaron, kills both the disobedient Israelite and the Midianite woman, apparently ending this tragic episode of disobedience.

ANCIENT CONNECTIONS SIDEBAR 4.4: BALAAM SON OF BEOR

The fame of Balaam son of Beor was apparently quite widespread, even to the extent that a much later writer referenced him, or perhaps a later diviner or sorcerer used his name to invoke a connection to the earlier Balaam. This is the conclusion suggested by the presence of the name "Balaam son of Beor" in an inscription discovered in the excavations at the city of Deir ʿAlla, near where the Jabbok River flows into the Jordan River. This Balaam was also a pagan diviner, sorcerer, and seer, and he received a special vision from his gods about an upcoming time of famine and darkness. The opening lines of the text read:

The misfortunes of the Book of Balaam, son of Beor.
A divine seer was he.
The gods came to him at night,
And he beheld a vision in accordance with El's utterance.
They said to Balaam, son of Beor:

"So will it be done, with naught surviving,
No one has seen [the likes of] what you have heard!"[15]

This inscription dates to the mid-eighth to seventh century BC, and thus was written hundreds of years after the events of Numbers, but it perhaps indicates that the fame of Balaam son of Beor continued to be known even in later centuries.[16]

The Obedient Generation (26:1–36:13)

THE GENERATIONAL TRANSITION—A NEW GENERATION AND NEW LEADERS (26:1–27:23)

After the plague in Numbers 25, in Numbers 26 Yahweh instructs Moses and Eleazar (who has replaced Aaron as the high priest and associate of Moses) to take another census. This second census occurs on "the plains of Moab by the Jordan across from Jericho" (26:3). This census identifies the new generation who will be the ones to conquer Jericho and complete the conquest of the Promised Land. The text is emphatic in noting that not one of the disobedient Israelites counted in the earlier census is still alive except Caleb and Joshua (and Moses) (26:64–65).

Numbers 27:1–11 presents a brief ruling that allows for daughters to inherit land if the family has no sons. Keep in mind that Israel does not have the land yet, for the conquest is still future. This request, therefore, seems to underscore the faith these daughters have that Israel would indeed receive their inheritance in the Promised Land, and they want to be sure they are included. On the other hand, these daughters are descendants of Makir, from the tribe of Manasseh, and in Num 32:33–42 Moses gives part of the territory east of the Jordan River to the tribe of Manasseh, and the descendants of Makir settle there. It may have been this soon-to-come assignment of inheritance territory that triggered the request by these daughters.

In 27:15–17 Moses makes a dramatic appeal to Yahweh to appoint a strong, capable leader to replace him, someone "who will go out before them and come back in before them, and who will bring them out and bring them in, so that the LORD's community won't be like sheep without a shepherd" (27:17). Although in Genesis,

---

[15] "The Deir ʿAlla Plaster Inscriptions," trans. Baruch A. Levine, *COS* 2.27:142.
[16] See the discussion in Cole, "Numbers," 1:380–81.

while blessing their sons, Joseph and Jacob both referred to Yahweh as a shepherd (Gen 48:15; 49:24), Moses's statement in Num 27:17 is the first usage of the shepherd imagery in regard to the human leaders of Israel, an imagery that will echo throughout the rest of the Old Testament and into the New Testament. In response to Moses's request, Numbers 27 concludes with the commissioning of Joshua as the future leader. The new leaders are now Joshua and Eleazar, replacing Moses and Aaron (27:22), although Moses will not die until Deuteronomy 34.

REMINDER OF OFFERINGS, FESTIVAL DAYS, AND SPECIAL VOWS (28:1–30:16)

Numbers 28–30 describes a number of offerings, festivals, and special vows, most of which have been presented before, either in Exodus or Leviticus or earlier in Numbers. The earlier part of the list (Numbers 28–29) is focused especially on the activities of the priests. It is probably placed here in this part of the story as a forward-looking affirmation that these worship activities would soon be taking place in the Promised Land, led by Joshua and Eleazar. Numbers 30 underscores the importance of keeping vows while describing certain situations where a husband or father can nullify the vows of his wife or daughter.

THE DEFEAT AND PLUNDER OF MIDIAN AND THE DEATH OF BALAAM (31:1–54)

In Num 31:1 Yahweh tells Moses that he has one more task for him to complete. Ironically, this task is to destroy the Midianites (his former in-laws) as a punishment for their part in trying to seduce the Israelites into worshipping Baal in Numbers 25. As Israel defeats Midian, the text notes the death of five kings of Midian, along with Balaam son of Beor (31:8). This episode also clarifies that the attempt to lead Israel away from Yahweh through the sexual seduction involved in Baal worship was indeed Balaam's advice (31:16). Recall that earlier in Numbers (10:29–32) Moses had invited his Midianite in-law Hobab to join Israel and to travel with them to the Promised Land, an invitation that Hobab rejected. Now, after the alliance of Midian with Moab, and their devious plan to lead Israel away from Yahweh, the Midianites are destroyed and plundered by the Israelites. We can only speculate on the fate of Hobab.

PREPARATIONS FOR ENTERING THE PROMISED LAND (32:1–36:13)

As described earlier in Numbers 21–22, Yahweh had led Israel to circle south of the Dead Sea and then to travel north in the Transjordan. After defeating the two kings

Sihon and Og, the Israelites move into the plains of Moab (21:21–22:1), still on the east side of the Jordan. Noting the fertility of the area east of the Jordan, the tribes of Reuben and Gad ask Moses if they can stay there and occupy the Transjordan as their Promised Land inheritance (32:1–5). After Moses rebukes them for refusing to go with the rest of Israel to conquer the land of Canaan, they reach a compromise. Reuben and Gad, along with part of Ephraim, would leave their families in the forti-fied cities of the Transjordan that had been captured by the defeat of Sihon and Og, while the men of fighting age would go with the rest of Israel into Canaan to conquer the Promised Land. After completion of the conquest, they would then return back across the Jordan River to their families (32:6–42).

Numbers 33:1–48 presents a review of the route that the Israelites have followed from the time they left Egypt until they arrive on the plains of Moab. Now, with the Promised Land just across the Jordan River, Yahweh reiterates what they are to do there. The Israelites are admonished to completely drive out all the inhabitants, destroying everything associated with the Canaanite pagan religion. Yahweh explic-itly instructs them to "destroy all their stone images and cast images, and demolish all their high places" (33:52). They are also to take possession of the land assigned to each tribe by lot. "If you don't drive out the inhabitants of the land," Yahweh warns, "[they] . . . will become barbs for your eyes and thorns for your sides; they will harass you in the land where you live. And what I had planned to do to them, I will do to you" (33:55–56).

Note that Yahweh does not necessarily instruct the Israelites to kill all the Canaanites but to drive them out of the land and to destroy everything associated with their pagan worship. His desire is that the Israelites, his special set-apart people, will be faithful in worshipping him alone. The consequences for not driving out the Canaanites, Yahweh mentions briefly but ominously at the end, is that he will do to the Israelites what he earlier desired for the Canaanites. That is, he will drive the Israelites out of the land, which will eventually take place in 722 BC and 587 BC.

Yahweh next describes to Moses and the Israelites the boundaries of the Promised Land, along with the appointment of leaders to help with the distribution of the land to each tribe. Yahweh also instructs Moses to give a number of the towns in the land to the Levites, along with the surrounding areas (34:1–35:5). Six of these Levitical towns, Yahweh adds, are to be cities of refuge, to where a person can flee if he has killed someone accidentally and then if the deceased person's family seeks vengeance (35:6–34).

Finally, now that the allotment of the Promised Land is being discussed, fur-ther clarification is needed regarding daughters who inherit land from their fathers because the families have no sons, an issue raised back in Num 27:1–11. The concern raised here in Num 36:1–4 is that if these women who have inherited tribal land marry outside the tribe, then, when they die, the inheritance of the land will pass into that other tribe. Yahweh presents them with the pragmatic answer: these women who inherit land must marry within their own tribe (36:5–9), something that they indeed do (36:10–12).

The book of Numbers concludes with the Israelites on the plains of Moab, just across the Jordan River from Jericho, making final arrangements about going into the land and about the distribution of the land. In Num 27:12–13 Yahweh indicated that Moses would die soon after the appointment of Joshua and before entering the land. As the book draws to a close, readers are left with forward-looking anticipation about the actual conquest and about the final transfer of power from Moses (when this great leader would actually die) to Joshua, the one who leads them into the Promised Land. The needed sequel is, of course, the books of Deuteronomy and Joshua.

Biblical Connections

Numbers is part of the narrative story that runs from Genesis 12 to 2 Kings 25. As part of the Pentateuch it is particularly connected to the exodus story and follows chronologically after the events at Mount Sinai in Exodus and the construction of the tabernacle, connecting frequently to many of those things in Exodus and Leviticus. Likewise, Numbers continues the theme of the unfolding fulfillment of Yahweh's promises to Abraham, Isaac, and Jacob. In particular, the large population seen in the two censuses taken in Numbers points to the fulfillment of the promise regarding numerous descendants. Likewise, Numbers also references or repeats the patriarchal land promise several times. Furthermore, the promise in Gen 12:3 to "bless those who bless you" and to "curse anyone who treats you with contempt" finds ironic and colorful fulfillment in the Balaam story of Numbers 22–24.

There are numerous references and allusions back to passages and events in Numbers made throughout the rest of the Bible. Often these references first occur in Deuteronomy, with Moses reflecting on the great deliverance Yahweh has just provided. Similarly, in texts where Israel's history is recounted or remembered, often the events of Numbers are included in this history (e.g., Psalms 105–106; 135–136; Nehemiah 9).

Frequently seen are references and allusions to the grumbling and disobedience of Israel in Numbers and the ensuing discipline and judgment of God. Indeed, one of the major themes in Numbers is the frequent grumbling, disobedience, faithlessness, and rebellion by Israel (see especially Numbers 11, 16, 20), climaxing with the refusal to enter the Promised Land (Numbers 13–14), each of which resulted in the discipline of God. Numerous times throughout Scripture these events are cited as warnings to the current audience, often referenced in some detail (Deut 1:26–46; 11:5–7; 33:8; Ps 78:14–55; 95:8–11; 106:13–33; 1 Cor 10:1–13; Heb 3:7–19; Jude vv. 5, 11).

Similarly, in Num 33:52 Yahweh explicitly instructs Israel to destroy the worship centers of the Canaanites, particularly mentioning the "high places" (Hebrew, *bamah*). The extent to which the later kings of Israel and Judah either destroy the "high places" as instructed in Num 33:52 or build or worship at the "high places" is a major criterion of how the kings are evaluated in 1–2 Kings. This is a major theme in 1–2 Kings, with more than thirty verses citing whether a king destroys the "high places," builds them, or worships there.

Sometimes, however, the events of Numbers are recalled to remind Israel of Yahweh's faithfulness and his great deliverance. In Deuteronomy, Moses declares:

> Do not forget . . . the LORD your God, who brought you out of Egypt. . . . He led you through the vast and dreadful wilderness, that thirsty and waterless land, with its venomous snakes and scorpions. He brought you water out of hard rock. He gave you manna to eat in the wilderness. (Deut 8:11–16 NIV; see also Neh 9:19–21)

The great victories over Sihon and Og (Num 21:21–35) are likewise repeatedly cited as evidence of how Yahweh has protected and empowered his people Israel, with the strong implication and expectation that he likewise could give them victory over the nations in the Promised Land (Deut 2:24–3:11; 29:7–8; 31:4–5; Neh 9:22; Ps 135:11–12; 136:17–19). Israel's victories over Sihon and Og were big news in that part of the world, and these victories are recounted with awe and respect by both foreigners and Israelites (Josh 2:10; 9:10; Judg 11:19–22).

The Nazirite vow of Num 6:1–21 is alluded to or implied several times. Not only Samson (Judg 13:5) but probably also Samuel (1 Sam 1:22) and John the Baptist (Luke 1:15) are Nazirites.[17]

As noted earlier, the bronze snake on a pole constructed by Moses in Num 21:8–9 was apparently preserved and is later inappropriately worshipped as a god by Israel. Second Kings 18:4 comments, "He [Hezekiah] broke into pieces the bronze snake that Moses made, for until then the Israelites were burning incense to it." In John 3:14–15

---

[17] Samuel's Nazirite status is perhaps suggested by the context, but 4QSam^a, one of the Dead Sea Scrolls manuscripts, includes the explicit explanation "I have dedicated him as a Nazirite" in Hannah's words (1 Sam 1:22).

Jesus alludes to this snake, especially the elevation of it up on a pole as a saving act for all who look on it in faith: "Just as Moses lifted up the snake in the wilderness, so the Son of Man must be lifted up, so that everyone who believes in him may have eternal life."

Balaam (Numbers 22–44) is referred to a number of times throughout Scripture, always in a negative way (Deut 23:3–5; Josh 13:22; 24:9–10; Neh 13:2; Mic 6:5; 2 Pet 2:15; Jude 11; Rev 2:14).

In Num 27:17 Moses introduces the motif of the leader of Israel being like a shepherd, a motif that will be repeated throughout Scripture, associated especially with David and then Christ (1 Sam 16:11, 19; 17:15, 34–37; 2 Sam 5:2; Ps 78:70–71; Isa 40:11; Ezek 34:1–24; John 10:1–18; Rev 7:17). Moses's specific fear is that the people of Yahweh might be shepherdless—that is, like "sheep without a shepherd" (Num 27:17). This specific image and phrase "sheep without a shepherd" is repeated several times throughout Scripture to depict people who are leaderless and lost (Ezek 34:5; Zech 10:2; Matt 9:36; Mark 6:34).

Gospel Connections

Several central theological themes run throughout Numbers that are foundational to—and further developed by or fulfilled in—the ministry, death, and resurrection of Jesus Christ. These include the following:

1. *The presence of God.* God wants to dwell in the midst of his people so as to relate to them, but their sin and his holiness often collide. Christ will become the answer to this by removing sin and making us holy, thus allowing the Holy Spirit to dwell within us.
2. *The revelation of God.* God speaks his word and conveys his will to his people. Christ is the ultimate revelation and Word of God.
3. *Holiness.* God is holy and demands that his people in his presence be holy (set apart, sanctified). Christ cleanses us from sin and then declares us to be righteous and holy, allowing us access to the presence of God.
4. *Exclusivity.* God demands that he alone be worshipped and that people worship him in the manner that he decrees. Jesus Christ stresses this as well, that he is "the way, the truth, and the life. No one comes to the Father except through me" (John 14:6).[18]

---

[18] This list of central theological themes in Numbers is developed from that of Cole, *Numbers,* 52–53.

Gordon Wenham points out that in the New Testament, Moses is often depicted as a type of Christ. John's Gospel, in particular, connects Jesus repeatedly to themes, images, and events in Numbers (often also overlapping with Exodus). Thus, Jesus is presented as the Shekinah glory, which was associated with the tabernacle (John 1:14; Num 9:15); the prophet or leader who is greater than Moses (John 5:46; 6:14; Num 12:6–8); the good shepherd (John 10:1–10; Num 27:17); the one lifted up who delivers from death, like the bronze serpent (John 3:14; Num 21:1–9); the Passover lamb with unbroken bones (John 19:36; Num 9:12); the provider of life-giving water (John 4:1–26; Num 20:2–11); and the manna from heaven (John 6:26–58; Num 11:7–9).[19]

In stressing the complete superiority of Jesus Christ, Heb 3:1–6 explains that Jesus is greater than even Moses. Citing Num 12:7, the author of Hebrews notes that while Moses was faithful as a servant in all God's house, Jesus was faithful as the Son over God's house.

Life Connections

At the heart of Numbers is the great disobedience of Israel, when, in spite of clear evidence that God would be with them and lead them to victory, the Israelites listened to the wrong leaders, became frightened about their own welfare, and refused to follow God into the Promised Land. Due to the mediation of Moses, God forgave them (Num 14:20) but not without consequences. That entire generation would wander in the wilderness until they died, and never would they be able to participate in God's great plan of living with him in the Promised Land. For Christians today, certainly the mediation of Christ provides forgiveness of our sins and maintenance of our relationship with him, but we are still called to obedience, and our repeated refusal to obey God and follow his leading can result in a similar removal from active participation in the unfolding plans of God. The lesson from Numbers is for us to trust God and obey, in spite of our fear.

Another important practical lesson to learn and apply from Numbers is in regard to Moses's marriage to the Cushite woman. This is clearly an interethnic marriage, and it finds unequivocal approval from God. In fact, God becomes angry at those who disapprove of it. This helps us realize that later prohibitions about intermarriage are against intermarrying outside of the faith and are not ethnic prohibitions. Also it is important to recognize that Moses is not some minor backgrounded character in the Bible. He is one of the most central, powerful, and important figures in the entire Bible. He marries a black African woman with God's approval. Certainly interethnic

---

[19] Wenham, *Numbers*, 51.

marriages today within the Christian faith are not prohibited and may even likewise find God's approval.

Interactive Questions

4-1. Samson is one of the characters in Israelite history who is designated as a Nazirite. Read Judges 13–16 and discuss the extent to which Samson keeps the Nazirite vow of Num 6:1–21 or violates it.

4-2. Explain how we might make contemporary application from the priestly blessing of Num 6:24–27.

4-3. In Numbers 9, what do the Israelites celebrate just before departure? Explain the significance of this celebration.

4-4. From the following texts, describe the mediatorial role of Moses: Num 11:1–3; 12:13–15; 14:13–25; 16:1–50.

4-5. Discuss the issue of interethnic dating and marriage in your church, school, or social setting context. Is it widely accepted? Or discouraged? What were the ethnic differences between Moses and the Cushite woman he marries in Numbers 12? Why do you think he married this woman? Do you see anything wrong with interethnic dating and marriage?

4-6. Why do the Israelites refuse to go and conquer the Promised Land (Numbers 13–14)? Wasn't it a good land? What kinds of things cause us to disobey God today?

4-7. Read Numbers 18. Explain the special role Yahweh gives to the Levitical priests.

4-8. Read Num 27:15–17 and discuss why the shepherd image is a good model for leaders.

4-9. Read Numbers 22–25 and discuss the actions and motives of Balaam.

4-10. Describe and evaluate the actions of the new priestly leaders Eleazar and Phinehas in Num 20:25–28; 25:1–13; 26:1–4; 27:18–23; and 31:1–54.

Recommended Resources

Ashley, Timothy R. *The Book of Numbers*. NICOT. Grand Rapids: Eerdmans, 1993.
Cole, R. Dennis. *Numbers*. NAC. Nashville: B&H, 2000.

———. "Numbers." In *ZIBBC*, edited by John H. Walton, 337–403. Grand Rapids: Zondervan, 2009.

Gane, Roy E. "Numbers." In *The Baker Illustrated Bible Background Commentary*, edited by J. Scott Duvall and J. Daniel Hays, 168–85. Grand Rapids: Baker, 2020.

Levine, Baruch A. *Numbers 1–20*. AB. New York: Doubleday, 1993.

———. *Numbers 21–36*. AB. New York: Doubleday, 2000.

Olsen, Dennis T. *Numbers*. Louisville: John Knox Press, 1996.

Satyavani, Puttagunta. *Seeing the Face of God: Exploring an Old Testament Theme.* Carlisle, UK: Langham, 2014.

Smoak, Jeremy D. *The Priestly Blessing in Inscription and Scripture: The Early History of Numbers 6:24–26*. Oxford: Oxford University Press, 2016.

Wenham, Gordon J. *Numbers*. TOTC. Downers Grove, IL: IVP, 1981.

5

Deuteronomy

"I have set before you life and death, blessing and curse. Choose life."
— Deuteronomy 30:19

Outline

I. The first speech of Moses: The historical prologue reviewing the recent relationship between Yahweh and Israel (1:1–4:43)
    A. Introduction (1:1–18)
    B. In spite of their rebellion, Yahweh was with the Israelites during the forty years of wilderness wandering (1:19–3:29)
    C. A current call to obey Yahweh—to enter the land and faithfully keep his commandments (4:1–43)
II. The second speech of Moses: The covenant terms by which the Israelites can live in the Promised Land with Yahweh in their midst and find rich blessings (4:44–28:68)
    A. Introduction (4:44–49)
    B. Basic principles and privileges of the covenant relationship (5:1–11:32)

              1.   The Ten Commandments (5:1–32)

              2.   The Israelites are called to love Yahweh, worship him only, obey his commandments, and never forget that he is the one who brought them out of Egypt (6:1–10:11)

              3.   Summary of the covenant situation: The Israelites are to love and obey Yahweh, for obedience results in blessings in the land while disobedience results in a curse (10:12–11:32)

    C. Specific principles and details of the covenant relationship (12:1–26:19)

              1.   Israel is called to worship Yahweh exclusively and joyfully (12:1–13:18)

              2.   The specifics of worship—clean and unclean food, tithing, canceling debts, freeing servants, holy days and festivals (14:1–16:17)

              3.   The proper function of legitimate human authorities (16:18–18:22)

              4.   Issues related to killing, especially murder and war (19:1–21:9)

              5.   Marriage and family issues (21:10–22:30)

              6.   Miscellaneous laws (23:1–26:19)

    D. Publicly recording the terms of the covenant and a nationwide oath of obedience (27:1–26)

    E. Blessings and curses as a result of obedience or disobedience (28:1–68)

III.   The third speech of Moses: Renewal of the covenant—the offer of life or death (29:1–30:20)

IV.   The postscript: The new leader Joshua, the Written *Torah*, the warning of apostasy, and the song and blessings of Moses (31:1–34:12)[1]

Author, Date, and Message

Author and Date

As explained in the introduction, this book follows the traditional understanding that Moses was the human author of Deuteronomy. Deuteronomy 1:1–5 provides the

---

[1] This outline has been developed and expanded from that in Hays and Duvall, *BIBH*, 107–8.

setting and context for how the material in Deuteronomy was produced. It is primarily a series of three speeches (1:5–4:43; 4:44–28:68; 29:1–30:20) made by Moses as mediator between Yahweh and Israel, on the plains of Moab, just east of the Jordan River, forty years after the exodus event (thus after the wandering in the wilderness), on the first day of the eleventh month. The date for Deuteronomy (i.e., the deliverance of Moses's speeches), therefore, would be forty years after the exodus event (either 1446 BC or 1270–1260 BC). References to Moses writing down this material occur in 27:2–4 and 31:9–26.[2]

Structurally, as noted above, Deuteronomy consists of three speeches of Moses (Deuteronomy 1–30) and a postscript (Deuteronomy 31–34). These speeches, however, are embedded into the pentateuchal narrative story. That is, Deuteronomy is a continuation of the narrative story that started in Genesis 12 with Abraham and has continued throughout the rest of Genesis and through Exodus, Leviticus, and Numbers. As we will see, however, the components of Deuteronomy—the topics discussed and the order of the topics—are quite similar to the content and formatting of international treaties from the latter half of the second millennium BC. Treaties and covenants are conceptually similar—a formal agreement between two parties. So, while placed into a narrative story and while communicated through a series of speeches, the book of Deuteronomy, as a covenant document between Yahweh and Israel, is structured in a fashion similar to typical international treaties of that time.

In Hebrew Bibles the title of this book can be translated as "These are the words," taken from the opening words of the book. This is an apt title reflective of the content, because the book of Deuteronomy is indeed the words of Yahweh as mediated through and spoken by Moses, words that hold the key to life or death, good or bad, blessings or curses. The Septuagint, the early Greek translation of the Hebrew Bible, titled the book *Deuteronomion*, which means "the second law," and the Latin Vulgate followed suit, titling the book *Deuteronomii*. English translations have followed this tradition by transliterating the title as Deuteronomy. Yet Deuteronomy is not really a "second law," but a second, renewed presentation of the terms of the covenant that was first given in Exodus at Mount Sinai. Most of the material in the book of the covenant of Exodus 21–23, along with the Ten Commandments of Exodus 20, appears in Deuteronomy, usually with additional details, explanation, and renewed emphasis on the importance of obeying.

---

[2] See the helpful discussion of the authorship and composition of Deuteronomy in Daniel I. Block, *Deuteronomy*, NIVAC (Grand Rapids: Zondervan, 2012), 30–33.

The Message of Deuteronomy

After Israel's disastrous refusal to obey Yahweh and conquer the Promised Land, followed by the consequential forty years of wandering until that disobedient generation died off, Yahweh has now brought Israel back to the border of the Promised Land. With this new generation poised to cross the Jordan and to conquer the Promised Land obediently, Yahweh renews the covenant with them he had originally made with their parents at Mount Sinai in Exodus. In essence, in the book of Deuteronomy Yahweh is presenting the Israelites with the terms by which they can live obediently in the Promised Land with Yahweh residing right in their midst. The purpose of this is so that they can experience blessing and the joyful good life that Yahweh's presence provides.

ANCIENT CONNECTIONS SIDEBAR 5.1: THE STRUCTURE OF DEUTERONOMY AND THE STRUCTURE OF TREATIES IN THE ANCIENT NEAR EAST

In their book *Treaty, Law and Covenant in the Ancient Near East*, Kitchen and Lawrence have collected and analyzed 102 different treaties and covenants from the literature across the ANE dating from the third millennium BC to the early first millennium BC. They demonstrate a remarkable amount of standardization in the structure (i.e., the components of the treaties and covenants and the order of these components) and that this standard form developed and changed over time. Thus the structure or form of treaties and covenants in the third millennium BC differs from those in the second millennium BC, which differ from those in the first millennium BC.[3] When placed in this context, the structure of Deuteronomy is very similar to the standardized structure seen in twenty different treaties (mostly Hittite) from the latter half of the second millennium BC (especially those Hittite treaties from the fourteenth and thirteenth centuries BC), but different in structure from the treaties dated to other eras.[4] One of these similar treaties is between the Hittite king Hattusili III and the Egyptian pharaoh Ramesses II. This treaty dates to 1259 BC, which makes it very close to the time of Moses, regardless of whether we place the exodus

---

[3] Kenneth A. Kitchen and Paul J. N. Lawrence, *Treaty, Law and Covenant in the Ancient Near East*, 3 vols. (Wiesbaden: Harrassowitz Verlag, 2012).

[4] Kitchen and Lawrence, 3:125.

at 1446 BC or 1270–1280 BC. Both the copy that the Hittites kept and the copy that the Egyptians kept have survived. Indeed, the Egyptian copy of this treaty was inscribed on the walls of the temple to Amon in the Karnak complex and on the walls of the Ramesseum mortuary temple, both in Thebes. Records of diplomatic correspondence from the court of Ramesses II indicate that this treaty was also read aloud publicly.[5] Although the other Hittite treaties of this era show a few slight variations, as does the book of Deuteronomy, the structure and content of Deuteronomy is remarkably akin to these Hittite treaties, as shown in table 5.1.[6]

Table 5.1: A Comparison of Deuteronomy and Hittite Treaties

Hittite Treaty Components[7]	Parallel Components in Deuteronomy
Title/preamble—identifies the parties of the treaty	1:1–5
Historical prologue—a description of past historical events that provide the legal or ideological basis for the treaty	1:6–3:29
Summary of laws/general stipulations	4–11
Specific laws/stipulations	12–26
Deposit of the document and reading instructions/witnesses	27:1–8 (stele with the written text; both a deposit of the document and a witness)
Ceremony with ritual oaths of obedience	27:1–26

---

[5] See the discussion in Gordon Johnston, "What Biblical Scholars Should Know about Hittite Treaties," in David C. Deuel, Richard S. Hess, and Richard E. Averbeck, eds., *Torah: Treaty, Law, and Ritual in the Hebrew Bible in Its Ancient Near Eastern Environment*, BBRSup (forthcoming, 2024).

[6] This chart has been developed from Kitchen and Lawrence, *Treaty, Law and Covenant*, 1:xxii–xxiv; 3:124. A similar but perhaps overly simplified chart was presented years ago by Meredith Kline in *Treaty of the Great King* (Grand Rapids: Eerdmans, 1963) and can also be seen in Joe M. Sprinkle, "Hittite Treaties and the Structure of Deuteronomy," *BIBH*, 109.

[7] While Deuteronomy contains the same components as the Hittite Treaties, the arranged order, identical in the first three categories, shows some variation in the order of later categories. Also, note that Deuteronomy cites three different witnesses (the public stele with written text, heavens and earth, the song of Moses) and places them in three different places.

Blessings	28:1–14
Curses	28:15–68
Epilogue (including oath)	29:1–31:8
Witnesses	30:19; 31:28 (heavens and earth)
Deposit of the document (usually in the temple) and reading instructions	31:9–30
Witnesses	31:30–32:47 (song)
No Hittite parallel	32:48–34:12 (death of Moses and his final blessings on the tribes of Israel)

This strongly suggests that Deuteronomy was written or at least "structured" in the second half of the second millennium BC. This fits with the range of dates we have proposed for Deuteronomy, assuming Mosaic authorship. It also suggests that as Yahweh presents the terms of his covenant with Israel, he places the written form of this covenant and its terms into a structured format that would have been recognizable as an international treaty or covenant format. It is quite likely that Moses, educated in the royal courts of Egypt, would have been familiar with such treaties.

While some of these treaties and covenants of the later second millennium BC are between kings who are somewhat equal (e.g., the Hittite king Hattusili III and the Egyptian pharaoh Ramesses II), most of them are between a more powerful lord or king (often referred to as the *suzerain*) and a less powerful person who is in a vassal-type relationship to the suzerain. In these treaties the powerful suzerain more or less dictates the terms by which he will protect the vassal. Often this requires that the vassal provide troops in time of war or promise not to attack their neighbors who are also under the suzerain's control. Remember that it is the format and structure that are parallel and not the details, which differ significantly in Yahweh's covenant treaty with Israel. These suzerainty treaties likewise follow the structure in table 5.1 but find even more parallels in Deuteronomy because the Yahweh-to-Israel relationship parallels the suzerain-to-vassal relationship in many regards. A few short excerpts from various suzerain-type Hittite treaties are offered here:

Title/preamble: "When the Sun-king, Suppliluliuma (I), the Great King, hero, the King of the Hatti-land . . . and Art[atam]la, King of the Hurri-land, concluded a treaty between them, at that time Tushratta,

King of the Mittani-land, showed hostility to the [Great] King, the King of the Hatti-land."[8]

Historical prologue: "When I reached the land of Nuhasse, I took over all of its territory. Sarrupsu went into hiding; (but) his mother, brothers, (and) his sons, I took captive and led away to the Hatti-land."[9]

Stipulations: "The people of the land of Hatti shall do nothing bad to the people of the land of Mittani, [and the people of the land of Mittani] shall do nothing bad to the people of the land of Hatti. . . . Do not be careless towards your treaty, do not seek (to extend) your border."[10]

Deposit of the document: "A duplicate of this tablet is deposited before the Sun-(goddess) of Ari[nn]a. . . . Also, in the land of Mitanni, (a copy) is deposited before the Storm-god. . . ."[11]

Witnesses: "We have invoked the gods of the secret and the gods who (are) lords of the oath. May they take their stand, take notice, and be witnesses. The Sun-(goddess) of Arinna . . . the Sun-god, Lord of heaven; Storm-god, Lord of Hatti; Seri. . . ."[12]

Curses: "Now if you, Ulmi-Tesub, do not observe the words of this tablet, and do not support me . . . then the Thousand gods shall blot out yourself, your wife, your offspring, your land, your house, your threshing-floor . . . and all your property."[13]

Blessings: "But if you observe the words of this tablet, and you support me . . . then shall these gods of the oath support yourself, your wife, your offspring, your land, your house, your threshing-floor . . . and all your property. And under the (good) hand of me, the Sun King, shall you live prosperously into old age!"[14]

---

[8] "Suppliluliuma I of Hatti and Shattiwaza of Mittani," in Kitchen and Lawrence, *Treaty, Law and Covenant*, 1:367.

[9] "Suppliluliuma I of Hatti and Shattiwaza of Mittani," 1:369.

[10] "Suppliluliuma I of Hatti and Shattiwaza of Mittani," 1:373, 375.

[11] "Suppliluliuma I of Hatti and Shattiwaza of Mittani," 1:377.

[12] "Suppliluliuma I of Hatti and Shattiwaza of Mittani," 1:377.

[13] "Tudkhalia IV of Hatti and Ulmi-Tesub of Tarhuntassa," in Kitchen and Lawrence, 1:639.

[14] "Tudkhalia IV of Hatti and Ulmi-Tesub of Tarhuntassa," 1:639.

Interpretive Overview

The First Speech of Moses: The Historical Prologue Reviewing the Recent Relationship between Yahweh and Israel (1:1–4:43)

INTRODUCTION (1:1–18)

The opening verses declare the nature of Deuteronomy—Moses is speaking to "all Israel," declaring everything that Yahweh has instructed him to say (1:1, 3). The phrase "all Israel" serves as an *inclusio*, occurring both in the opening verse of the book (1:1) and in the closing verse (34:12). The time frame given in 1:3 ("in the fortieth year") identifies Deuteronomy as the sequel to Numbers. Indeed, the defeat of Sihon and Og, described in Num 21:21–35, is cited in Deut 1:4 as an important preceding event.

In 1:6–8 Moses starts off his speech by reminding the Israelites that Yahweh had told them while back at Horeb/Mount Sinai (Horeb and Sinai refer to the same place and are used interchangeably; in Deuteronomy, Horeb is the preferred name) that he was giving them the land in fulfillment of his covenant promises to Abraham, Isaac, and Jacob. The land is a major theme in Deuteronomy; indeed, the Hebrew term translated as "land" occurs more than 125 times. Possessing the land is stressed as the fulfillment of the Abrahamic covenant promise in the opening chapter (Deut 1:8) and in the closing chapter (34:4). In 1:9–18 Moses references the appointment of leadership to assist him (see Exod 18:13–26), but the point here seems to have been to remind them that "the LORD your God has so multiplied you that today you are as numerous as the stars of the sky," once again citing a fulfillment of Yahweh's promise to Abraham and the patriarchs (1:10; Gen 15:5; 22:17; 26:4). This fulfillment continues to drive the story, as it has been doing throughout the Pentateuch since Genesis 12.

IN SPITE OF THEIR REBELLION, YAHWEH WAS WITH THE ISRAELITES DURING THE FORTY YEARS OF WILDERNESS WANDERING (1:19–3:29)

Moses next recounts the terrible events of Numbers 13–14, when Israel refused to obey Yahweh and go into the Promised Land. Because of this disobedience, Israel was sent out into the wilderness to wander for forty years until that disobedient generation died off (1:19–2:23).

Yet Yahweh in his grace did not abandon them. Moses reminds them that Yahweh "has watched over your journey through this immense wilderness. The LORD your God has been with you these past forty years, and you have lacked nothing" (2:7).

The powerful presence of Yahweh has sustained and protected Israel, even as they wandered in the wilderness.

Moses then reminds Israel of their recent defeat of two powerful kings, Sihon and Og (2:24–3:11). Note that these two victories were ones that his current audience (the new generation) had experienced. While their parents had seen the spectacular victory of Yahweh over Egypt, the current Israelite adults had been only children then (or not yet born). But the victories over Sihon and Og were ones they personally experienced and were still fresh in their minds. Thus, Moses mentions those victories twice (1:4; 2:24–3:11).

Moses also lets Israel know that he will not be able to go into the land with them but that Joshua will follow him as their leader and take them into the land. He mentions this twice as well (1:37–38; 3:21–28).

A Current Call to Obey Yahweh—to Enter the Land and Faithfully Keep His Commandments (4:1–43)

After summarizing the previous forty years, Moses moves to the present and exhorts Israel to obey Yahweh *now* and to be obedient by entering the land (4:1–40). Terms relating to "today" or "now" are used throughout this section (4:1, 20, 39, 40). In 4:1–8 Moses points to the benefits of obedience, especially the wonderful life in the land that lies ahead. Indeed, "that you may live . . . in the land" opens and closes the entire unit in an *inclusio* (4:1, 40). He also underscores that Israel's relationship with Yahweh is to be a testimony to the nations (4:6–8), highlighting that the purpose of Yahweh in giving this *torah* to Israel had an important missiological component, in accordance with his promise that through Abraham there would be blessings to the nations and to "all the peoples on earth" (Gen 12:3; 18:18). In 4:9–31 Israel is warned about the danger of idolatry, and the importance of teaching their children and grandchildren to be faithful is stressed.

Several other important themes run throughout this section. The dramatic encounter with Yahweh at Mount Sinai/Horeb (Exodus 19, 24) is revisited (Deut 4:10–15; 32–36). The important creed-like statement of Yahweh being the one who brought Israel up out of Egypt is repeated twice (4:20, 37). The importance and uniqueness of Yahweh's close personal presence with Israel is underscored (4:7, 29–31, 36–37). Throughout this unit Moses provides insight into the character of Yahweh, mentioning such things as his anger and his jealousy (4:21, 24), his compassion and mercy (4:31), his love (4:37), and his rule over heaven and earth (4:36–39). The Ten Commandments (Hebrew, "the ten words") are referenced in 4:13 in the context of the encounter at Mount Sinai/Horeb as being the essence of the covenant. Revisiting Yahweh's history with the Israelites as their great deliverer and sovereign ruler underscores the fact that Yahweh's relationship with his people is not, and will not be, based on just warm, fuzzy feelings, but is grounded in his historical acts of deliverance, the concrete demonstration of his covenant loyalty.

This unit serves to close out the opening historical prologue and call to obedience and to introduce the Ten Commandments, which will be presented in the next chapter. Indeed, the essence of 4:1–40 is an expansion and more detailed explanation of the first two of the Ten Commandments (5:6–8).

WORD STUDY
THE "COMMANDMENT" TERMINOLOGY OF DEUTERONOMY

Deuteronomy 4:1–8 employs all six central Hebrew words that are used throughout Deuteronomy dozens of times to refer to the terms of the covenant that Yahweh is revealing to Israel through Moses. (These terms are also quite frequent in Psalms; Psalm 119 uses all six of these words repeatedly.)

> "Now, Israel, listen to the **statutes** [*hoq*] and **ordinances** [*mishpat*] I am **teaching** [*lamad*] you to follow, so that you may live, enter, and take possession of the land the LORD, the God of your ancestors, is giving you. You must not add anything to **what I command** [*dabar* and *tsavah*; i.e., the "words that I command"] you or take anything away from it, so that you may keep the **commands** [*mitsvah*] of the LORD your God I am giving you." (4:1–2)

> "Look, I have **taught** [*lamad*] you **statutes** [*hoq*] and **ordinances** [*mishpat*] as the LORD my God has **commanded** [*tsavah*] me." (4:5)

> "What great nation has righteous **statutes** [*hoq*] and **ordinances** [*mishpat*] like this **entire law** [*torah*] I set before you today?" (4:8)

The Hebrew term *hoq* (occurring twenty-one times in Deuteronomy) refers to a decree or statute issued by a high authority such as a king. *Mishpat* (occurring thirty-seven times in Deuteronomy) has more of a legal connotation; that is, it implies a judgment, a decision in a case, or a statement of justice. In the human realm this ruling could come from a king, a judge, or someone else in authority (e.g., Deut 16:18–20). In Deuteronomy these two words are repeatedly paired together (4:1, 5, 8, 14; 5:1, 31; 6:1, 20; 7:11; 11:32; 12:1; 26:16–17) and used as an umbrella-like phrase to refer to an inclusive, wide range of material Yahweh presents through Moses to Israel concerning Israel's expected behavior and lifestyle.

The verb *tsavah* simply means "to command," and the associated noun *mitsvah* means "commandment." These two words stress the point that all these terms of the covenant in Deuteronomy are to be obeyed. They are not suggestions; they are commandments from Yahweh. These two related terms (*tsavah* and *mitsvah*) are used more widely than *hoq* and *mishpat*, with the verb *tsavah* occurring in Deuteronomy eighty-eight times and the noun *mitsvah* occurring forty-six times. Sometimes *mitsvah* is added to the pair (*hoq* and *mishpat*) to create a triad, likewise referring to and including large portions of Deuteronomy (e.g., 8:11). In this case, when *mitsvah* is used with the other two terms (*hoq* and *mishpat*), sometimes *mitsvah* appears first, in singular form ("*the* commandment"), followed by the plurals of *hoq* and *mishpat*, implying that *mitsvah* can serve as an inclusive singular summary of the other two in their plurality (e.g., 6:1, "This is the **command**—the **statutes** and **ordinances**—the Lord your God has **commanded** me to teach you").

Likewise stressing that these statutes, ordinances, and commands come from Yahweh (via Moses) is the frequent use of *dabar* ("word") in these contexts. Recall that Deuteronomy opens with "These are the **words**" (1:1). Furthermore, the Ten Commandments are referred to as "the ten **words**" (4:13; 10:4; many English translations render these as "the Ten Commandments," but the Hebrew word is the plural of *dabar*, thus, "the ten words"). In addition, as we will see, the plural of *dabar* is often connected to *torah* ("the words of the *torah*").

Frequently appearing in the same context as the terms for words, statutes, ordinances, and commandments is the Hebrew word *lamad*, which means "to teach" or "to learn" (e.g., 4:1, 5, 10, 14; 5:1, 31; 6:1; 17:19). This underscores that these words of Yahweh—the statutes, ordinances, and commandments—are to be taught and learned. That is, they are not to be left isolated, inscribed into stone, but incorporated into their lives and their character.

Related to the emphasis on teaching and learning is the use in Deuteronomy of *torah*, which often means "teaching" or "instruction."[15] Likewise, as noted earlier, in Deuteronomy *torah* is often connected with the plural of *dabar* ("words") in the phrase "the words of the *torah*" (17:19; 27:3, 8, 26; 28:58; 31:12). In

---

[15] For a discussion on the use of *torah* in Deuteronomy see García López, "*Tôrâ*," *TDOT* XV:640–45. For a good, general discussion on *torah* see Martin J. Selman, "Law," in *Dictionary of the Old Testament: Pentateuch*, 497–515.

addition, the word *torah* is closely associated with the other terms (*hoq, mishpat, mitsvah*) and is sometimes used as a summary or a collection word that includes the others (e.g., 4:8; 30:10). In Deut 1:5 (at the beginning) and in 31:9–12 (toward the end) *torah* is a "comprehensive expression for what Moses wrote."[16] The "teaching, instruction" meaning is still there, but throughout Deuteronomy the stress is that this teaching, the very word of Yahweh, is authoritative *and must be obeyed*. Thus, the teaching aspect of *torah* takes the concept of statutes, ordinances, and commandments from being merely rules and guidelines in a law collection and adds the understanding that these statutes, ordinances, and commandments are to be grasped and understood, integrated into all of life to build the foundational character of the people of Yahweh (cf. Ps 1:2).

The Second Speech of Moses: The Covenant Terms by Which the Israelites Can Live in the Promised Land with Yahweh in Their Midst and Find Rich Blessings (4:44–28:68)

INTRODUCTION (4:44–49)

Deuteronomy 4:44–45 summarizes the unit that follows by stating, "This is the law [*torah*] Moses gave the Israelites. These are the decrees, statutes, and ordinances Moses proclaimed to them after they came out of Egypt." As discussed above, note that the Hebrew word translated as "law" is *torah*, and it normally carries nuances of "teaching" or "instruction."

The recent victories over Sihon and Og are mentioned again, for the third time, in Deuteronomy (see 1:4; 2:24–3:11). These Yahweh-empowered victories occurred in Numbers 21 but are mentioned several times in Deuteronomy (see also 29:7; 31:4) because they represent the best recent direct evidence of how Yahweh could give the Israelites victory.

BASIC PRINCIPLES AND PRIVILEGES OF THE COVENANT RELATIONSHIP (5:1–11:32)

The Ten Commandments (5:1–32)

The Ten Commandments form a basic foundational summary for the entire collection of "decrees, statutes, and ordinances" that follow in Deuteronomy 6–26. Likewise,

---

[16] García, 642.

it was this text, the Ten Commandments, that Yahweh delivered to the Israelites from out of the fire at Mount Sinai and that Yahweh himself wrote down, as Moses reminds Israel in Deut 5:22. Thus it is appropriate for them to be presented first, at the head of the covenant stipulations.

In Deut 5:1–5 Moses stresses that this covenant, integrally related to these commandments, is not just a covenant made with their parents (the previous generation), but one made with them (the current generation). Once again, "today" is the focus (5:3).

Moses presents 5:6–21 as a direct quote from Yahweh. In 5:6 Yahweh identifies himself as "I am the LORD [Yahweh] your God, who brought you out of the land of Egypt, out of the place of slavery." This creed-like statement appears not only throughout Deuteronomy but throughout the rest of the Old Testament. It is, in fact, one of Yahweh's favorite self-identifying statements of who he is. That is, his identity with regard to his relationship with Israel is tied to the exodus, Yahweh's great act of gracious deliverance and salvation. Furthermore, his call to obey him and to keep his commandments, as presented in the following verses, is grounded on the fact that he is the one who saved them and delivered them from slavery in Egypt.

The first commandment is "Do not have other gods besides me" (5:7), a significant and foundational starting point, for central to the entire covenant is Yahweh's insistence on absolute loyalty and faithfulness to him alone. This is a major theme throughout Deuteronomy, and it sets the tone for the remaining Ten Commandments and the rest of the book.

The Ten Commandments presented in Deut 5:6–21 are almost identical to the Ten Commandments revealed earlier in Exod 20:1–17 (see the discussion in chapter 2 for additional explanation on specific commandments). The first four of the Ten Commandments specify how the Israelites were to relate to Yahweh, while the following six commandments give guidance for how they were to relate to each other. One important difference between the Ten Commandments in Exod 20:1–17 and in Deut 5:6–21 concerns the Sabbath observance (the fourth commandment). Exodus 20:8–11 connects the Sabbath rest to Yahweh's rest after his great act of creation. Deuteronomy 5:12–15 relates Sabbath obedience to Yahweh's deliverance of Israel from slavery in Egypt. Both accounts stress that the Sabbath is holy.

Running throughout the Ten Commandments, in both Exod 20:1–17 and Deut 5:6–21, is the undergirding stress on faithfulness—to Yahweh, to neighbors, to spouses, to parents, and to people in general. Both accounts state that Yahweh wrote down the Ten Commandments on two stone tablets (twice, actually, since Moses broke the first set), and this is declared repeatedly throughout Deuteronomy and Exodus (Deut 4:13; 5:22; 9:9–17; 10:1–5; Exod 24:12; 31:18; 32:15–16; 34:1–5, 27–28). The mention of two tablets probably does not mean that the Ten Commandments are split up onto two tablets (i.e., commandments 1 through 5 on one and 6 through 10 on the other, as popularly depicted) but that there were two copies made, in keeping with the practice in the ANE of making two copies of important treaties, one for each member of the treaty.[17]

The Israelites Are Called to Love Yahweh, Worship Him Only, Obey His Commandments, and Never Forget That He Is the One Who Brought Them Out of Egypt (6:1–10:11)

In this section Moses looks to the future after Israel has taken possession of the land, and he challenges Israel to stay faithful to worship Yahweh and him alone. In essence Moses is expanding on practical aspects of keeping the first commandment ("Do not have other gods besides me").

In Deut 6:4–5, at the beginning of this section and providing clear overall basic orientation, is the famous Jewish prayer known as the Shema: "Hear, O Israel: The LORD our God, the LORD is one. Love the LORD your God with all your heart and with all your soul and with all your strength" (NIV). The title *Shema* comes from the first Hebrew word in 6:4 (*shema*), which means "to hear and to obey." This verse is no doubt the most quoted Old Testament passage in modern Judaism. Traditionally, Jews are to recite this verse every morning and evening.

Deuteronomy 6:4–5 is both an affirmation of who Yahweh is and a call to love and obey him with all of one's being. Note that in Hebrew the word for "heart" (*lebab*) is used here figuratively, not so much as the seat of emotion, as in English, but as the seat of volitional decision-making. The idea conveyed is "Love the LORD your God with all your decision-making."

As in Deuteronomy 4, the importance of teaching these commandments to their children and passing true faith in Yahweh to each successive generation is stressed (6:7–9, 20–25). Much of the material in 6:1–9 is also repeated in Deut 11:1–20.

---

[17] Johnston, "What Biblical Scholars Should Know about Hittite Treaties."

CONTEMPORARY CONNECTIONS: CURRENT JEWISH USE OF *TEFILLIN* AND *MEZUZOT*

In Deut 6:6–8, to assist with remembering the commandments of Yahweh and in passing that faith to the next generation, Moses states, "These words. . . . Bind them as a sign on your hand and let them be a symbol on your forehead." While Moses is probably speaking figuratively, Judaism has traditionally taken it quite literally, as many Orthodox Jews do today. Before they begin their prayers, many adult Jewish males will strap on *tefillin*, two small black leather pouches, one for the forehead and one for the forearm. These pouches are filled with rolled-up texts from the Torah, typically Exod 13:1–10; 13:11–16; Deut 6:4–9; and 11:13–21. Similarly, Moses tells Israel, "Write them on the doorposts of your house" (6:9). In Jewish tradition today, many homes have a small, thin box (called *mezuzah*; plur., *mezuzot*) mounted on their doorframes. Rolled up and placed inside this box are small pieces of parchment with Deut 6:4–9 and 11:13–21 written on them.

Recall our word study of "good" (*tov*) and "evil/bad" (*ra'*) in Genesis, and recall the repeated use of "good" (*tov*) in Genesis 1. This theme is picked up in Deut 6:18, where *tov* occurs three times: "Do what is right and good [*tov*] in the Lord's sight, so that you may prosper [*tov*; i.e., be good for you] and so that you may enter and possess the good [*tov*] land the Lord your God swore to give your ancestors." Implications continue throughout Deuteronomy that moving into the abundant, fruitful Promised Land has symbolic allusions of returning to the garden of Eden, a "good" (*tov*) place where once again Yahweh's people will be living near his presence.[18]

In Deut 7:6 Moses reminds the Israelites that they are a treasured possession to Yahweh, chosen and holy (recalling Exod 19:4–6). To stay holy and special, it will be important that they not intermarry with the pagan inhabitants of the land, for such intermarriages will introduce pagan gods into the family (7:1–6; see esp. 7:4). Note that the issue here is theological difference and not ethnic difference. The Israelites were forbidden to marry people who did not worship Yahweh exclusively; race or

---

[18] Duvall and Hays, *God's Relational Presence*, 56 (see chap. 1, n. 4); Daniel I. Block, "A Place for My Name: Horeb and Zion in the Mosaic Vision of Israelite Worship," *JETS* 58 (2015): 244; Oren Martin, *Bound for the Promised Land: The Land Promise in God's Redemptive Plan*, NSBT 34 (Nottingham, UK: Apollos, 2015), 83–86.

ethnicity was not a criterion. In fact, ethnically speaking, outside of religion, the Canaanites were rather close to the Israelites. Both groups spoke similar languages, and they were probably indistinguishable in appearance.

Although introduced in Deut 6:10–12, in Deuteronomy 8 Moses warns once again that after the Israelites move into the Promised Land and enjoy the rich prosperity of the land, they will be tempted to forget Yahweh and to worship the gods of their pagan neighbors. Indeed, the theme of "do not forget Yahweh" and "Remember Yahweh" runs throughout this section (6:12; 8:2, 11, 14, 18, 19; 9:7). The grim consequences of forgetting Yahweh and turning to other gods are cited as well (8:19–20).

In Deuteronomy 9 Moses explains that Israel was not chosen as a special people by Yahweh because of their righteousness or due to anything that they have done. They were chosen only because of his love and good grace. The Canaanites, likewise, are being driven out due to their own wickedness, not due to Israel's righteousness (9:4–6). As an example of their unworthy behavior, Moses recounts the terrible golden calf episode of Exodus 32, reminding the Israelites that only due to his intercession and Yahweh's gracious compassion was judgment on them averted (9:7–10:11).

Summary of the Covenant Situation: The Israelites Are to Love and Obey Yahweh, for Obedience Results in Blessings in the Land While Disobedience Results in a Curse (10:12–11:32)

This section reiterates the call for Israel to love Yahweh and to serve him obediently, further demonstrating the close connection between loving Yahweh and obeying him. In 10:14–19 Moses stresses that not only is Yahweh a great and awesome God but that he loves and cares about the well-being of all people, including vulnerable people described by the triad of the fatherless, the widow, and the residing foreigner (10:17–18).

Throughout this larger unit are repeated allusions to Yahweh's fulfillment of the covenant with Abraham, Isaac, and Jacob (6:10, 23; 7:8, 12–14; 9:27). Deuteronomy 10:22 continues to reference the fulfillment of this covenant, noting that when Israel's ancestors went into Egypt, they were but seventy in number but that now they are "numerous, like the stars of the sky" (cf. Gen 15:5; 22:17; 26:4).

Deuteronomy 11 wraps up this large section (Deuteronomy 5–11) by repeating and summarizing much of what has been stated in earlier chapters. Once again Israel is called to love Yahweh, obey his commandments, and worship him only. Once again, the current generation about to go into the Promised Land is exhorted to pass the faith on to their children. The choice Israel has before them—obedience or disobedience, especially as it regards worshipping Yahweh alone or worshipping other gods—has serious consequences and will result in either blessings (if they are obedient) or curses (if they are disobedient). Yahweh tells them that after they enter the land, they will gather on Mount Gerizim and Mount Ebal and proclaim both the blessings and the curses aloud. Much of this material on blessings and curses, including the exhortation to make the blessing and curses proclamation on the two mountains, is repeated in Deuteronomy 27–28. In Joshua 8 the Israelites obediently make this proclamation on those two mountains.

ANCIENT CONNECTIONS SIDEBAR 5.2: WHO CONTROLS THE RAIN?

Although the Canaanites currently living in the land worshipped a pantheon of gods, one of the primary gods they venerated was Baal, a fertility god who, they believed, had control over thunderstorms and thus over rainfall.[19] This characterization of Baal is evident in the Baal Myth (from Ugarit), which states:

> For now Baʿlu [Baal] (can) send his rain in due season,
> Send the season of driving showers;
> (can) Baʿlu [Baal] shout aloud in the clouds,
> Shoot (his) lightning-bolts to the earth.[20]

Worship of Baal, the Canaanites maintained, was required to guarantee adequate rainfall, and therefore proper veneration of Baal was essential to any successful agricultural activity. Once in the land, most of the Israelites will become farmers, making them dependent on rainfall. Yahweh lets them know up front that if they worship him alone, trusting him instead of Baal to provide the rain, it will rain abundantly. If, on the other hand, the Israelites turn to Baal to provide rain, worshipping him instead of Yahweh, then they will see only drought. Indeed, rainfall versus drought is one of the central aspects of the blessings versus curses that Yahweh declares (Deut 11:10–17; 28:12, 24). This reality will be played out in some detail later in Israel's history in 1 Kings 17–18 when King Ahab, king of Israel, makes Baal his primary god. In accordance with Deuteronomy, the prophet Elijah consequently proclaims a major drought, which devastates the land. After Yahweh demonstrates his power over Baal on Mount Carmel—that Yahweh is God and Baal is nothing—and after the people obediently destroy the prophets of Baal, the drought ends and it rains.

---

[19] Catherine L. McDowell, "The Canaanites and Canaanite Religion," *BIBH*, 29–30.
[20] "The Baʿlu Myth," trans. Dennis Pardee, *COS* 1.86:260.

SPECIFIC PRINCIPLES AND DETAILS OF THE COVENANT RELATIONSHIP (12:1–26:19)

Israel Is Called to Worship Yahweh Exclusively and Joyfully (12:1–13:18)

Having reviewed the history between Yahweh and Israel, followed by the presentation of the most basic principles and stipulations of the covenant intertwined continuously with the call to obedience, Moses now expands on those basic principles and stipulations, adding more details and examples that relate to the covenant Yahweh is renewing with Israel. In general, the discussion in Deuteronomy 12–26 roughly follows the order of the Ten Commandments given in Deuteronomy 5. Deuteronomy 12:1–13:18, for example, expands on the implications of the first three commandments, discussing who Yahweh is and how he is to be worshipped.

While the Canaanites had high places, sacred trees, and other worship sites scattered across the land, the Israelites are commanded to destroy all of these and to worship Yahweh alone, only at the place he would specify and at which he would dwell (12:1–7). This stress on location underscores the continuing connection between worship and the presence of Yahweh. Throughout Deuteronomy 12 are several references to a specific place Yahweh will choose as a dwelling for his name (12:5, 11, 21). Later in the biblical story we learn that this place will be Jerusalem. Note that throughout this chapter, proper worship is to be done joyfully in the very presence of Yahweh (12:7, 12, 18), who currently dwells in the tabernacle, but who will later dwell in the temple. Thus, the use of "name" does not suggest a replacement of the real, intense presence of Yahweh with some esoteric and vague concept of Yahweh who really dwells only in heaven. Yahweh still will dwell in the tabernacle and then later in the temple in a real and intense manner, and it is there that all worship of Israel is to be directed. The addition of the term *name* adds additional connotations of presence (recall Exodus 3 and 6, where his name *Yahweh* is explained) and probably also suggests nuances of ownership.[21]

Idolatry is extremely serious, Yahweh declares throughout Deuteronomy 13. All advocates of the false gods that might tempt Israel to turn away from Yahweh must be removed, including false prophets (13:1–5), close relatives (13:6–11), or even an entire village or town (13:12–18).

---

[21] Duvall and Hays, *God's Relational Presence*, 50–54 (see chap. 1, n. 4); Sandra L. Richter, *The Deuteronomistic History and the Name Theology*, BZAW 318 (Berlin: De Gruyter, 2002); and "The Place of the Name in Deuteronomy," VT 57 (2007): 342–66.

The Specifics of Worship—Clean and Unclean Food, Tithing, Canceling Debts, Freeing Servants, Holy Days, and Festivals (14:1–16:17)

In Deut 14:1–21 Moses reminds the Israelites that they are a holy people (14:2) and that this status as holy will affect how and what they eat. The rest of this section then discusses clean and unclean foods (similar to Lev 11:1–47). The point is that Yahweh, and not the surrounding culture, will determine what is clean and what is not clean. Furthermore, the purpose of these rules seems to be to keep the Israelites conscious at all times of their holy status (14:2, 21).

The fourth commandment (Sabbath observance) is the basic foundational principle that is expanded on in Deut 14:22–16:17. In these verses Yahweh explains that life for the Israelites in covenant with him is to be governed by similar "holy rhythms." Not only weekly Sabbath observance is required but also regularly scheduled tithing (14:22–29). The Israelites are to set aside one-tenth of the produce from their fields and herds as a tithe (14:22). Furthermore, 14:23–26 specifies that each Israelite family is to eat this tithe joyfully as a special meal in the presence of Yahweh. The Israelites are also reminded to use this tithe to help support the Levites, who do not have much inherited land on which to grow crops. Every three years (again, note the cyclical rhythm), the Israelites are to bring their tithe (crops and animals) together and store it in their towns, using it to support the Levites and to feed the vulnerable underclass, defined by the familiar triad of residing foreigners, the fatherless, and widows (14:28–29; 26:12–13).

Repeating some material from Exodus and Leviticus, Deut 15:1–16:17 continues to lay out the regularly scheduled rhythms of life for Yahweh's people. This included regularly scheduled cancellation of debts and provision for the poor (15:1–8), the regular annual sacrifice of firstborn animals (15:19–23), and the celebration of three annual worship festivals—the Passover, the Festival of Weeks, and the Festival of Shelters (16:1–17). When compared with Exodus, two new emphases emerge from this unit: (1) all of these sacrifices and activities must be done at the place Yahweh chooses for his name (16:2, 6, 7, 11, 15); and (2) the command not to come before Yahweh empty-handed that was applied to the Festival of Unleavened Bread (Exod 23:15) is now applied to the Festival of Unleavened Bread, the Festival of Weeks, and the Festival of Shelters (Deut 16:16–17).

The Proper Function of Legitimate Human Authorities (16:18–18:22)

In this section Moses focuses on human authorities. The fifth of the Ten Commandments (honoring parents) dealt with the most basic, fundamental authority under which one lived. Here in this unit Moses now expands the understanding of living under authority by discussing other authority structures—judges and courts (16:18–17:13); the king (17:14–20, still future at the time of Moses); priests and Levites (18:1–8); those who engage in prohibited occultic practices (18:9–14); and prophets (18:15–22).

Yahweh is concerned that Israel's legal system carry out true justice for all people, regardless of social or economic status (16:18–17:13). He himself provides the model (10:17–18), for Yahweh "shows no partiality and accepts no bribes. He defends the cause of the fatherless and the widow, and loves the foreigner residing among you" (NIV). Based on his model of justice, he tells the judges of Israel, "Do not deny justice or show partiality to anyone. Do not accept a bribe. . . . Pursue justice and justice alone" (16:19–20; see 1:16–17). In a later section (19:15–21), Yahweh underscores that in trials, judges must investigate the crime thoroughly, corroborating multiple witnesses, and punishing any witnesses who lie.

In Deut 17:14–20, Moses, anticipating the future monarchy, lays out Yahweh's guidelines for choosing the king and for how the king should live. First, the king must be an Israelite, especially one whom Yahweh himself chooses. Then Moses lists three basic prohibitions guiding how the king should live, all three of which were in stark contrast to the regular practices of monarchs across the ANE:

1. The king must not acquire a great number of horses, especially from Egypt. (This is probably a reference to having a large standing chariot army, as the Egyptians did.)
2. The king must not accumulate numerous wives. (Ramesses II, for example, had eight royal wives and a large number of lesser wives—some estimate 200 to 300. He fathered over 110 sons who lived to adulthood.)[22]
3. The king must not accumulate large quantities of silver and gold for himself.

Later in Israel's history, King Solomon will violate all three basic royal prohibitions, in addition to leading the people into idolatry (1 Kgs 10:14–11:13).[23]

As mediator between Yahweh and the people, as well as the one who spoke the very words of Yahweh, Moses is the model of a true prophet. In 18:15–22 Moses explains that one is a true prophet if what he prophesies in the name of Yahweh comes

---

[22] "Rameses' Queens," in *Egypt: Land and Lives of the Pharaohs Revealed*, ed. Belinda Bollinger et al. (Willoughby, AU: Global, 2005), 364–65.

[23] See Hays, "Has the Narrator Come to Praise Solomon or to Bury Him?," 149–74 (see chap. 2, n. 34).

true. Moses then prophesies that Yahweh would raise up another prophet like himself who will also speak the words of Yahweh, conveying his commandments to Israel. This sets the pattern for all the true biblical prophets to come (Elijah, Elisha, Isaiah, Jeremiah, etc.) and is ultimately fulfilled by Jesus Christ himself.

Issues Related to Killing, Especially Murder and War (19:1–21:9)

The sixth commandment was the prohibition of murder, and Deut 19:1–21:9 deals with numerous issues related to killing people. It includes a provision of refuge cities to protect those who commit accidental homicides (19:1–13). Continuing the theme of justice and impartiality, next comes a discussion on the importance of honest testimony in court, corroborated by multiple witnesses (19:15–21). Deuteronomy 20:1–20 describes the rules for warfare, in particular the rules for besieging and capturing cities. The rules for capturing cities in the land, where the Israelites would settle, are different (much harsher) than the rules for capturing cities outside of the land. This reiterates the warning that the people in the land posed a serious threat of leading the Israelites away from Yahweh. This section concludes with a discussion of how to deal with unsolved murders (21:1–9).

ANCIENT CONNECTIONS SIDEBAR 5.3: LAW COLLECTIONS IN THE ANCIENT NEAR EAST

Available in museums around the world today are the literary records of countless law codes and collections that were written in Mesopotamia in the 500-plus years before Moses. This includes Ur-Namma (c. 2100 BC) and Lipit-Ishtar (c. 1930 BC), written in Sumerian, and the Laws of Eshnunna (c. 1770 BC), the Laws of Hammurabi (c. 1750 BC), and the Hittite Laws (c. 1650–1500 BC), written in Akkadian. These collections did not function like our modern law codes do today in that they were not primarily provided as guidelines for judges in the courtroom. They did "provide models of judicial wisdom" and were used by the monarchs who sponsored them to demonstrate their judicial wisdom and thus to legitimize their reigns,[24] both before the gods and their subjects.

Many of the laws and guidelines in Deuteronomy, especially regarding things such as marriage and marriage violations, inheritance issues, murder, and

---

[24] Roy E. Gane, *Old Testament Law for Christians: Original Context and Enduring Application* (Grand Rapids: Baker, 2017), 126.

property damage find similar parallels in the law collections of the ANE. Thus it appears that in some cases Yahweh was often drawing on widely accepted norms of behavior. For example, consider the following "laws" from the Laws of Hammurabi:

> If a man destroy the eye of another man, they shall destroy his eye. If one break a man's bone, they shall break his bone. . . . If a man knock out a tooth of a man of his own rank, they shall knock out his tooth.[25] (Compare Deut 19:19–21; Lev 24:19–20.)

> If a man comes forward to give false testimony in a case but cannot bring evidence for his accusation, if that case involves a capital offense, that man shall be killed.[26] (Compare Deut 19:15–21.)

On the other hand, the collection of laws and guidelines in Exodus, Leviticus, Numbers, and Deuteronomy reflect some significant differences from the other law collections in the ANE as well. The Old Testament laws are given to Israel in the context of being the terms of the covenant that they had with their one God, Yahweh. Thus, this teaching (the *torah*) presented in the rules and guidelines also reflects the morality that the one God Yahweh desires for his people, a morality that he himself reflects in his own character. This is without parallel in the ANE.[27]

Marriage and Family Issues (21:10–22:30)

The seventh commandment prohibited adultery, and in 21:10–22:30 Moses addresses various issues related to marriage and family, some of which also overlap with the previous sections dealing with family (honoring parents) and killing (prohibition against murder). The first issue presented is how to marry a woman who is captured after a battle (21:10–14). In general, this guideline focuses on protecting the captured woman. That is, she is to be treated as a wife, not as a slave. Also, the fact that Moses addresses how one can marry a captured woman underscores the fact that interethnic

---

[25] Robert Francis Harper, ed. and trans., *The Code of Hammurabi: King of Babylon about 2250 B.C.* (Chicago: University of Chicago Press, 1904), 196–97, 200.

[26] "The Laws of Hammurabi," trans. Martha Roth, *COS*, 2.131:337.

[27] Gane, *Old Testament Law for Christians*, 129. For a list of additional differences, see Gane, 129–33.

marriage is not prohibited—all these captured women would be ethnically different from the Israelites—but only intermarriage with the Canaanite inhabitants of the land is prohibited, especially when the Canaanites continue to maintain their pagan practices and beliefs. The rest of this unit covers inheritance rights of the firstborn (21:15–17), how to deal with rebellious sons (21:18–21), guidelines for executing convicted murderers (21:22–23), the responsibility everyone has for caring for the welfare of others (22:1–4), the importance of maintaining natural distinctions (22:5–12), and inappropriate sexual actions and relationships (22:13–30).

Miscellaneous Laws (23:1–26:19)

The eighth commandment (prohibition of stealing) and the tenth commandment (prohibition of coveting) are at the core of building an unselfish community that seeks the well-being of everyone. This seems to be the unifying factor in several of the guidelines and stipulations in this section. Yet the collection is quite diverse, and some of the texts appear to relate to some of the other commandments as well. The major issues discussed in this unit are acceptance and exclusion from the worshipping assembly (23:1–8); ritual uncleanness (23:9–14); runaway slaves (23:15–16); temple prostitution (23:17–18); interest on loans (23:19–20); making vows (23:21–23); eating your neighbors' produce in the field (23:24–25); divorce (24:1–4); securities required for loans (24:6, 10–13); care and justice for the hired worker, the poor, and the residing foreigner (24:14–22); appropriate punishment for guilty people (25:1–3); compassion on working animals (25:4); levirate marriage—that is, when a man dies, his brother is to marry his widow (25:5–10);[28] honesty in commercial dealings (25:13–16); an exhortation to remember and avenge the treachery of the Amalekites (25:17–19);[29] and tithing out of one's firstfruits—once again including food provisions for the orphans, widows, and residing foreigners, as well as the Levites (26:1–15). This section concludes with the now-familiar call to keep Yahweh's commandments with all one's heart and soul, along with Yahweh's promise to honor Israel above all the nations if they do (26:16–19).

As part of the firstfruits offering, the Israelites are to recite a creed-like statement in the presence of Yahweh, provided in 26:5–10. This statement summarizes their

---

[28] Note how this plays out in the book of Ruth, including the hearing at the gate and the exchange of sandals.

[29] This recalls the events in Exod 17:8–13, restating Exod 17:14. These texts will also echo into the story of 1 Samuel 15 and 1 Samuel 30.

salvation history, starting with Abraham ("my father was a wandering Aramean"), focusing on Yahweh's great salvific act of delivering them from Egypt and bringing them into the bountiful promised land.

JUSTICE AND CARE FOR THE ORPHAN, THE WIDOW, AND THE RESIDING FOREIGNER

The book of Deuteronomy consistently identifies those who were vulnerable in the society with a repeated triad of terms: "the orphan, the widow, and the residing foreigner." The Hebrew word the CSB translates as "resident alien" is *gēr*, a term that refers to someone from a different ethnic and geographical group who was temporarily residing or perhaps migrating into or through the land. Likewise, during the exodus and the wandering period, these people lived among the Israelites and traveled with them. The NIV translates this term as "foreigner," while ESV translates it as "sojourner." As mentioned previously, we have opted to translate this throughout this book as "residing foreigner." Normally, within Israel, the *gēr* did not own land. These three groups tended to be at a socioeconomic and legal disadvantage within the typical power structures of the ancient world, where land ownership, being part of the local ethnic majority, and having a local, established family patriarch were critical components in exerting and protecting one's rights. Deuteronomy addresses this specific triad six times (10:17–18; 14:28–29; 16:11–14; 24:14–22; 26:1–15; and 27:19), underscoring their importance in Yahweh's plan for how Israel should live in the Promised Land.

The instruction starts by revealing Yahweh's character and his attitude toward these three groups of people. Moses declares:

> "For the LORD your God is the God of gods and Lord of lords, the great, mighty, and awe-inspiring God, showing no partiality and taking no bribe. He executes justice for the fatherless and the widow, and loves the resident alien, giving him food and clothing. You are also to love the resident alien, since you were resident aliens in the land of Egypt." (10:17–19)

Yahweh uses himself as the model for his people to follow. He shows no partiality or favoritism in his care for this vulnerable group. In fact, he *loves* the residing foreigner and takes care of him. The implication is that Yahweh wants his people to act as he does toward this group.

Several texts in Deuteronomy stress the provision of food and the inclusion of this triad in the rituals and festivals that involved meals. The Levites, who also did not have land, are sometimes included along with this triad, when food is involved. In Deut 14:28–29 and 26:12–13 Yahweh tells the Israelites to take the tithe from every third year and store it in their towns to provide for the Levites, along with providing for the residing foreigner, the orphan, and the widow. In Deut 16:9–15 Yahweh tells the Israelites to celebrate the Festival of Weeks and the Festival of Shelters with joy, along with the residing foreigner, the orphan, and the widow (16:11, 14).

Deuteronomy 24:14 warns the Israelites against taking advantage of hired workers, whether they are resident aliens or local Israelites. Then Yahweh explicitly states, "Do not deny justice to a resident alien or fatherless child, and do not take a widow's garment as security. Remember that you were a slave in Egypt, and the Lord your God redeemed you from there" (24:17–18).

Next, and still in the context of justice, Yahweh orders that when reaping their fields, gathering their grapes, and harvesting their olives, the Israelites are not to go over the process a second time to ensure they harvested everything thoroughly. Grain and fruit that were missed in the first pass are "to be left for the resident alien, the fatherless, and the widow" (24:19; this is similar to Lev 19:9–10; 23:22). The Hebrew text does not actually include the phrase "it is to be left for" but only states that "it is for" or "it belongs to." The idea that the Hebrew seems to convey is "Do not pick the forgotten sheaf, the remaining olives and grapes; *they belong to* the resident foreigner, the orphan, and the widow." This implies that the people living in the land but who, for various reasons, did not have ownership of the land, would still qualify to share in the blessings that the land provided, along with the land owner.[30] The last half of 24:19 adds the beneficial consequences for the landowners who followed this—"so that the Lord your God may bless you in all the work of your hands." The seriousness of Yahweh in regard to this vulnerable triad can also be seen in its inclusion among the twelve curses in Deuteronomy 27: "The one who denies justice to a resident alien, a fatherless child, or a widow is cursed" (v. 19).

---

[30] Christopher Wright, *Deuteronomy*, NIBC (Peabody, MA: Hendrickson, 1996), 260–61.

Publicly Recording the Terms of the Covenant and a Nationwide Oath of Obedience (27:1–26)

Throughout Deuteronomy, Moses has been the one speaking and relaying the commandments of Yahweh to the Israelites. In Deuteronomy 27 he is joined by "the elders of Israel" (27:1) and "the Levitical priests" (27:9), signifying a broad leadership approval of the covenant relationship. In 27:1–8 they instruct the Israelites to write "all of the words of this law" (27:3; Hebrew, *torah*; i.e., teaching, instruction) on stone pillars (stele) covered with plaster and to set them up in public view on top of Mount Ebal. This placed the terms of the covenant in a public place for all to see, but it also served as a witness for the agreement with Yahweh that Israel had just formalized.

Back in Deut 11:26–32 Yahweh stated that he was putting before Israel the option of blessings or curses and that when they entered the Promised Land they were to go up on Mount Ebal and Mount Gerizim and proclaim both options, the curses from Mount Ebal and the blessings from Mount Gerizim (which Joshua and the people do in Josh 8:30–35). Here in Deuteronomy 27, with Mount Ebal in focus (where the stele with the written record of the covenant terms was placed), a basic summary of the twelve curses is to be proclaimed by the Levites to all the people. Most of the curses flow right out of the Ten Commandments. The first curse, of course, is on the one who makes an idol (27:15). There are also four curses relating to forbidden sexual relations (27:20–23) and two curses relating to murder (27:24–25). Curses will also fall upon those who dishonor their parents (27:16), move boundary stones (27:17), mislead the blind (27:18), and deny justice to resident aliens, the fatherless, and widows (27:19). The final, summary curse is on the one "who does not put the words of this law [Hebrew, *torah*] into practice" (27:26). After the proclamation of each curse, all the people were to respond publicly with "amen," a Hebrew term expressing an affirmation of the truth and trustworthiness of the statement.

ANCIENT CONNECTIONS SIDEBAR 5.4: THE IMPORTANCE OF NOT MOVING YOUR NEIGHBOR'S BOUNDARY STONES

As the formerly enslaved, now semi-nomadic Israelites prepare to move into the Promised Land and become a nation of resident small farmers, Yahweh gives them important rules regarding the critical status of property lines and the boundary stones that delineated those property lines. Deuteronomy 19:14

commands, "Do not move your neighbor's boundary marker," and the curse for this appears in 27:17: "Cursed is anyone who moves their neighbor's boundary stone" (NIV; cf. Prov 23:10–11). Throughout the ANE it was common practice to delineate property boundaries with small stone markers, which were often inscribed with the owner's name as well as with appropriate divine curses on anyone who moved them. Laws prohibiting tampering with these boundary stones are often included in the law collections of the ANE.[31] Similarly, in *The Instruction of Amenemope*, a document of Egyptian wisdom literature, the reader is warned:

> Do not displace the surveyor's marker on the boundaries of the arable land,
>> Nor alter the position of the measuring line;
> Do not be covetous for a single cubit of land,
>> Nor encroach upon the boundaries of a widow. . . .
> Take care not to topple over the boundary marks of the fields,
>> Not fearing that you will be brought to court.[32]

Blessings and Curses as a Result of Obedience or Disobedience (28:1–68)

The conditional nature of Yahweh's covenant with Israel is spelled out in Deuteronomy 28 and includes two contrasting options with two diametrically opposed consequences: "Now if you faithfully obey the LORD your God and are careful to follow all his commands I am giving you today . . . All these blessings will come and overtake you. . . . But if you do not obey the LORD your God by carefully following all his commands and statutes I am giving you today, all these curses will come and overtake you" (28:1–2, 15). The wonderful blessings are listed in 28:3–14 and the horrific curses, somewhat parallel to the blessings but much longer and in more graphic detail, are listed in 28:16–68. Indeed, Yahweh goes to great lengths to make it crystal clear just how important it will be to stay faithful to him, keep his commandments, and worship him only while they live in the land with him living in their midst.

---

[31] Eugene E. Carpenter, "Deuteronomy," *ZIBBC* 1:487–88; Michael A. Grisanti, "Deuteronomy," *BIBBC*, 199.

[32] "The Instruction of Amenemope," in Simpson, ed., *The Literature of Ancient Egypt*, 229 (see intro., n. 17).

The Third Speech of Moses: Renewal of the Covenant—the Offer of Life or Death (29:1–30:20)

In Moses's third and final speech, he first sums up many of the preceding chapters. Once again, he tells the story of the exodus, the wilderness wandering, and the recent victories over Sihon and Og, emphasizing Yahweh's constant faithfulness (29:1–8). Next, repeating the theme that occurs repeatedly throughout the book, Moses exhorts Israel to commit to the covenant and to following all the commandments of Yahweh, who is right there in their presence (29:9–18).

Next, however, Moses seems to prophesy the sad but true reality that in the future the Israelites will turn away from Yahweh to worship other gods, breaking the covenant. Yahweh will consequently banish them from the land (29:19–29). Then, sounding a lot like the prophets Isaiah and Jeremiah, Moses declares that after this terrible time of exile out of the land, Yahweh will have compassion on them and restore them to the land. These prophesied events lay out the story line that the rest of the Old Testament will follow. Israel (and Judah) will turn away from Yahweh and worship other gods. They will be banished from the Promised Land and exiled away from the land. Then Yahweh in his grace will bring them back and restore them (30:1–10). The restoration in the Old Testament, however, was only partial, and the full restoration is still in the future, awaiting the final return of Christ.

In 30:11–20 Moses returns to the present tense, stating "today" (CSB) or "now" (NIV). The terms of Yahweh's covenant are neither confusing nor difficult to obey (30:11–14), and he summarizes them clearly in 30:15–16. First he declares, "See, today I have set before you life and prosperity [Hebrew, *tov*], death and adversity [Hebrew, *ra*]." Recall our discussion of "good" (*tov*) and "evil/bad" (*ra*) in Genesis 1–3, where these two opposites were also connected to life and death. In essence Yahweh is offering Israel a chance to return to the garden situation, where they will have life and that life will be *tov*, living with the blessings that come with the close presence of Yahweh.

Moses repeats a short warning regarding disobedience in 30:17–18, and then in 30:19 he calls on "heaven and earth" as metaphorical witnesses to the terms of the covenant offer. Heaven and earth are also called to be witnesses in Deut 4:26; 31:28; and 32:1. Later in Israel's history, when the prophet Isaiah declares that Israel has violated the terms of this covenant agreement, he will call on these witnesses, heaven and earth, to bear testimony against Israel, testifying that Israel did in fact agree to keep the covenant (Isa 1:2). Note the similarities:

Pay attention, heavens, and I will speak;
listen, earth, to the words from my mouth. (Deut 32:1)

Listen, heavens, and pay attention, earth,
for the LORD has spoken. (Isa 1:2)

The Postscript: The New Leader Joshua, the Written Torah, *the Warning of Apostasy, and the Song and Blessings of Moses (31:1–34:12)*

The death of Moses overshadows this entire section. Allusions to his upcoming death occur frequently (31:1–2, 14, 16, 27, 29; 32:48–52; 33:1; 34:1–12), and, indeed, his death serves as an *inclusio*, alluded to in the opening verses, 31:1–2, and described in the closing verses, 34:1–12. Yahweh clearly does not want the covenant relationship he has with the Israelites to die with Moses, and in this closing unit Moses reminds Israel of Yahweh's provision for its continuation. First, Yahweh reassures the Israelites that he himself will continue to be present with them, to lead them into the land and to drive out their enemies before them (31:1–6, 8), even without Moses as the mediator. Joshua is then formally appointed by Yahweh as the new leader of Israel (31:7–8, 14–15, 23). Both Moses (31:7) and Yahweh (31:23) tell Joshua to "be strong and courageous," an exhortation that is repeated several more times in Joshua 1 (vv. 6, 7, 9, 18), connecting the opening of the book of Joshua to the closing of Deuteronomy.

Yet while the transition in human leadership is important to the covenant, more critical to the ongoing relationship is the written "law of Moses," the *torah* or teaching that Yahweh has been transmitting through Moses. Starting with the Ten Commandments and expanding on them, several times earlier throughout Deuteronomy there are references to the written form of Yahweh's *torah*, his "statutes, ordinances, and commands" (4:13; 5:22; 10:1–5; 17:18–19; 27:1–8). Here at the end, this is stressed (31:9–13), as Moses writes down the *torah* and gives it to the priests. Thus, in reality, Joshua does not replace Moses entirely. He replaces him as the military leader and civic judge, but Joshua does not become the new mediator between Yahweh and Israel. The role of mediator between Yahweh and his people—especially the mediation of Yahweh's spoken word, a role that Moses played dramatically throughout Exodus, Leviticus, Numbers, and Deuteronomy—is now transferred, not to Joshua, but to the written word, the *torah*.

Recall that throughout our study of the story of Yahweh's covenant relationship with Israel, a study that covered Exodus, Leviticus, Numbers, and Deuteronomy, Israel has been repeatedly disobedient and rebellious. Here at the conclusion to the Pentateuch, as Israel plans to cross the Jordan River and take possession of the Promised Land, the optimistic reader might hope that this disobedient behavior would stay in the past. Yahweh, however, knows better, and during the actual commissioning of Joshua (Deut 31:14–22), Yahweh predicts the future apostasy of Israel, when they would break this covenant and lose the blessings of his powerful indwelling presence ("I will abandon them and hide my face from them," v. 17).

Yahweh then instructs Moses to write down a song and teach it to the Israelites (31:19–22). This song, to be learned and sung by everyone in Israel, was not only an attempt to keep Israel faithful by repeating the stern warnings of Yahweh, but it was to serve as a witness against them when, in the future, they would break the covenant and reject Yahweh. Within this final unit of Deuteronomy, this somber song features prominently. Quite lengthy, it is recorded and cited in 32:1–43. At the conclusion of the song, Moses, sounding a bit more optimistic than Yahweh, exhorts Israel to take the song—and the words of the *torah*—and to obey them. He concludes, "For they are not meaningless words to you but they are your life, and by them you will live long in the land you are crossing the Jordan to possess" (32:47).

Immediately after that, Yahweh instructs Moses to go up on Mount Nebo, where he can see the Promised Land. There he will die, without entering the land, because of his earlier disobedience in striking the rock (Num 20:1–13; Deut 3:21–29).

Like the patriarch Jacob in Gen 49:1–28, in Deuteronomy 33 Moses blesses the tribes of Israel right before he dies. The opening verse (33:1) refers to Moses as "the man of God," a term which in later Israelite history will be used of the true prophets of Yahweh. With the exception of the blessing on Levi and Joseph, each blessing is very brief. In 33:5 and 33:26 (see also 32:15) Israel is ironically referred to as *Jeshurun*, a rarely used poetic term meaning "the Upright One."[33]

In Deut 34:1–4 Moses climbs Mount Nebo, and from there Yahweh shows him the Promised Land. Yahweh then restates that possessing the land is in fulfillment of the covenant with Abraham, Isaac, and Jacob, paralleling the opening in Deut 1:8 as an *inclusio*. References to the Abrahamic or patriarchal covenant have appeared several times in Deuteronomy, reminding the readers that Yahweh's promise to Abraham will continue to move the story forward, even after the disobedience and rebellion of Israel (1:8; 6:10; 9:5, 27; 29:13; 30:20; 31:20; 34:4). Placed at the end of Deuteronomy, following the grim predictions of Israel's future apostasy, Yahweh's promise to Abraham, Isaac, and Jacob provides a strong ray of hope for the future.

---

[33] Jack R. Lundbom, *Deuteronomy: A Commentary* (Grand Rapids: Eerdmans, 2013), 924. Outside of these three occurrences in Deuteronomy 32–33 this term only appears in Isa 44:2.

Moses, now once again called the servant of Yahweh, dies and is buried (34:5–8). Other than Yahweh, Moses has been the dominant character in the pentateuchal story since Exodus 2. Appropriately, Deut 34:10–12 closes out Deuteronomy and the Pentateuch with a glowing epitaph for Moses, while pointing forward in hope to the coming of the great future prophet, Jesus Christ:

> No prophet has arisen again in Israel like Moses, whom the LORD knew face to face. He was unparalleled for all the signs and wonders the LORD sent him to do against the land of Egypt . . . and for all the mighty acts of power and terrifying deeds that Moses performed in the sight of all Israel.

Biblical Connections

The material in Deuteronomy is presented to Israel after the exodus and wandering and just before their conquest of the Promised Land. As a covenant document, in essence Deuteronomy presents the terms by which Israel can live in the Promised Land and live a life characterized by blessings resulting from Yahweh dwelling in their midst. The key question emanating from Deuteronomy throughout the rest of the Old Testament is this: Will the Israelites be faithful to the covenant expressed in the terms of Deuteronomy and thus live the good, blessed life in the land? The sad answer is no.

As laid out in Deuteronomy 28–32 the story of Israel will follow a pattern of "blessing, sin, exile (curse instead of blessing), and restoration or blessing." This pattern—the Deuteronomistic view of Israel's history—describes the plotline of the story that runs throughout the Old Testament and into the New Testament, which views Israel as still in exile and yet which proclaims the time of restoration through Jesus Christ.[34]

Whether or not Israel will obey the terms in Deuteronomy is a central issue in the narrative story from Joshua to 2 Kings, throughout which the blessings or curses experienced by Israel are directly linked to the obedience or disobedience of the Israelites and their leaders. Individual kings are evaluated by how well they kept or didn't keep the terms in Deuteronomy. The Old Testament Historical Books, along with the Prophets, stress repeatedly that the invasions and destruction brought by the Assyrians in 722 BC on Israel and by the Babylonians in 587/586 BC on Judah, along

---

[34] See C. Marvin Pate et al., *The Story of Israel: A Biblical Theology* (Downers Grove, IL: IVP, 2004).

with the exile out of the land, were the direct consequence of disobeying the terms in Deuteronomy. Indeed, allusions and direct references to Deuteronomy abound throughout the so-called Deuteronomistic history (Joshua to 2 Kings, including Ruth, as in the Christian canon) and are too numerous to list.[35] A few examples, however, will give the reader a feel for the extensive reliance on Deuteronomy that runs throughout this section.

Consider the small book of Ruth. In the canonical story, Joshua, obedient to Yahweh and the *torah* of Deuteronomy, is successful and takes possession of the land, leaving Israel with the same admonitions at the end of the book of Joshua as Moses did at the end of Deuteronomy. Judges, on the other hand, is a disaster, as the Israelites turn away from Yahweh to worship other gods and are thus oppressed by a range of different foreign enemies in accordance with the curse warnings of Deuteronomy 28. The question at the end of Judges is "Who will deliver Israel from this mess?" The answer is "David," whose story is told in 1–2 Samuel. The book of Ruth introduces David, the coming great deliverer. In this context, note the frequent connections to Deuteronomy. First, as the family of Naomi moves out of the Promised Land, terrible things happen (all the men die), and after she (and Ruth) returns to the land, she experiences blessing (safety, peace, joy, a grandson). In fact, the story of Ruth involves (1) the treatment of one who is both a widow and a residing foreigner; (2) the harvesting of overlooked, left-behind sheaves in the field; and (3) issues of levirate marriage, including the settlement of the case before the elders of the city and using shoes to seal the agreement. All these issues are addressed in the short passage of Deut 24:16–25:10, which is, no doubt, the background for the story of Ruth.[36]

Boaz, who acts in obedience to Deuteronomy's guidelines regarding widows and residing foreigners, shows compassion and generosity to Ruth and consequently receives rich blessings from Yahweh. Ironically, Ruth is also a Moabite, and Moabites were forbidden to enter the assembly of Yahweh due to their hostility against Israel during the exodus and wandering era. Indeed, Deut 23:3–6 declares, "No Ammonite or Moabite may enter the Lord's assembly. . . . Never pursue their welfare or prosperity as long as you live." Yet by embracing Naomi's people and Naomi's God and by

---

[35] See the long list compiled by Gary Edward Schnittjer, *Old Testament Use of Old Testament: A Book-by-Book Guide* (Grand Rapids: Zondervan, 2021), 75–77.

[36] Berman writes, "My claim is that the book of Ruth constitutes a legal homily whose plot unfolds according to the sequential order of the legal materials found in Deuteronomy 24,16–25,10, and is a comment upon them." Joshua Berman, "Ancient Hermeneutics and the Legal Structure of the Book of Ruth," *ZAW* 119 (2007): 23.

taking an oath in Yahweh's name to move with Naomi back into the Promised Land (Ruth 1:16–17), Ruth not only finds acceptance, but she becomes the matriarchal ancestor of King David and, likewise, Jesus Christ (Ruth 4:21–22; Matt 1:5).

Throughout 1–2 Samuel and 1–2 Kings, the monarchs are judged by the narrator in accordance to how well they obey the terms in Deuteronomy. This is often played out in contrasting actions, such as between David and Saul, or between David and Solomon. For example, Deut 25:17–19 instructs the Israelites that after they settle in the land, they are to destroy the Amalekites. Saul's final and fatal failure as king is his refusal to destroy these Amalekites (1 Sam 15:1–35), a story that concludes with "And the LORD regretted he had made Saul king" (15:35). David, on the other hand, destroys the Amalekites, even before he becomes king (30:1–20).

Likewise, as mentioned earlier, Deut 17:16–17 specified that the king was not to (1) accumulate lots of chariot horses, especially from Egypt, which implies that the king was forbidden from keeping a large standing chariot force; (2) accumulate many wives; and (3) accumulate lots of personal silver and gold. In 1 Samuel 8, after David defeats the Moabites and captures a thousand chariots (implying the capture of at least 2,000 chariot horses), he hamstrings all but 100 of the horses. Likewise, he takes all the silver and gold he captures and dedicates it to Yahweh (2 Sam 8:4, 11). Solomon, on the other hand, violates all three of these commands from Deuteronomy 17 excessively and blatantly (12,000 horses from Egypt; unimaginable, opulent amounts of silver and gold; 1,000 wives and concubines) and worships foreign gods (1 Kgs 10:14–11:8). The narrator concludes, "Solomon did what was evil [*ra*'] in the LORD's sight, and unlike his father David, he did not remain loyal to the LORD. . . . The LORD was angry with Solomon, because his heart had turned away from the LORD" (1 Kgs 11:6, 9).

Deuteronomy is also reflected often in Psalms, especially the "Torah" Psalms (1, 19, 119) and the "Wisdom" Psalms (111:10; 34:8–12). Throughout Psalms, references to *torah* (normally translated as "law" in NIV and as "instruction" in CSB) have the book of Deuteronomy in mind.[37]

Deuteronomy lies at the heart of the message and theology of the Prophets. The Old Testament Prophets basically proclaim three central things to Israel and Judah: (1) You have broken the covenant. Repent before it is too late! (2) Since you did not repent, judgment is coming. (3) Beyond the judgment there is a future deliverance and restoration (a new covenant, a new exodus, a new indwelling of Yahweh). When the prophets accuse Israel of breaking the covenant, it is the Mosaic

---

[37] Block, *Deuteronomy*, 34.

covenant, as defined by Exodus-Deuteronomy, and especially Deuteronomy, to which they refer. The prophets are like Yahweh's prosecuting attorneys, standing before Yahweh the judge with Deuteronomy in their hands, calling on the witnesses heaven and earth (Isa 1:2; Jer 2:12), accusing Israel and Judah of flagrantly violating and breaking (i.e., abrogating) the covenant by their idolatry, their extensive acts of social injustice (especially against the residing foreigner, the widow, and the fatherless), and their hypocritical acts of worship. Likewise, because Israel and Judah refuse to repent and turn back to obeying the covenant of Deuteronomy, the Prophets declare the coming judgment, in fulfillment of the curses described in Deuteronomy 28.[38]

Because of Yahweh's grace and his love, however, which was inextricably interconnected to the promises in his covenant with Abraham (as well as his covenant with David), the Prophets proclaim a future time of restoration and deliverance, a spectacular deliverance that will even overshadow the exodus event. This deliverance will involve a "new covenant" (Jer 31:31–34). In stark contrast to the covenant in Deuteronomy, this new covenant will be written on their hearts instead of on stone. Indeed, Yahweh will put his *torah* right in their midst ("minds," NIV).

Although most of the Prophets rely heavily on Deuteronomy, it is in Jeremiah that the connections are the most frequent and the most obvious. The language of Jeremiah is so similar to the language of Deuteronomy that many nonevangelical scholars have concluded that the same person (or group of people) must have written both documents. Of course, it is much more likely that it is Jeremiah's reliance on Deuteronomy as the legal definition of the covenant terms that Israel has violated that creates such similar language between Jeremiah and Deuteronomy. A few select examples are listed here:

> "If you no longer oppress the resident alien, the fatherless, and the widow . . . or follow other gods . . . I will allow you to live in this place, the land I gave to your ancestors" (Jer 7:6–7). Compare with Deut 24:17–22; 26:12–15; 27:19, which has "the resident alien, the fatherless, and the widow" in the exact same order.

> "Let a curse be on the man who does not obey the words of this covenant, which I commanded your ancestors when I brought them out of the land

---

[38] J. Daniel Hays, *The Message of the Prophets: A Survey of the Prophetic and Apocalyptic Books of the Old Testament* (Grand Rapids: Zondervan, 2010), 62–74.

of Egypt" (Jer 11:3–4). Compare with Deut 28:15–68—the curses (punishment) for failure to keep the terms of Deuteronomy.

"The house of Israel and the house of Judah broke my covenant I made with their ancestors" (Jer 11:10). Compare with Deut 31:16, which uses the exact same terminology, when Yahweh predicts, "They will . . . break the covenant I have made with them."

"Judah mourns. . . . Their nobles send their servants for water. They go to the cisterns; they find no water; their containers return empty. . . . The ground is cracked since no rain has fallen on the land" (Jer 14:2–4). Compare with Deut 28:12, where abundant rain is part of the blessing, and 28:22–24, where drought is one of the terrible curses.

"Look, I am setting before you the way of life and the way of death" (Jer 21:8). Compare with Deut 30:19, which reads, "I have set before you life and death, blessing and curse" (see also Deut 30:15).

"After the prophet Hananiah had broken the yoke bar from the neck of the prophet Jeremiah, the word of the LORD came to Jeremiah: 'Go say to Hananiah, "This is what the LORD says: You broke a wooden yoke bar, but in its place you will make an iron yoke bar"'" (Jer 28:12–13). Compare with Deut 28:48, where Yahweh says Israel's enemies will place an iron yoke on them.

Such allusions and direct references continue throughout Jeremiah and, indeed, throughout most of the prophetic literature. Even as the Old Testament canon is closing, Malachi is making references back to Deuteronomy. He warns, "I will come to you in judgment . . . against those who oppress the hired worker, the widow, and the fatherless; and against those who deny justice to the resident alien" (Mal 3:5), a direct allusion to Deut 24:14–22; 26:12–15; 27:19. In the final verses of Malachi, the prophet is still calling on the people to obey the terms of Deuteronomy: "Remember the instruction [*torah*] of Moses my servant, the statutes and ordinances I commanded him at Horeb for all Israel" (Mal 4:4).

In the New Testament Gospels, the testing of Jesus (Matt 4:1–11; Luke 4:1–13) is introduced with language reminiscent of Moses and Israel in the wilderness. (Jesus is led into the wilderness to be tested; he fasts forty days and nights) Moses also fasts for forty days and nights (Exod 34:28), and this is mentioned five times in Deut 9:1–10:11 (9:9, 11, 18, 25; 10:10), stressing that this happened twice: once just before receiving the Ten Commandments and once after the terrible golden calf incident, when Moses prayed before Yahweh for forty days and nights in intercessory prayer for Israel. The implication of the allusion is that Jesus is probably not just praying and fasting as a personal preparation for his upcoming ministry but that he is praying as an intercessor for Israel (and perhaps for his people in general—the "true Israel"). The devil tempts Jesus three times (once to provide food for himself in the wilderness, as in the pentateuchal story), and each time Jesus responds with a quote from Deuteronomy (8:3; 6:13; 6:16), using Deuteronomy as a God-spoken guideline for behavior and strength to overcome testing. Unlike Israel, who in Exodus-Deuteronomy repeatedly failed their testing in the wilderness, Jesus emerges from the testing as completely obedient and faithful to God.

References to texts in Deuteronomy (and parallel texts in Exodus and Leviticus) also abound throughout the Gospels. This is especially true, for example, in the Sermon on the Mount (Matthew 5–7), where Jesus repeatedly states, "You have heard it said . . ." and then quotes from Deuteronomy, followed by his further explanation or expansion on the text in Deuteronomy. This is also true of the texts relating to the Sabbath controversies.

Recall that Deut 18:15–19 not only prophesied that Yahweh would raise up a prophet like Moses in the future, but it stressed the importance of listening to and obeying this prophet. Several New Testament texts allude to this passage (John 1:21; 5:45–47; 6:14; 7:40; Acts 3:22–23), likewise often underscoring the importance of listening to and obeying this prophet (i.e., Jesus).

Paul, when explaining the relationship between law and grace, and when discussing the future of Israel, connects to Deuteronomy frequently. In Romans, for example, although not used as prominently as Isaiah is, Deuteronomy is one of the books that Paul quotes and to which he alludes frequently. This is particularly true of Romans 10, which cites Deuteronomy 30:12–14 several times, climaxing with the citation of 30:14 (Rom 10:8), "**The message is near you, in your mouth and in your heart**." Paul pulls these citations of Deuteronomy 30 together and concludes in 10:8–9, "This is the message of faith that we proclaim: If you confess with your mouth, 'Jesus is Lord,' and believe in your heart that God raised him from the dead, you will be saved." As Paul continues, explaining that Israel's current rejection of God's revelatory and salvific word is not historically unusual, he cites Deut 32:21 (Rom 10:19) and 29:4 (Rom 11:8). In the closing of Romans, as Paul reiterates that the inclusion of the Gentiles (i.e., "the nations") is not something new but something foretold in Scripture, he cites Deut 32:43 (Rom 15:10): "**Rejoice, you Gentiles** [this Greek word *ethnē* can also be translated as 'nations'], **with his people!**"

Gospel Connections

Embedded in the biblical theme of blessing, sin, exile, restoration of blessing, the Old Testament Prophets proclaimed that since Israel has failed to keep the terms of the Mosaic covenant, especially as defined by Deuteronomy, judgment (the curses of Deuteronomy) is coming. They continued, however, to offer future hope of restored blessing based on Yahweh's gracious promises seen especially in the Abrahamic covenant and in the Davidic covenant. Paul picks up this theme of the contrast between the conditional terms of the Mosaic covenant (Deuteronomy) and the unconditional promises to Abraham, and he frames it as the contrast between law and grace, between the works of the law and faith (Rom 3:21–4:25; Gal 3:1–22). Paul puts this law/grace theme at the heart of the gospel, proclaiming that one cannot be saved by keeping the law (the terms of Deuteronomy) but only by grace through faith.

Deuteronomy 27:26 ("Anyone who does not put the words of this law into practice is cursed") is a concluding, summary statement for all the curses listed in Deuteronomy 27. It also serves as an introduction to the long list of curses in Deut 28:15–68. Paul alludes to this verse in Gal 3:10 ("**Everyone who does not do everything written in the book of the law is cursed**"), concluding that "all who rely on the works of the law are under a curse." Paul then declares that "Christ redeemed us from the curse of the law [i.e., the curses in Deuteronomy 27–28] by becoming a curse for us" (Gal 3:13). To demonstrate this Paul then cites Deut 21:23: "**Cursed is everyone who is hung on a tree**" (Gal 3:13b).

Paul also points out that the law (terms of Deuteronomy) was not in conflict with God's promises to Abraham (Gal 3:21), but that "the law, then, was our guardian until Christ, so that we could be justified by faith. But since that faith has come, we are no longer under a guardian" (Gal 3:24–25).

The book of Hebrews, which cites and alludes to the Old Testament more than any other New Testament book (except perhaps Revelation), specifically cites and alludes to Deuteronomy numerous times. Often it is to a theme that occurs in Deuteronomy but one that occurs also in Exodus, Leviticus, or Numbers, and sometimes in other books, such as Psalms, which reference the pentateuchal books as well. Thus, texts such as Heb 3:5 ("Moses was faithful as a servant in all God's household"), allude back to Deut 34:5–12. Likewise, references to Jesus as mediator of a new covenant (Heb 8:6; 9:15; 12:24) carry contrastive allusions to Moses as the mediator of the old one (Exodus-Deuteronomy). Indeed, in the contrast between the new covenant and the old covenant, Deuteronomy (along with Exodus) forms the primary point of reference for the old covenant. Other references to Deuteronomy in the book of Hebrews include Heb 10:28 (Deut 17:6); 10:30 (Deut 32:35–36); 12:15 (Deut 29:18); 12:21 (Deut 9:19); and 13:5 (Deut 31:6–8).[39]

Likewise, James has several texts that imply a background understanding of Deuteronomy. This includes references to looking after "orphans and widows" (Jas 1:27; compare Deut 10:17–18; 14:28–29; 16:11–14; 24:14–22; 26:1–15; and 27:19), not showing favoritism (Jas 2:1–13; compare Deut 1:16–17 and 10:17), references to the Ten Commandments (Jas 2:11; compare Deut 5:6–21; Exod 20:1–17), and paying field workers their wages (Jas 5:4; compare Deut 24:14–15).

Life Connections

Deuteronomy is filled with constant reminders that we can trust God completely, even during the most difficult times. God reminds Israel of the great things he has done for them in their past, and then he asks them to trust him for the future. Likewise, we should take time to reflect on what God has done for us in the past, how he has saved us from sin, guided us, and so on, and this should encourage us to trust him for the future. In addition, just reading how he delivered the ancient Israelites and provided for them should also reassure us that he can care for us when we trust him.

In Deuteronomy we also see God telling Israel, "I am offering you life!" Indeed, he also offers us life, a life of blessing in close relationship to him. But to receive this life that God offers, we have to approach and worship God according to his stipulations. The Israelites could not embrace the Canaanite cultural methods of worshipping various gods and expect to receive the good life from God. Likewise, God tells us that we can approach him and find the good life in him only through Jesus Christ.

In this book we are also reminded of how important it is, and what a blessing it is, to live in the presence of God. As Christians we are indwelt by the powerful Holy Spirit, and through the blood of Jesus Christ we can fellowship closely with God dwelling in us, finding joy in worshipping and serving him.

Deuteronomy also reminds us how important it is to pass our faith on to our children and our children's children. It is important that parents and grandparents consciously share with their children and grandchildren how God has worked in their lives. Likewise, we can learn much from the regular rhythm of worship activities (e.g.,

---

[39] George H. Guthrie, "Old Testament in Hebrews," in Ralph P. Martin and Peter H. Davids, eds., *Dictionary of the Later New Testament and Its Developments* (Downers Grove, IL: IVP, 1997), 848–49.

Sabbath, festivals, Jubilee) that God decreed in Deuteronomy. The Christian life is best lived and passed on to the next generation, if it is placed within a regular cycle of worship, celebration, and remembrance.

This wonderful book also lets us see how much God cares about those who are socioeconomically or culturally vulnerable and how he wants his people to have the same care and compassion. It is a clear reminder that the Christian life is not about the individual but about loving and serving God and others.

Finally, we cannot miss the character of God that is revealed throughout Deuteronomy. We see his love and compassion for his people as well as his anger at sin. We see his patience, holiness, concern for justice, and all-powerful sovereign rule over all the world. We also see just how much he wants to have a close, personal relationship with his people.

Interactive Questions

5-1. Explain the situation for the Israelites that is implied in Deuteronomy 6. Then discuss how we can apply Deuteronomy 6 today to stay faithful during times of cultural upheaval and challenge.

5-2. Discuss the commands in Deuteronomy to care for the orphan, the widow, and the residing foreigner. Why are these three grouped together? Why are they vulnerable? Identify similar vulnerable groups in our society today and discuss what it would mean for us to care for and provide justice for these groups.

5-3. In the Ten Commandments, discuss the vertical aspect (5:6–12) and the horizontal aspect (5:13–21). How do these two aspects relate? Explain briefly how each of these commandments should be applied in your context today.

5-4. Using a concordance, identify the times in Deuteronomy that Abraham is mentioned, and discuss the role that Yahweh's covenant with Abraham plays in Deuteronomy.

5-5. Read Deut 4:9, 23, 31; 6:12; 8:11–14, 19, and discuss why Yahweh seems to be so concerned that the Israelites would "forget" him and what he had done for them. In today's Christian world, is there a danger of us forgetting God? Does the memory of God and his saving actions ever disappear from generation to generation?

5-6. Discuss the tithing requirements of Deut 14:22–28. Does this have any application for us today? If so, how?

5-7. What was the meaning and purpose of the three annual celebrations described in Deut 16:1–17 (Passover, Festival of Weeks, Festival of Shelters)? What annual celebrations do we in the church celebrate today?

5-8. Choose four texts from Deuteronomy in which Yahweh says something about being the Lord who brought Israel up out of Egypt. Explain why Yahweh repeatedly states this and identifies himself with this affirmation.

5-9. What does Deut 30:19–20 mean for Christians today?

5-10. From Deuteronomy 28 and Leviticus 26, using the categories of (a) economic, (b) political, and (c) personal or family, compare and contrast the blessings and the curses of Leviticus 26 and Deuteronomy 28. Present your material in a three-column chart, followed by a concluding summary paragraph at the end.

Recommended Resources

Arnold, Bill T. *The Book of Deuteronomy, Chapters 1–11*. NICOT. Grand Rapids: Eerdmans, 2022.

Block, Daniel I. *Deuteronomy*. NIVAC. Grand Rapids: Zondervan, 2012.

Christensen, Duane L. *Deuteronomy 1:1–21:9*. 2nd ed. WBC. Nashville: Thomas Nelson, 2001.

———. *Deuteronomy 21:10–34:12*. WBC. Nashville: Thomas Nelson, 2002.

Craigie, Peter C. *The Book of Deuteronomy*. NICOT. Grand Rapids: Eerdmans, 1976.

Grisanti, Michael A. "Deuteronomy." In *The Baker Illustrated Bible Background Commentary*, edited by J. Scott Duvall and J. Daniel Hays, 187–205. Grand Rapids: Baker, 2020.

Kitchen, Kenneth A., and Paul J. N. Lawrence. *Treaty, Law and Covenant in the Ancient Near East*. 3 vols. Wiesbaden: Harrassowitz Verlag, 2012.

Lundbom, Jack R. *Deuteronomy: A Commentary*. Grand Rapids: Eerdmans, 2013.

Schnittjer, Gary Edward. *Old Testament Use of Old Testament: A Book-by-Book Guide*. Grand Rapids: Zondervan, 2021.

Wright, Christopher. *Deuteronomy*. NIBC. Peabody, MA: Hendrickson, 1996.

Appendix

How to Interpret and Apply the Old Testament Law

All Scripture is inspired by God and is profitable for teaching,
for rebuking, for correcting, for training in righteousness.

—2 TIMOTHY 3:16

Introduction

Throughout our study of the Pentateuch, we have encountered hundreds of "laws" (specific commands and instructions) addressed to the Israelites from God.[1] For many Christians today, interpreting and applying these Old Testament laws can be quite challenging. Obviously, these laws are important—they comprise a substantial

---

[1] The material in this section, with some slight modification and updating, is from J. Daniel Hays, "Applying the Old Testament Law Today," *BSac* 158 (January–March 2001): 21–35. The same basic approach and similar material is in Hays and Duvall, *BIBH*, 1079–88. A more thorough discussion, along with numerous examples, can be found in Duvall and Hays, *Grasping God's Word*, 383–401 (see chap. 1, n. 5).

portion of God's written revelation to us—but how can Christians today apply them? In the Pentateuch we encounter some strange laws:

Exod 34:26: "You must not boil a young goat in its mother's milk."

Lev 19:19: "Do not . . . put on a garment made of two kinds of material."

Furthermore, we as modern Christians violate numerous Old Testament laws with some regularity. For example:

Deut 22:5: "A woman is not to wear male clothing, and a man is not to put on a woman's garment."

Lev 19:32: "You are to rise in the presence of the elderly."

Deut 14:8: "And pigs . . . are unclean for you. Do not eat their meat or touch their carcasses."

While we tend to ignore those laws, there are some Old Testament laws that we embrace as the moral underpinnings of Christian behavior. These are more familiar to most of us:

Lev 19:18: "Love your neighbor as yourself."

Exod 20:13: "Do not murder."

Deut 5:18: "Do not commit adultery."

So why do we adhere to some laws and ignore others? Which laws are valid, and which are not? Many Christians today are puzzled by these questions and are left wondering about what to do with this part of the Bible. Some take the default approach of simply skimming through the numerous laws of the Pentateuch, skipping over all of the laws that do not seem to apply. These laws they choose to ignore altogether. Then when they occasionally encounter one that seems to make sense in today's world, they grab it, underline it, and use it as a guideline for living. Surely this random approach to interpreting the Old Testament law is inadequate. But how should we interpret the law?

The Traditional Classification Approach

For many years a popular approach to interpreting the Old Testament law has been to emphasize the distinction between moral, civil, and ceremonial laws. *Moral laws* are defined as those that deal with timeless truths regarding God's intention for human ethical behavior. "Love your neighbor as yourself" is a good example of a moral law. *Civil laws* are those describing aspects that are related to the nation's legal system. These laws deal with the courts, economics, land, crimes, and punishment. An example of a civil law can be found in Deut 15:1: "At the end of every seven years you must cancel debts." *Ceremonial laws* are defined as those that deal with sacrifices, festivals, and priestly activities. For example, Deut 16:13 instructed the Israelites to "celebrate the Festival of Shelters for seven days when you have gathered in everything from your threshing floor and winepress."

Under this traditional approach, the distinctions between moral, civil, and ceremonial laws are critically important because they allow the Christian to know whether the law still applies to them. Moral laws, according to this system of interpretation, are universal and timeless. They still apply as law to Christian believers today. Civil and ceremonial laws, on the other hand, applied only to ancient Israel. They do not apply at all to believers today. Through the years this system has been helpful to many, providing a methodology whereby texts such as "love your neighbor as yourself" could still be claimed as law for the Christian while all of the texts dealing with sacrifices and punishments could be dismissed as invalid.[2]

In recent years, however, a growing number of evangelical scholars have begun to question this approach (see note 4 in this chapter). One of the major objections is that these critical distinctions appear to be rather arbitrary. That is, there are no clear distinctions between the so-called moral, civil, and ceremonial laws in the biblical text. For example, "love your neighbor as yourself" (Lev 19:18) is followed in the very next verse by "You are to keep my statutes. Do not crossbreed two different kinds of your livestock, sow your fields with two kinds of seed, or put on a garment made of two kinds of material" (Lev 19:19). Gordon Wenham notes, "The arbitrariness of the distinction between moral and civil law is reinforced by the arrangement of the material in Leviticus. Love of neighbor immediately precedes a prohibition on mixed breeding; the holiness motto comes just before the law on executing unruly children (19:18–19; 20:7–9)."[3] Should we apply Lev 19:18 as law but dismiss 19:19 as nonapplicable altogether? The text gives no indication whatsoever that any kind of hermeneutical shift has taken place between the two verses. Indeed, the so-called

---

[2] For a defense of this approach see Willem A. VanGemeren, "The Law is the Perfection of Righteousness in Jesus Christ: A Reformed Perspective," in *The Law, the Gospel, and the Modern Christian*, ed. Wayne C. Strickland (Grand Rapids: Zondervan, 1993), 13–58.

[3] Wenham, *Leviticus*, 34 (see chap. 3, n. 12).

moral, civil, and ceremonial laws are jumbled together without textual indicators of any difference between them.

In addition, it is often extremely difficult to determine whether a law falls into the *moral* category or into one of the others. Because the various laws presented in Exodus to Deuteronomy defined the covenant relationship between God and Israel, these laws, by nature, were theological. In some sense all of the law has theological content. The question then becomes "Can a law be a theological law but not a moral law?" For example, consider again the commandment in Lev 19:19, "Do not . . . sow your fields with two kinds of seed, or put on a garment made of two kinds of material." As we discussed in the chapter on Leviticus, one of the central themes running throughout that book is the holiness of God. Indeed, the discourse by God in Leviticus 19 is prefaced by the commandment "Be holy because I, the LORD your God, am holy" (19:1). Part of this theme is the teaching that holy things must be kept separate from profane things. While we may not understand all the nuances of the command against mixing cloth material or mixing seed, we do know that it relates back to the holiness of God. In fact, all of the laws relating to separation appear to connect to the overarching principle of God's holiness and the separation required because of that holiness. How can this law not be a moral law?

Or consider Num 5:5–31, which describes how a woman suspected of adultery is to be tried by the priest. Surely, adultery is a moral issue. Is this law then a timeless universal law for us? In Numbers 5, the priest is to make the accused woman drink some *bitter* water. If she gets sick, then she is guilty. Should this be practiced by Christians today? On the other hand, if we do not practice it, are we saying that it is not a moral law—that adultery is not a moral issue?

In addition, the traditional classification system of dividing laws into the categories of moral, civil, or ceremonial tends to dismiss the civil and ceremonial laws as not at all applicable to Christians today. These two categories include large portions of Exodus, Leviticus, and Deuteronomy. On the other hand, we read in 2 Tim 3:16–17 that "*all* Scripture is inspired by God and is profitable for teaching, for rebuking, for correcting, for training in righteousness" (italics added). This text strongly implies that all of those Old Testament laws have some teaching value, that there is some meaning in those laws that does indeed apply to Christians today. Therefore, it certainly seems that this traditional approach involving distinctions between moral, civil, and ceremonial laws is too ambiguous, too inconsistent, and too narrow to be a valid approach to interpreting Scripture.

The Principle Approach

A valid approach to the Old Testament law is one that can be used consistently with all of the laws and guidelines in the Pentateuch, allowing the Christian to apply all of the various types of covenantal stipulations encountered in Exodus to Deuteronomy. Furthermore, it should employ a method that does not require arbitrary, nontextual distinctions between verses. One approach that meets these criteria and has been widely advocated in recent years is the Principle Approach (sometimes called the *paradigmatic approach*).[4] The Principle Approach stresses the following: (1) The Old Testament laws are embedded in the narrative story that runs from Genesis 12 to 2 Kings 25, and thus the narrative context must be taken into account; and (2) these Old Testament laws are also an integral part of God's covenant God made with Israel at Mount Sinai; thus they must be interpreted within the context of being the terms and stipulations of this specific covenant.

The Narrative Context

As mentioned above, the Old Testament law is firmly embedded in Israel's theological history, especially the narrative story that runs from Genesis 12 to 2 Kings 25. The law is not presented by itself as some disconnected but timeless universal code of behavior. Rather, it is presented as part of the theological narrative that describes how God delivered Israel from Egypt and then entered into a covenant with them at Mount Sinai. The books of Exodus, Numbers, Leviticus, and Deuteronomy are all part of this narrative, integrally connected to the story of Israel's exodus, wandering, and conquest. Our interpretative approach to the law should take this into account. Connecting texts to their contexts is a basic tenant of proper interpretive method. Indeed, our methodology of interpreting Old Testament law should be like

---

[4] For example, see Daniel I. Block, "Preaching Old Testament Law to New Testament Christians," in *The Gospel According to Moses* (Eugene, OR: Cascade, 2012), 104–36; *Deuteronomy*, 37–38 (see chap. 5, n. 2); Christopher J. H. Wright, *Old Testament Ethics for the People of God* (Downers Grove, IL: IVP, 2004), 315–24; *Deuteronomy*, 13–14 (see chap. 5, n. 30); John Goldingay, *Models for Interpretation of Scripture* (Grand Rapids: Eerdmans, 1995), 92; Robert Chisholm, *From Exegesis to Exposition* (Grand Rapids: Baker, 1998), 223–24, 255; Wenham, *Leviticus*, 33–35; Hartley, *Leviticus*, lxxiii (see chap. 3, n. 13); William W. Klein, Craig L. Blomberg, and Robert L. Hubbard Jr., *Introduction to Biblical Interpretation*, rev. ed. (Nashville: Thomas Nelson, 2004), 345–46; and Andreas J. Köstenberger and Richard D. Patterson, *Invitation to Biblical Interpretation* (Grand Rapids: Kregel, 2011), 162–67.

our methodology of interpreting Old Testament narrative, because the law is contextually part of the narrative. This does not diminish the force and power of the text, for narratives in the Scripture are also authoritative.

The Covenant Context

As we have noted throughout this book, the various laws and guidelines that God gives to Israel in Exodus, Leviticus, Numbers, and Deuteronomy are presented and recorded as the terms and stipulations of the Mosaic covenant. This is an important, if not obvious, hermeneutical connection, for our understanding of the status of the Mosaic covenant should then bear heavily on our interpretive approach to the law. In light of this, several important observations about the nature and status of the Mosaic covenant merit discussion.

1. THE MOSAIC COVENANT IS CLOSELY ASSOCIATED WITH ISRAEL'S CONQUEST AND OCCUPATION OF THE LAND

The Mosaic covenant is neither geographically neutral nor universal. This covenant provides the framework by which Israel can occupy and live prosperously with God in the Promised Land. As we noted earlier, the close connection between the covenant and the land is stressed repeatedly in the book of Deuteronomy.

2. THE BLESSINGS FROM THE MOSAIC COVENANT ARE CONDITIONAL

This is a point we have noted several times, especially in our discussion of Deuteronomy. A constant warning runs throughout the story from Exodus to Deuteronomy explaining to Israel that obedience to the covenant will bring blessing but that disobedience to the covenant will bring punishment and curses. Leviticus 26 and Deuteronomy 28 are particularly explicit regarding the conditional nature of the covenant blessings.

3. THE MOSAIC COVENANT IS NO LONGER A FUNCTIONAL COVENANT

The New Testament affirms that the old Mosaic covenant has ceased to function as a valid covenant. Hebrews 8–9 makes it clear that Jesus came as the mediator of a new covenant that replaced the old covenant: "By calling this covenant 'new,' he has made the first one obsolete" (Heb 8:13 NIV). This has important implications for our understanding of the law. The Old Testament law represented the terms by which Israel could receive blessings in the land under the old (Mosaic) covenant. If the old covenant is no longer valid, how can the laws that make up that covenant still be valid? If the old covenant is obsolete, should we not also view the system of laws that comprise the old covenant as obsolete?

Paul argues forcefully that Christians are not under the Old Testament law. For example, in Gal 2:15–16 he writes, "We . . . know that a person is not justified by the works of the law, but by faith in Jesus Christ" (NIV). In Rom 7:4 Paul states that "you also were put to death in relation to the law through the body of Christ." Likewise, in Gal 3:25 he declares, "Now that this faith has come, we are no longer under a guardian" (NIV). Paul argues vigorously against Christians returning to a first-century Jewish understanding of the Old Testament law. Yet note that Paul still views all of Exodus-Deuteronomy as Scripture, and he cites texts from the Pentateuch frequently. He treats these texts as authoritative and instructive Scripture, just not as law, the terms and stipulations of the old covenant.

On the other hand, how are we to understand the words of Jesus in Matt 5:17? The Lord states, "Don't think that I came to abolish the Law or the Prophets. I did not come to abolish but to fulfill." First, note that the phrase "the Law or the Prophets" is a reference to the entire Old Testament. So, in this verse Jesus is not speaking about just the Mosaic law. Also note that the antithesis is not between "abolish" and "observe," but between "abolish" and "fulfill." Jesus does not claim that he has come to observe the law or to keep the law; rather, he has come to fulfill it. Matthew uses the Greek word translated as "fulfill" numerous times, and it normally means "to bring to its intended meaning." Jesus is *not* stating that the law is eternally binding on New Testament believers. This would clearly be against New Testament teaching. What Jesus was saying is that he did not come to sweep away the righteous demands of the law but to fulfill these righteous demands. Furthermore, the Law, as well as the Prophets, had prophetic elements in it, particularly in pointing to the ultimate demands of holiness due to the presence of God. Jesus, as the climax of salvation history, fulfills all the righteous demands and all of the prophetic foreshadowing of the Law and of the Prophets. In addition, Jesus thus becomes the final interpreter of the law. Indeed, he is the authority over the meaning of the law, as other passages in Matthew indicate, many of which follow immediately on the heels of 5:17. Some of the Old Testament laws Jesus restates (Matt 19:18–19), but some he modifies (Matt 5:31–32). Some laws he intensifies (Matt 5:21–22, 27–28), and some he changes significantly (Matt 5:33–37, 38–42, 43–47). Furthermore, some laws he appears to abrogate entirely (Mark 7:15–19). Jesus is not advocating the continuation of the traditional first-century Jewish approach of adherence to the law. Neither is he advocating that we dismiss the law altogether. He is proclaiming that we must reinterpret the meaning of the law in light of his coming and in light of the profound changes that the new covenant brought.[5]

Thus, we have seen that the law is integrally connected to the Mosaic covenant, which is, in turn, integrally connected to the land and the conditional promise of blessing for Israel in the land. We as Christians are not related to the land, nor are we related to the conditions for being blessed in the land. The old Mosaic covenant is obsolete, having been replaced by the new covenant. Therefore, we would suggest that the law, which defines the old covenant, is likewise no longer applicable *as law* over us.

Embedded in the narrative, however, these "laws" are still inspired Scripture and thus still very much have applicability to us, just as narrative text does. The best way that we can interpret and apply all of these laws is by using the Principle Approach.

The Procedures for Using the Principle Approach

The procedures for employing the Principle Approach to the Old Testament laws can be described in five basic steps.

Step 1. Identify What the Particular Law Meant to the Biblical Audience

Probe into the text and study it thoroughly. Remember that the Old Testament law is part of a larger narrative. Read and study it as you would a narrative text. Identify the historical and literary contexts. Are the Israelites on the bank of the Jordan preparing to enter the land (Deuteronomy), or are they back at Mount Sinai at the beginning of the exodus (Exodus, Leviticus)? Is the law you are studying given as a response to a specific situation that had come up, or is the law describing the requirements for Israel

---

[5] For similar views on Matt 5:17–48, see D. A. Carson, "Matthew," *The Expositor's Bible Commentary* (Grand Rapids: Zondervan, 1984), 142–44; R.T. France, *Matthew* (Grand Rapids: Zondervan, 1989), 194–95; and Donald A. Hagner, *Matthew 1–13*, WBC (Dallas: Word, 1993), 104–6.

after they move into the land? What other laws are in the immediate context? Is there a connection between these laws? Probe into the nature of the individual law you are studying. Try to identify how this specific law relates to the old covenant. Does it govern how the Israelites were to approach God? Does it govern how they relate to each other? Does it relate to agriculture or commerce? Is it specifically tied to life in the Promised Land? Now determine what this specific, concrete expression of the law meant for the Israelites, the immediate Old Testament audience. Identify clearly what the law demanded of them.

Step 2. Determine the Differences between the Biblical Audience and Us

In this step the goal is to determine the differences between us today as Christians and the immediate Old Testament audience. For example, we are under the new covenant and not under the old covenant as they were. Thus, we are no longer under the law as the terms of the covenant. Also, we are not Israelites preparing to dwell in the Promised Land with God dwelling in the tabernacle or temple. We are Christians with God dwelling within each of us. We do not approach God through the sacrifice of animals. We approach God through the sacrifice of Jesus Christ. We live under a secular government and not under a theocracy as ancient Israel did. We do not face pressure from Canaanite religion but rather from non-Christian worldviews and philosophies. Additionally, many of us do not live in agrarian societies.

Step 3. Develop Universal Principles from the Text

Behind the expression of the meaning for the original audience lies a universal, timeless principle. Each of the Old Testament laws presents a concrete, direct meaning for the Old Testament audience, a meaning that is tied within the old covenant context. But that meaning is usually based on a broader universal truth, one that is applicable to all of God's people, regardless of when they live and under which covenant they live. In this step we want to ask the questions, "What is the universal principle that is reflected in this specific law? What is the broad principle that God has behind this text that allows for this specific ancient application?" In developing these principles, the following guidelines are helpful: (1) The principle should be reflected in the text, (2) the principle should be timeless, (3) the principle should correspond to the broad theology of the rest of Scripture, (4) the principle should not be culturally tied, and (5) the principle should be relevant to both Old Testament and current New Testament audiences. These principles often will be directly related to the character of God and his holiness, the nature of sin, or concern for other people.

Step 4. Correlate the Principle with Related New Testament Teaching

Cross into the New Testament with the universal principle and filter it through the New Testament, especially through any New Testament text that addresses the principle or the specific Old Testament law being studied. Some of the Old Testament laws (especially many of the Ten Commandments) are restated in the New Testament as commandments for Christians. When the old covenant was abrogated, the Old Testament law ceased to be law for us. However, when the New Testament repeats it as a commandment, we are to obey it as a commandment of Christ. In addition, as noted earlier, occasionally the New Testament will qualify the Old Testament law, either modifying it or expanding it. For example, if we are interpreting Exod 20:14, "Do not commit adultery," our universal principle will be related to the sanctity of marriage and the need for faithfulness in marriage. As we pass into the New Testament, we must incorporate Jesus's teaching on the subject. In Matt 5:28 Jesus states, "But I tell you, everyone who looks at a woman lustfully has already committed adultery with her in his heart." Jesus expands the range of this commandment, applying it not only to *acts* of adultery but also to *thoughts* of adultery. In developing a concrete expression of Exod 20:14 for today's audience, we must incorporate Jesus's comments on that law. The commandment for us becomes "You shall not commit adultery, in act or in thought." But keep in mind that we are now seeking to obey this as Scripture and New Testament commandment, and not as Old Testament law.

Step 5. Apply the Universal Principle in Our Individual Lives

Take the expression developed in step 4 and apply it to specific situations that Christians encounter today. It doesn't do any good to go through this entire academic process if we do not obey the Scripture and actually apply the principle that we develop. So, in step 5 we will take the expression that we developed in step 4 and apply it to specific situations that we as individual Christians encounter today.

An Example: Leviticus 5:2

As an example of how to use the Principle Approach in interpreting and applying the Old Testament law, let's study Lev 5:2 and take it through these five steps.[6] The text reads as follows: "Or if someone touches anything unclean—a carcass of an unclean wild animal, or unclean livestock, or an unclean swarming creature—without being aware of it, he is unclean and incurs guilt."

First, as we give this text a close reading and try to place it in context, we observe that the individual apparently does become aware that he has made this unclean contact and is now unclean. The action required to correct the unclean status in this verse is described a few verses later, in 5:5–6. Thus, we should add this text as well to our study of 5:2. Leviticus 5:5–6 reads:

> "If someone incurs guilt in one of these cases, he is to confess he has committed that sin. He must bring his penalty for guilt for the sin he has committed to the LORD: a female lamb or goat from the flock as a sin offering. In this way the priest will make atonement on his behalf for his sin."

STEP 1. IDENTIFY WHAT THE PARTICULAR LAW MEANT TO THE BIBLICAL AUDIENCE

Recall that Leviticus in general deals with the Israelites' situation when the holy, awesome God comes to dwell in their midst. With the all-righteous and holy God dwelling nearby in the tabernacle, the Israelites are faced with numerous challenges. How can they approach God if he is holy and they are sinful? How can they deal with sin and unclean things with the holy God living among them? Leviticus answers these questions, and the verses we are studying are part of that answer. Our verses (Lev 5:2, 5–6) fall into the literary subsection of 4:1–5:13, a section dealing with purification offerings—how to make oneself pure again after becoming ritually unclean. While Leviticus 4 focuses primarily on the leaders, Leviticus 5 deals with regular people. Verse 2 explains that if the Israelites touch anything that has been defined as unclean (dead animals or unclean animals), even by accident, they are defiled and now unclean. With this status of "unclean," they are not allowed to approach God and worship him. To do so, they must first be purified (made clean). Leviticus 5:5–6 explains how to do this: they must confess their sin and then bring the priest a sacrifice, either a lamb or

---

[6] This example is taken from Duvall and Hays, *Grasping God's Word*, 396–99.

a goat. The priest would then sacrifice that animal on their behalf, and they would be made clean again, now able to approach and worship God.

Step 2. Determine the Differences between the Biblical Audience and Us

We as Christians today are not under the old covenant. Our sin is now covered by the death of Christ and not by the sacrifice of animals. Furthermore, through Christ we have direct access to the Father, and we no longer need human priests as mediators.

Step 3. Develop Universal Principles from the Text

The overarching principle behind these verses is the constant reality that God is holy. Since he is holy, and since he dwells among his people, his holiness demands that his people keep separate from sin and unclean things. If his people do become unclean, they must be purified by a blood sacrifice.

Observe the important elements of this universal principle. It is reflected in the text of Lev 5:2, 5–6 but is expressed in more general terms than what was stated in step 1. Furthermore, this general principle fits well into the overall theology of Leviticus as well as the rest of Scripture. Finally, it is expressed in a way that is universally applicable to both Old Testament and New Testament people.

Step 4. Correlate the Principle with Related New Testament Teaching

Crossing into the New Testament we recognize that God no longer dwells among his people (we Christians) by residing in the tabernacle. Now he lives right within each Christian through the indwelling Holy Spirit. His presence, however, is still holy and still makes demands on us for holiness. He calls on us to avoid sin and to stay separate from unclean things.

Yet the New Testament redefines the terms *clean* and *unclean*. Consider what Jesus says about this in Mark:

> "Nothing that goes into a person from outside can defile him but the things that come out of a person are what defile him." . . .
>
> And he said, "What comes out of a person is what defiles him. For from within, out of people's hearts, come evil thoughts, sexual immoralities, thefts,

murders, adulteries, greed, evil actions, deceit, self-indulgence, envy, slander, pride, and foolishness. All these evil things come from within and defile a person." (7:15, 20–23)

Jesus is redefining for the new covenant people what makes people unclean. We are not made unclean by touching dead animals. We become unclean through our unclean thoughts, unclean speech, or sinful actions.

Likewise, under the new covenant, and because of the atoning death of Christ, Christians now deal with sin and uncleanness differently. We are not required to bring an animal sacrifice to atone for our sin and to restore us to "clean" status. The sins of Christians are covered by the atoning sacrifice of Christ. The death of Christ washes away all our sin and changes our status from unclean to clean. Confession of sin, however, is still important under the new covenant (1 John 1:9).

So, a concrete expression of the theological principle for Christians today would be this: Stay away from sinful actions and impure thoughts because the holy God lives within you. If you do commit unclean acts or think unclean thoughts, confess this sin, receive forgiveness, and be made clean through the death of Christ.

STEP 5. APPLY THE UNIVERSAL PRINCIPLE IN OUR INDIVIDUAL LIVES

In this step we try to find specific ways that we can apply the principle of step 4 in our lives today. There are numerous areas of application. One area of application, for example, is the issue of Internet pornography. This text in Leviticus tells us that the holiness of God, who dwells within each of us as Christians, demands that we lead clean lives. Watching Internet pornography clearly falls within the category that the New Testament defines as unclean. This action is a violation of God's holiness and thus hinders a Christian's ability to approach, worship, or fellowship with God. Thus, we are called to stay away from Internet pornography, recognizing that it makes us unclean and offends the holiness of God, who dwells within us, disrupting our fellowship with him. However, if we do fall into this sin, we should confess this sin, and through the death of Christ we can be forgiven and our fellowship with God be restored.

Numerous other applications are possible, especially regarding issues such as greed, envy, slander, and anger, among others.

BIBLIOGRAPHY

Block, Daniel I. "Preaching Old Testament Law to New Testament Christians." In *The Gospel According to Moses*, 104–36. Eugene, OR: Cascade, 2012.

Gane, Roy E. *Old Testament Law for Christians*. Grand Rapids: Baker, 2017.

Hays, J. Daniel. "Applying the Old Testament Law Today." *BSac* 158 (January-March 2001): 1–15.

———. "How to Interpret the Old Testament Law." In *Read the Bible for Life*, edited by George Guthrie, 95–110. Nashville: B&H, 2010.

———. "How to Interpret and Apply the Old Testament Law." In *The Baker Illustrated Bible Handbook*, edited by J. Daniel Hays and J. Scott Duvall, 1079–87. Grand Rapids: Baker, 2011.

———. "Old Testament—Law." In *Grasping God's Word*, 4th ed, edited by J. Scott Duvall and J. Daniel Hays, 383–403. Grand Rapids: Zondervan, 2020.

Imes, Carmen Joy. *Bearing God's Name: Why Sinai Still Matters*. Downers Grove, IL: IVP, 2019.

Sprinkle, Joe M. *Biblical Law and Its Relevance: A Christian Understanding and Ethical Application for Today of the Mosaic Regulations*. Lanham, MD: University Press, 2006.

Strickland, Wayne G., ed. *Five Views on Law and Gospel*. Grand Rapids: Zondervan, 1999.

Wright, Christopher J. H. *Old Testament Ethics for the People of God*. Downers Grove, IL: IVP, 2004.

———. *Deuteronomy*. NIBC. Peabody, MA: Hendrickson, 1996.

SUBJECT INDEX

AUTHOR INDEX

SCRIPTURE INDEX